Praying Your Way Out of Bondage

Prayers from Exodus and Leviticus

BOOKS BY ELMER TOWNS

Knowing God Through Fasting

Praying the Psalms

Praying the Proverbs, Song of Solomon, and Ecclesiastes

Praying the Book of Job

Praying the Book of Revelation

Praying the Gospels

Praying the Book of Acts and the General Epistles

Praying Paul's Letters

Praying the New Testament

Praying Genesis

Praying Your Way Out of Bondage:
Prayers from Exodus and Leviticus

Praying For Your Second Chance:
Prayers from Numbers and Deuteronomy

AVAILABLE FROM DESTINY IMAGE PUBLISHERS
www.desinyimage.com

PRAYING YOUR WAY OUT OF BONDAGE

PRAYERS FROM EXODUS AND LEVITICUS

Book Ten in *Praying the Scriptures* Series

Elmer L. Towns

DESTINY IMAGE® PUBLISHERS, INC.
P.O. Box 310, Shippensburg, PA 17257-0310

"Speaking to the Purposes of God for this Generation and for the Generations to Come."

This book and all other Destiny Image, Revival Press, Mercy Place, Fresh Bread, Destiny Image Fiction, and Treasure House books are available at Christian bookstores and distributors worldwide.

For a U.S. bookstore nearest you, call **1-800-722-6774.**

For more information on foreign distributors, call **717-532-3040.**

Reach us on the Internet at **www.destinyimage.com.**

ISBN 10: 0-7684-2759-2

ISBN 13: 978-0-7684-2759-2

For Worldwide Distribution, Printed in the U.S.A.

1 2 3 4 5 6 7 8 9 10 11 / 13 12 11 10 09

DEDICATED TO STEVE AND SHIRLEY JONES

I meet early every Sunday morning for prayer with approximately 15 to 20 people. This is my most important meeting each week, for these people pray for me. I couldn't do what I do without their intercession.

When I was told I had cancer, it was hard to accept because I had always been in excellent health. The first people I told outside my family were Steve and Shirley Jones because I know they intercede and their prayers get through.

Today I'm again in good health as this book is finished. The cancer is gone, praise the Lord! I just had an annual CAT scan and the doctor said, "You're clean as a whistle."

Thank you, Steve and Shirley, for praying for me; thank you prayer team. The Lord is Jehovah Rapha, the God who heals...Hallelujah!

With respect,
Elmer Towns

CONTENTS

PRAYERS FROM EXODUS

PREFACE

Praying the Scriptures is an exciting way to read the Word of God. Most simply read the Bible, which enlightens your mind, but in this volume you'll pray your way through Scripture, which touches the mind, emotions, and the will. If you pray with all your heart, you'll be transformed into the image of Christ (see 2 Cor. 3:18).

The word *Exodus* means "way out." This is an exciting story of how God provided a way out of bondage for His people in Israel who were slaves in Egypt. Over 550,000 men, plus their families, walked triumphantly away from their oppressive masters.

Just as God gave deliverance to His people from tyranny, so today God delivers His people from the bondage to sin. Jesus said, "Whoever commits sin is a slave to sin" (John 8:34). Then Jesus went on to say, "If the Son shall make you free, you'll be free indeed" (John 8:36). The Lord transforms His people so they can worship Him, serve Him, and live their lives in freedom as a testimony to His power and sovereignty. *Lord, change my life as I read this book so I can freely worship You and serve You.*

Every person on this earth has an enemy, whether they realize it or not. Satan is a roaring lion who seeks to eat us up (see 1 Peter 5:8). Satan wants people to worship and serve him, and when he's finished chewing them up, he'll throw them on the garbage heap of humanity. He'll do that to you, just as he tried to do to Israel.

God's people entered Egypt in a favored position under Joseph. They were given the choice land in the Nile delta. They worked as herdsmen for Pharaoh, but over the next 300 years, they became the slaves of the Egyptians. Hard, cruel slave drivers beat them mercilessly to build the monuments of Egypt. When God's people cried to God, He sent Moses to deliver them. This book describes the spiritual battle between the demonic forces of darkness in Egypt against the delivering power of God. It's a historical war story of spiritual warfare.

But Exodus is not just about old, dry history. It's a picture of your battle today against the powers of spiritual darkness. Just as God delivered Israel from Egypt, He'll also deliver you from sin's slavery. How did God deliver approximately three million people from slavery? The same way God does it today! God lives among His people to show Himself strong. Today, God wants to live in your body to show Himself strong to the world. "Greater is He who is in you than he who is in the world" (1 John 4:4).

This book continues the series *Praying the Scriptures*. I began writing this series five years ago (2004). Previous books released in this series:

Praying the Book of Genesis

Praying the Psalms

Praying Proverbs, Ecclesiastes and the Song of Solomon

Praying the Book of Job

*Praying the Gospels**

*Praying the Acts and General Epistles**

*Praying Paul's Letters**

*Praying the Book of Revelation**

Praying the New Testament (* joined into one volume)

I've translated the Scriptures from the original text into modern English—thought for thought—and then turned each passage into a prayer to God. It's a process I've called transliteration.

To the first few volumes I've added footnotes and explanations to help readers with technical material. Later in the series I've incorporated technical backgrounds into stories that interpret the biblical passage for the readers. Read the story how Moses may have learned Jewish genealogy. If that is not the way it happened, then God revealed the information directly to him, as God revealed the story of Creation.

The practical applications come in the prayers that are added. If you just read the Scriptures, then you only learn what God has said. But when you pray the Scriptures, you also involve your emotions and will. Praying the Bible stirs your emotions and commits your will to serve God. Isn't that what the Bible is all about?

As you read *Praying Your Way Out of Bondage: Prayers From Exodus and Leviticus,* may you experience your own deliverance from the bondage of sin and may you prepare to enter your personal Promised Land.

Sincerely yours in Christ,
Elmer L. Towns
Written from my home
at the foot of the Blue Ridge Mountains

INTRODUCTION

*C*RACK!

The elderly shepherd snapped to attention. He called out into the darkness, "Who's there?" He heard nothing, so he got up to walk all the way around his sheep to make sure they were all safe. Seeing nothing, he went back to his warm fire.

The elderly shepherd was completely exhausted; the fierce sun had sapped his strength, now he faced a frigid desert night. He just wanted to wrap up in his tunic and sleep. The long, dark shadows from the nearby mountains had covered him, everything was black. Moses knew he had to eat, so he had earlier built a small fire.

It had been 20 years since Moses had fled Egypt with an arrest warrant on his head. Moses was no longer sleeping in a palace; tonight he would sleep on the ground between some rocks, out of the wind.

Moses' half brother Pharaoh Thutmosis III had sought to arrest Moses out of revenge because Moses had killed an Egyptian slave.

Killing a slave should have been a little thing because the royal family condemned slaves to death all the time, but Thutmosis used Moses' crime as an excuse to eliminate any threat to the throne after his father, Rameses II, died.

There was no breeze that evening, so the smoke from the fire went straight into the sky—high enough to be seen a long way off. Unknown to Moses, an escaped Hebrew slave was trying to cross the Sinai Desert. Many had tried it, but most died in the desert. In the providence of God, this escapee saw the smoke and knew it was a sign of life. When the escapee got close enough to see the fire in the distance, he yelled out a greeting. It was dangerous walking into a shepherd's fire unannounced.

"SHALOM!"

"What...?" Moses again snapped his head to listen. It was a dialect he recognized. He heard the Hebrew language, and he yelled back, *"SHALOM."* After Moses greeted the escapee and heard the story of his escape, one old shepherd then fed an older escapee a simple shepherd's meal. Then they sat around the fire to talk. It was then Moses noticed the unusual walking stick that the old man had.

"What's that carved in the staff?" Moses pointed to the intricate carvings—curious carvings—at the top of the 6-foot shepherd's staff.

"It's the rod of God," the older escapee answered.

"How do you know it's God's rod?" Moses lifted an eyebrow as he asked the obvious question.

The older man pointed to the top, "This has the genealogy of our people from Abraham to the present." The palm of his hand caressed the signet at the very top of the rod. He whispered, "There's Abraham's signet, this rod belonged to Abraham." It was as if the old man didn't want anyone to hear him.

"There's Isaac's...his birthright son's signet is right below Abraham's." Then he pointed to Ishmael's on the back of the rod, the son who did not receive the promises of God.

Moses took the rod to finger each signet carefully. Because he knew the Hebrew language, he recognized the name of Jacob, and the twelve sons of Jacob's small signets were all there.

"Each of the twelve had his own signet rod to start a new family—a new tribe," the old man said.

"Where are these rods now?" Moses asked the elderly man.

"Many are in Egypt with the families. A new name was added with each generation."

"Are all twelve family rods in Egypt?" Moses asked.

"No," the old man shook his head and told the story that one of the twelve sons who came to Egypt with Jacob didn't stay. "After a few years, Issachar left Egypt to go back and live in the desert. He lived in the land of Uz. He died, but his son Job lives there now. He's the richest man in the area."

"I know that name," Moses answered. "I've heard a man named Job lives a week's journey from here."

Around the campfire that evening, Moses found out that Job possessed Issachar's family rod but that he took great pride in family ancestry. Job had many of the records stretching for hundreds of years, all the way back to Adam.

"I've heard stories about this Job," Moses began to talk to the old man. "Soon I'm going to see if everything I've heard about him is true."

A Few Months Later

When Moses first saw the house, it was the most beautiful thing he had seen in years—at least the most beautiful thing since he left the palace in Egypt. The path to the house was paved with tile, right through blowing sand—a tile path. Animals filled the pens, all symbolically in a row: cattle, sheep, and various other animals. Servants were scurrying around everywhere, carrying water, working with the animals.

This is not a man's home, thought Moses, this is a small city.

When Moses saw the owner in the garden, Job, he saw that he stood erect but was short and bald with a wiry frame. There was a strong will living in his body, almost 200 years old.

After greetings and an evening meal, Moses told Job why he had come. "I must know more about my heritage. I must know about our people."

Then Moses told Job about how God delivered him as a child. Job had heard this story of how Pharaoh was killing Hebrew babies, but a faithful Jewish mother hid Moses in a basket in the Nile River. Hatseput, the daughter of Pharaoh, found Moses and raised him as her own child.

Moses told Job,

"I was trained in all the wisdom and literature of Egypt, but I murdered a man and had to flee for my life." Then Moses explained he had become a shepherd—hiding from Pharaoh—in the desert for approximately 20 years.

Then it was time for Job to tell his story. God had prospered him, and he was rich, but not as rich as he was now. "I had a much smaller home, but one day satan entered Heaven to challenge my love for God." Job explained that satan challenged God,

"Take away all Job's wealth, and he will curse You."

"God allowed satan to do that to me. I lost all my wealth...my home...my cattle...everything, yet I said, 'The Lord gives, and the Lord takes away; blessed be the name of the Lord' (Job 1:20-22).

"Because satan couldn't get me to deny my faith, he said to God that if he could take away my health, I would curse God to His face. I lost my health, but I did not curse God. I blessed Him."

Moses listened carefully to the story, asking questions to understand what happened. It was as though Moses wanted to know the story exactly so he could write it down. Then Job explained,

"The end result is that God gave me more children, more wealth, and miraculously said that I would live twice the age of 70, my age when all my calamities happened. I am now 180 years old."

When Moses found out that Job had memorized the history of mankind as it had been told to him, he had not forgotten a single name; it was then Moses said,

"You must tell me everything so I can write it down. We Jews cannot lose our past." Moses went on to explain, "If God's people—the Jews—do not remember how God has blessed us and led us in the past, then we won't know how to live for Him in the future."

Time is nothing to a shepherd; his sheep are everything. So Moses had time to listen to Job, and he wrote down everything he heard from the old patriarch. Later, Moses would have time to sit and write as he watched his sheep. But now at the dinner table, the moment was sacred. Moses wanted to learn everything he could about God and about His people. Moses was unaware that God was preparing him personally for what God wanted Moses to write. He wrote down the words of God. Thousands of years later Jesus would remind us Moses wrote the first five books of the Old Testament.

Notes

Notice how both Moses and his half brother, Thutmosis III, 1504-1450 B.C., have the name and the root Moses in their name—to draw up.

Many have claimed Moses couldn't write, but that's not true. "Moses was learned in all the wisdom of the Egyptians, and was mighty in words and deeds" (Acts 7:22). Did you notice the part about Moses knowing words? It suggests he knew many languages. The Gospels declare Moses wrote Scripture (Matt. 19:7; Matt. 22:24; Mark 1:44; Mark 12:19,26; Luke 2:22; Luke 20:28,37; Luke 24:27; John 7:19,22; John 8:5).

Exodus 1

ISRAEL IN EGYPT

These are the sons of Israel who came to Egypt with Jacob, each man brought his entire household with him: Reuben, Simeon, Levi, Judah, Issachar, Zebulun, Benjamin, Dan, Naphtali, Gad, and Asher. There were a total of 70 descendents; Joseph was already in Egypt.

Joseph died as did all the other sons of that generation. The descendents of Israel were fruitful and multiplied abundantly and grew into a powerful minority, and the land became filled with them.

A new king came into power who knew nothing about what Joseph did for the Egyptians. He said, "Look, the descendents of Israel are becoming too large and powerful for us. Let us deal wisely with them or they will continue to multiply and when war comes, they will join our enemies to fight against us."

So they put slave masters over the Israelites and forced them into slave labor. Israeli slaves built the cities of Pithom and Raameses. But the more the Egyptians oppressed them, the more the Israelites multiplied until the Egyptians hated and feared the Israelites. As a result, they worked them relentlessly. They had to dig clay, make bricks, and do all types of field work, because the Egyptians worked them mercilessly.

The Egyptian king issued a decree to the Hebrew midwives, "Where you see a Hebrew woman giving birth, if it is a boy kill him; but if it is a girl, let her live." The king had given the order to Shiphrah and Puah. But they were God fearers, so the order of the king was not carried out. The king summoned them and demanded, "Why are the boys allowed to live?" The midwives answered Pharaoh, "The Hebrew women are stronger than the Egyptian women. When they go into labor, they give birth before the midwife arrives."

Lord, you prospered Israel and they continued to grow and became powerful. Because the midwives feared You, they became founders of families. Then Pharaoh commanded, "Throw every baby boy into the river that is born, but let the girls live."

Lord, satan has always hated the little children;
When he can't enslave their minds, he slaughters them.

The abortion industry is evil and does satan's work;
I pray for children—born and unborn—to live
And come to know You, and serve You.

Amen.

Exodus 2:1-25

THE BIRTH OF MOSES
A HEBREW DELIVERER IS BORN

A man from the family of Levi married a woman from the same family. She conceived, and when a fine son was born, she hid him for three months. When she was no longer able to hide the boy, she took a reed basket and sealed it with tar, put the child in the basket, and set it floating among the reeds of the river. Miriam, the child's sister, watched from a distance to see what would happen to him.

The daughter of Pharaoh came to bathe in the river, accompanied by her attendants. When she saw the basket floating among the reeds, she sent a servant girl to get it. When she opened it to look inside, the baby wept. She was captured by her compassion for the baby and said, "This must be one of the Hebrew children."

Miriam, the baby's sister, said to Pharaoh's daughter, "Would you like me to find a Hebrew woman to nurse him for you?" Pharaoh's daughter answered, "Yes...." So Miriam called the baby's own mother to do it. Then Pharaoh's daughter told her, "Take this baby and nurse him for me. I will pay you." So Moses' mother nursed the baby. Then when the child was grown, she brought him to Pharaoh's daughter, and the boy was raised in the palace as the son of Pharaoh's daughter. She called him Moses (to pull out of the water) explaining, "Because I pulled him up out of the water."

Lord, You accomplish Your will through the circumstances of life;
Thank You for saving baby Moses.

Lord, work through the circumstances of my daily life
So I may accomplish Your will in my life.

When Moses was 40 years old, he went to visit his kinsmen. He saw
them straining at forced labor. When an Egyptian struck a
Hebrew, one of his family relatives, Moses looked both ways and
because no one was watching, he killed the Egyptian and buried
the body in the sand.

The following day Moses saw two Hebrew men fighting. Moses separated them and said to one, "Why are you fighting your brother?"
The man answered, "Who made you a judge over us? Will you
kill me the way you killed the Egyptian yesterday?" Moses was
frightened knowing the fact was known. When Pharaoh heard it,
he was ready to execute Moses, but Moses fled to the Sinai
Desert to live in the land of Midian.

One day Moses was sitting at a well when the seven daughters of Reuel
the priest of Midian came to draw water. They tried to fill the
trough with water for their sheep, but some shepherds tried to
take their water and run them off. Moses protected the women
and watered their sheep. When they got home, Reuel asked,
"Why have you come home so soon?" They answered, "An
Egyptian defended us from the shepherds, and then he drew
water for our sheep." Reuel asked them, "Where is he, why did-
n't you invite him to come eat with us?"

Moses stayed with Reuel, and eventually Reuel gave Moses Zipporah as
his wife. She gave birth to a son, and Moses named him
Gershom (a foreigner here). Moses said, "I am a foreigner in a
foreign land."

Eventually the king of Egypt died, but the Israelites still were persecuted
with extreme labor.

Lord, the people of Israel cried out, and their cry came up to You;
You heard their groanings and remembered the covenant
You made with Abraham, Isaac, and Jacob.

Amen.

The Story of a Deliverer for the Hebrews Is Born

Date: 1571 B.C. ~ Place: Egypt

"I'm not getting married," Amram told another Hebrew slave. He hated the Egyptians for taking away his freedom. Pharaoh Thutmose II had forgotten all the good things that Joseph did for Egypt, saving them from starvation in the great famine almost 420 years ago.

Amram and other unmarried Hebrew males were rounded up and forced to build the great public buildings of Egypt. "I'll not marry," the strong young Amram told everyone. "I wouldn't bring children into a world to be slaves."

"Look at that wall," Amram complained that conditions were getting worse. The bricks at the bottom were evenly measured; the straw used to make the bricks was evenly cut from the fields. Higher up the wall, the bricks contained straw pulled by hand. The Hebrews had been punished, and they were forced to pull straw by hand to make bricks. Finally, the bricks at the top of the wall were made with trash and stubble swept from the streets. It was almost impossible for the Hebrew slaves to make bricks.

After the success of gathering young Hebrew men, next the Egyptians arrested families...old people...children; all Hebrews were rounded up into slavery camps. They were thrown into compounds resembling prisons.

29

The previous Hyksos Pharaohs were Semitics; racially and linguistically, Hyksos were similar to the Hebrews. God's people prospered because the Hyksos Pharaohs brought a number of Asians into government jobs. That's after Joseph became Minister of Agriculture.

Then the 18th dynasty began with Pharaoh Ahmoses I in 1570 B.C. Motivated by racial hatred, Pharaoh turned against the Hebrews and other Asians, proclaiming, "If an enemy invades us, the Hebrews will fight with our enemy."

Amram sloshed in a mud pit all day, mixing clay, then lifting heavy buckets of clay to fill molds so the bricks would dry in the sun. Several times each day, he slipped and fell in the slimy mess, then a torturous whip on his back reminded him of his daily quota. "I'll work...I'll suffer...I'll die," was all Amram expected in life.

Then he met Jochebed, the most beautiful girl he had ever seen. Because love is eternal, and even lives in a slave camp, Amram fell in love with Jochebed.

Jochebed was also an unmarried Hebrew slave, also from the tribe of Levi. Because love doesn't understand the limits of slavery, they were married, and because love is driven by the passion of intimacy, the couple had two children, Aaron and Miriam. Shortly after that Amram heard,

"THROW ALL THE NEW BOY BABIES IN THE NILE," the slave drivers' booming voices announced to the Hebrews. Pharaoh was stepping up a holocaust against them. The burial detail dragged away the corpses each day of those who died in servitude—it was mostly the aged—now Pharaoh would eliminate baby boys. Fearing a possible genocide against a future child, Amram said,

"We'll not have any more children," the husband whispered to his wife Jochebed; but because love is driven by its passion, she became pregnant again. God in Heaven saw the pure motives of this married couple and had plans for their child.

"What a beautiful boy," Jochebed remarked after a boy was born to them. All the slave families knew about the new baby boy, but no one told the

Egyptians about the boy. The Hebrews protected one another. After several narrow escapes when the Egyptians almost discovered the baby—his crying—Jochebed knew she couldn't keep him alive in the compound.

Jochebed wove long green marsh grass into a basket, then coated it with tar to make it waterproof. She set the basket floating in the Nile, telling her daughter, Miriam, "The Egyptians treat this river like god. If they find this baby in the river, they'll let him live, thinking the child came from their god."

The young feet of Miriam ran nimbly along the river's edge, following the basket as it floated in the river's current. The tide swept it near some marble steps where Hatseput, the daughter of Pharaoh Thutmosis II, came to bathe. The princess had elegant marble tubs in the palace, but Hatseput came to the river for ceremonial purification, because the Nile was one of Egypt's many gods.

"Look, there's a basket," a maid told the princess Hatseput.

"Fetch it!" As the princess removed the lid to the basket, the baby cried, "Waaa...waaa...waaa...." What woman can refuse a crying baby? Hatseput instantly loved the baby even though the maid correctly guessed, "It must be a Hebrew baby." As the little boy snuggled into Hatseput's arms, then smiled at her, he captured her heart. Miriam, the older sister to the baby boy, approached the royal party with an inspired idea,

"I know a woman who would nurse your baby for you."

The two mothers met and exchanged the baby. The adoptive mother, Hatseput, had received from God a divine love for her new son; she gave the baby to the birthmother, Jochebed, whose natural motherly love would sovereignly provide him with a Hebrew foundation faith. The baby would have the best of both worlds, access to the privileges of Egypt, and access to the Hebrew heritage of his fathers. Hatseput gave him legal freedom to live, and from the child she received the meaning of life. Jochebed gave him the nourishment to grow and from him received the hope of freedom for her people.

31

"I'll name him Moses." Hatseput thought that was a good name because it meant *drawn from the water,* but the name was also adapted from her father, who was named Ahmosis II.

Moses went to school in the palace with Thutmosis III, younger brother to Hatseput. Little Thutmosis was being carefully trained by the finest teachers in the world to rule the Egyptian kingdom, and Moses was being equipped by God to rule His earthly Kingdom—their curriculum: language, reasoning, persuasion, history, natural science, astronomy, and numbers.

When Pharaoh died, Hatseput was elevated to the title Pharaoh. She shared the throne with her brother Thutmosis III, they were co-regents until she died; then the cruel brother scratched her name off every monument and defaced the buildings she built.

Moses was 40 years old when his adoptive mother died; then the Egyptian empire struggled through upheaval, a revolution that would influence his future. One day Moses saw a cruel taskmaster mercilessly whipping a Hebrew slave.

"Stop..." Moses demanded, snatching the whip from his hand. "I'll give you a taste of this whip." He began beating the Egyptian slave master, and as religious vengeance is sometimes blinded to reason, Moses beat the man to death. The horrified slaves watched the son of Pharaoh bury the bleeding Egyptian corpse in the sand.

The next day Moses visited the same work area as the previous day. Two slaves were fighting; the Egyptian slave masters laughed and let them fight. When Moses pulled the two men apart, they quit fighting, realizing the son of Pharaoh had separated them. One of the two men was the slave Moses had delivered the previous day. Without any gratitude to Moses—but now motivated by fear—he yelled,

"Are you going to kill me like you killed the Egyptian slave master yesterday?"

Moses looked up to see anger in the face of the other slave masters who had been watching the two Hebrews fighting. One slave master will always protect another, and if there is any rebellion against them—they meet violence with greater violence, lest the slaves get out of hand. The slave master ran to tell Thutmosis II what Moses had done.

A pharaoh could overlook the death of anyone, for he treated his people like beasts of burden. Many pharaohs had been responsible for many deaths, but Thutmosis used the occasion of Moses murdering a slave driver to rid himself of a rival in the palace. He had eliminated the memory of Hatseput; now he would eliminate a son of Hatseput. But before Tutmosis III could arrest Moses, he fled across the Red Sea into the desert.

Moses escaped to the land of the Ishmaelites, his distant blood relatives through Ishmael, son of Abraham. His road of escape led Moses to a well, where he saw some shepherds teasing a group of young girls trying to water their sheep. When Moses took the side of the girls, the shepherds ran off.

"I'll dip water for your sheep," Moses told the girls. When the girls returned home earlier than usual, their father Jethro asked "Why?" They told him about the strong Egyptian who helped them.

"Go invite him home for a meal."

Moses not only ate a meal, he was also invited to live in the tribe with them. They were a Bedouin tribe living in tents, following their sheep through the Sinai Peninsula. Within time, Moses married Zipporah, the daughter of Jethro, the priest of the people.

Moses was approximately 40 years old when he left Egypt. He possessed the greatest education in the world, but all he was doing was humbly leading sheep. That was because God wanted to add character to his head knowledge. What better teacher than sheep to make Moses patient, he spent 40 years learning leadership from animals called "dumb."

My Time to Pray

- Lord, You equip Your servants differently. You prepared Moses with a secular Egyptian training and with a biblical foundation from his mother.

- Thank You for my past that equipped me for service. Now I want to serve You as best I can, with the training that equipped me for service.

Exodus 3

GOD CALLS MOSES

Moses spent his life tending the sheep of Jethro, his father-in-law, a priest of Midian. As Moses led his sheep to the backside of the desert, he came to Sinai, the mountain of God in the Horeb range.

Lord, You spoke to Moses through the angel of the Lord in a burning bush, but the fire did not consume the bush. Moses went to see why the bush was not burned up. You saw that Moses had come to examine the bush. You called to Moses, "Moses…, Moses…" He answered, "Here am I." Lord, You said, "Don't come any closer, this is holy ground. Take your sandals off."

Lord, You said to Moses, "I am the God of your fathers, the God of Abraham, Isaac, and Jacob." Moses covered his face because he was afraid to look in Your face. You said, "I have seen the oppression of my people in Egypt. I have heard their cry to be released from their task masters. I know their pain. Therefore, I have come down to deliver them from the Egyptians and lead them to a large, spacious land that flows with milk and honey; now occupied by the Canaanites, the Hittites, the Amorites, the Perizzites, the Hivites, and the Jebusites.

Lord, You told Moses, "The anguish of the people of Israel has come to Me, and I have seen the oppression of the Egyptians, so I am going to send you to Pharaoh to deliver My people out of Egypt."

Moses said, "I am not a good representative to go to Pharaoh to deliver Your people."

Lord, You told Moses, "I will be with you. When you have brought My people out of Egypt, you will serve Me on Mount Sinai—this mountain."

Moses argued with God, saying, "When I come to the people of Israel to tell them, 'The God of your fathers has sent me to deliver you,' they will ask me Your name. What is Your name? What shall I say to them?"

Lord, You said to Moses, "'I AM THAT I AM,' is who I AM. You shall say to the leaders of Israel, 'I AM has sent me to you.'" Then You, Lord God, told Moses to announce, "The Lord God of your fathers, the God of Abraham, Isaac, and Jacob has sent Me to you. I AM is My eternal name. This is how you will remember Me from generation to generation."

Lord, when Moses gave excuses to escape serving You,
  You told him to use the power of Your name.

Lord, may I never give excuses to not follow You,
  May I use the power that is available to me.

Lord, You told Moses, "Go gather together the leaders of Israel and tell them, 'Adonai (Master), the God (Elohim) of your fathers, the God of Abraham, Isaac, and Jacob has appeared to me.' This is what He told me to tell you: 'I have seen your oppression by the Egyptians. I will lead you to the land of the Canaanites, the Hittites, the Amorites, the Perizzites, the Hivites, and the Jebusites. It is a land flowing with milk and honey.'"

Lord, You told Moses, "Get the leaders of the people of Israel to go with you to tell the king of the Egyptians, 'We want to go three days' journey into the desert to sacrifice to the Lord our God.'"

Lord, You told Moses, "The king of Egypt will not let the people of
Israel go unless he is forced to do so. So I will stretch my hand
toward Egypt to do miracles to make him willing to release My
people. After that, he will let them go. I will make the Egyptians
disposed toward the people of Israel so that the Egyptians will
not send them away empty handed. Every woman will ask her
Egyptian neighbor for articles of gold, silver, and clothing that
will dress the sons and daughters of Israel. That way, you will
plunder the Egyptians."

Lord, at first this looks like taking things
Under false pretenses;
But the Israelites were collecting the back wages
The Egyptians owed them for work done as slaves.

Lord, You always look after the needs of Your children;
Take care of me as You provided for Israel's new start.

Amen.

Exodus 4:1-31

GOD SENDS MOSES TO EGYPT

Moses answered God, "The twelve leaders of the tribes of the Israelites won't listen to me, nor will they believe me. They will rationalize, 'God did not appear to you.'"

Lord, You asked Moses, "What is in your hand?" Moses answered, "A shepherd's staff." You, Lord, told him, "Throw it on the ground." When Moses obeyed, it turned into a poisonous serpent. Moses recoiled. Then You, Lord, said, "Reach out and take up the snake by its tail." When Moses obeyed, it became a staff again. Lord, You told Moses, "This miracle will make the Israelite leaders believe that I—the Lord God of their fathers—have appeared to you and sent you to them."

Lord, You told Moses, "Place your right hand into your coat." When Moses obeyed and removed his hand, it was leprous, as white as snow. Then You told Moses, "Place your right hand back into your coat." Moses obeyed, and when he withdrew the hand, it was restored to healthy flesh. Then You said, "If they won't believe you because of the first miracle, use the second to convince them. If they won't believe the two miracles, then take fresh water from a river, pour it onto the ground and it will turn to blood on the dry land."

Moses still doubted if he could do the task. He gave another excuse, "I am a poor speaker. I stutter. My words come out slowly."

Lord, You answered Moses, "Who made your mouth? Who makes a person dumb, deaf, or blind? Isn't it I, Your Lord? Go do what I tell you, and I will be with your mouth."

Moses still refused saying, "Please, Lord, send someone else." God's anger boiled against Moses.

Lord, may I never offer excuses to You
So that You get angry at me.

Lord, I yield to Your will for my life,
I will wholeheartedly do what You command.

Lord, You asked Moses, "Don't you have a brother—Aaron—he is a good speaker. He is coming now to meet you. He will be happy to see you. You will speak to Aaron and give him the words to say. You will be the spokesman to the people, he will be your mouth. You will be My representative to him. Now, take this rod—the rod of God—for you will need it to do miracles."

Moses left the sheep and returned to his father-in-law, Jethro, and asked him, "Please let me go return to my brethren in Egypt to see if they are still alive." Jethro said, "Go in peace."

Lord, You reassured Moses, "Go back to Egypt because all the ones who wanted to execute you are dead."

Moses put his wife and sons on a donkey and headed to Egypt. He had the rod of God in his hand.

Lord, You told Moses, "When you appear before Pharaoh, do all the miracles I showed you. But I will harden Pharaoh's heart so that he will not let my people go. Then tell Pharaoh, 'God says, "Israel is my firstborn son, and you will not let my son go to worship Me, but you have refused to let him go. Therefore, I will kill your firstborn son."'"

Lord, You met Moses at the place of lodging and would have killed him, if his wife Zipporah had not taken a sharp stone and circumcised the sons. She threw the foreskins at Moses' feet saying, "You are a bloody bridegroom because of circumcision."

Lord, You told Aaron, "Go meet Moses in the desert." When they met,
Moses told Aaron everything that You, Lord, told him to do,
including the miracles You had ordered him to do. Then Moses
and Aaron gathered all the leaders of Israel. Aaron told them
everything that You, their God, had told Moses. Moses then did
Your miracles for them, and they believed. When the leaders
heard that You, their God, were coming to deliver them, they
bowed their heads in worship.

Lord, I worship You for Your help in my life,
Just as the Israeli leaders worshiped You.

May I always be grateful for Your presence in my life;
Lord God, thank You for delivering me.

Amen.

Exodus 3:1–4:18

The Story of God's Call to Moses

Date: 1491 B.C. ~ Place: Mount Sinai

"WHAT'S THIS?" Moses yelled audibly, but no one was there to
hear him—at least that's what 80-year-old Moses thought. He
didn't know that God was near to hear everything he said. Moses was
shocked to see a bush was burning with a crackly fire. But he shouldn't
have been surprised. Dry bushes in the desert burst into flame when
rubbed together by a hot wind, which produced spontaneous combus-
tion. Sometime they burst into flames, then burned to ashes. But this
bush was different—it didn't burn up.

Moses didn't know the bush represented the God of Israel. He didn't realize, "God is a consuming fire." Moses didn't know God's indignation was burning against the Egyptians.

"Why is this not burning up?" Moses cautiously crept closer to inspect this phenomenon. Then he heard a voice from the bush call his name,

"Moses...Moses..." his Hebrew training told him this could only be God, for God was calling him his Hebrew name. The 80-year-old answered, "Here am I."

The audible voice of God told Moses, "Don't come any closer...take off your shoes...you're standing on holy ground."

Moses had been searching for sheep on Mount Sinai, the mountain of God. This is the mountain where God will later give Moses the Ten Commandments. This is the mountain where thunder, lightning, fire, and smoke will announce God's presence.

When God told Moses not to come any closer, Moses fell with his face to the ground in obedience to the voice. The voice terrified Moses, then he heard God say,

"I am the God of your fathers, of Abraham, Isaac, and Jacob." God told Moses that He had seen the affliction of His people in Egypt, He heard their cry, and He knew their suffering. God told Moses,

"I am come down to deliver My people from Egypt, and will lead them to the Promised Land, flowing with milk and honey." Then God added the part that scared Moses,

"I will send you to Pharaoh to deliver My people from bondage."

Moses rejoiced in God's promise of deliverance, but the part about his return to Pharaoh frightened him. With the heat of the burning bush on his head, and his perspiring face in the sand, Moses argued with God, giving Him excuses why he shouldn't return to Egypt to free the Hebrew slaves,

"Who am I to do this job?" Moses told God, "I'm not good enough to do this task." Moses remembered he killed a man in Egypt. He didn't want to face Pharaoh again with a death sentence hanging over his head. God answered Moses' excuse.

"I'll go with you to deliver My people." When God tells someone He will go with the person, that should be enough. But Moses had another excuse why he shouldn't go. Even though he had the best education Egypt could give, Moses was not trained in Hebrew tradition. He said,

"When I tell the people of Israel that God sent me to deliver them, they will ask me your name. I do not know your name!"

God answered Moses, "My name means I AM THAT I AM. Go tell the Hebrews that JEHOVAH—the name that means the Self-Existing One—has sent you to them."

Moses still was not sure. He was 80 years old, and he was a loser. He had spent 40 years tending sheep in the desert. The Hebrews wouldn't remember him. The Hebrews in Egypt wouldn't follow him. Each of the 12 tribes had an elder, and the Hebrews followed the elder of each tribe. Moses told God,

"They won't listen to me; they won't believe You appeared to me; they won't follow me."

God saw the answer to Moses' excuse, He saw the rod of God in Moses' hand. God asked Moses, "What is in your hand?" It was his trusty walking stick that reminded him of Abraham, Isaac, and Jacob. Moses had gotten the shepherd's staff, the rod of God, in an unusual way. This was the staff with the signet of Abraham, Isaac, and Jacob carved into its top.

Moses had fought off wild animals with the stick and lifted fallen sheep with the staff. God commanded Moses, "Throw the stick on the ground."

The stick became a serpent instantly as it touched the sand. As the snake coiled to strike, Moses recoiled out of striking range, for it was a poisonous serpent.

"Take the snake by the tail," God instructed.

Moses knew a snake must be held behind its head; that way it couldn't strike you. He also knew it was dangerous to reach for its tail. Moses was afraid to touch the snake but had greater fear to disobey God. When he grabbed the snake, it became a stick again.

"Put your right hand in your bosom," God instructed Moses, and when he obeyed; his hand was covered with white leprous flakes. Leprosy—the flaking disease that makes a person unclean—the disease that eats away flesh, bringing premature death. Moses momentarily froze with thoughts of death. Then God instructed him,

"Replace your hand in your bosom," the hand became healthy, lively flesh like it had been. Moses fell on his face.

"O God, I know You can do miracles," he wept before God, but still he didn't want to return to Egypt. Moses offered yet another excuse to God, another excuse that was big in Moses' mind. "I can't speak—I stutter—they won't understand me."

God promised to be with Moses' mouth so he could speak to others. Every time God told Moses to go do the job, Moses had an excuse. Every time God answered Moses' excuse, Moses came up with another. Finally, Moses pleaded with God,

"Send someone else."

The anger of God burned against Moses, for God does not expect to be rejected. God expects faith and obedience. Then God said,

"Your brother Aaron is coming to see you, I will use his mouth to speak for you; but you must be the leader."

> Lord, Moses was Your choice to lead Israel,
>   But in unbelief Moses offered excuses.
>
> When You have a job for me to do,
>   I will not offer excuses, but I'll obey.
>
> Tell me what You want me to do;
>   I'll do it without excuses.
>
>   Amen.

Exodus 5

MOSES AND AARON SPEAK TO PHARAOH

Moses and Aaron came to meet Pharaoh and told him, "Here is what the Lord God of Israel says, 'Let My people go so they can worship Me in the desert.'"

Lord, the bottom line is always worship;
You want to free us from any habits and sins,
So we have a new freedom to worship You.

Lord, I pray for people in slavery
Everywhere and for all reasons,

That they may be free from their bondage
So they can worship You freely.

Pharaoh replied, "Who is this God that I should obey when He says, 'Let Israel go'? I don't know this God, and I won't let Israel go."

Moses and Aaron answered, "The God of the Hebrew people has met with us. We must go three days' journey into the desert to sacrifice to the Lord our God, otherwise He may send a plague on us or strike us with the sword."

The king of Egypt answered Moses and Aaron, "How dare you take these people away from their work! Get back to work. The population of the land has grown, yet you want them to stop work." That day Pharaoh ordered the slave masters and foremen to no longer provide straw for the bricks the Hebrews were making. "Make them gather their own straw, but they must produce the same amount of bricks. They spend too much time doing nothing, that's why they are begging to go sacrifice to their gods. Give them more work to keep them busy."

Lord, Pharaoh's attitude reminds me of satan's domination;
satan wants us in his bondage for his own pleasure.

Lord, I pray for freedom for me and others;
May we enjoy freedom to worship You.

The slave masters and foremen told the people what Pharaoh said. The Hebrews were sent to gather straw wherever they could find it, but their daily quota was not reduced. The slave masters kept pressing them to make their quotas as before. The foremen flogged them when they didn't meet their quotas.

The leaders of the Hebrews complained to Pharaoh, "Why are you treating your servants this way? No straw was given to us, yet the slave masters tell us to make our quota of bricks."

Pharaoh told them they were lazy because they asked to go into the desert to sacrifice to God. "Get back to work; no straw will be given to you, now get back to work—yet you must produce the full amount of bricks daily."

As the Hebrew leaders left, they met Moses and Aaron standing in the road and said to them, "The Lord will punish you because you have made Pharaoh and his servants hate us. You have put a sword in their hand to kill us."

Moses went into the presence of the Lord and said, "Lord, why have You treated Your people so badly? Why did You send me to Pharaoh? Ever since I went to Pharaoh to speak in Your name, Pharaoh has treated Your people terribly. You haven't delivered them as You promised."

Lord, may I never blame You for evil that befalls me,
      Nor for the bondage of satan,
      Nor for the adverse circumstances of my life.

Lord, help me see Your divine hand
      Working in the circumstances of my life.

Amen.

Exodus 6

PROMISE OF DELIVERANCE

Lord, You said to Moses, "Now you will see what I will do to Pharaoh. When he feels My mighty hand, he will drive Israel from Egypt. I am the Lord. I appeared to Abraham, Isaac, and Jacob by the name of God Almighty, *El Shaddai,* but I did not appear to them by My name Jehovah, I AM I AM. I have established My covenant to give them the land of Canaan, the land where their fathers wandered about and lived as foreigners. I have heard the groanings of the people of Israel whom the Egyptians persecute. I will deliver them and lead them to the Promised Land."

> *Lord, teach me the power of Your personal name;*
> > *I know You are the great I AM, You are God,*
> > *I worship You for Your greatness and power,*
> > *I cling to You for Your love and compassion when I hurt.*

Lord, You told Moses, "Say to the people of Israel, 'I am the Lord and redeem you by an outstretched arm and great judgments. I will take you as My people, and I will be Your God. Then you will know I am the Lord Your God who delivered you from the persecution of the Egyptians. I will bring you into the land which I swore to give to Abraham, Isaac, and Jacob. The land will be your inheritance; I am the Lord.'"

When Moses told the people of Israel what You said, they wouldn't listen because their spirit was crushed and their slavery was so terrible.

Lord, You told Moses, "Go tell Pharaoh, 'Let the people of Israel leave this land.'"

Moses answered You, Lord, "The people of Israel haven't listened to me, why should Pharaoh listen to me? I am a poor speaker."

Lord, You told Moses and Aaron, "Give an order to the people of Israel and Pharaoh that my people—the people of Israel—must come out of the land of Egypt."

These are the heads of their fathers' houses: The sons of Reuben, the firstborn of Israel, were Hanoch, Pallu, Hezron, and Carmi. And the sons of Simeon were Jemuel, Jamin, Ohad, Jachin, Zohar, and Shaul the son of a Canaanite woman. These are the names of the sons of Levi according to their generations: Gershon, Kohath, and Merari. And the years of the life of Levi were 137. The sons of Gershon were Libni and Shimi according to their families. And the sons of Kohath were Amram, Izhar, Hebron, and Uzziel. And the years of the life of Kohath were 133. The sons of Merari were Mahali and Mushi.

Now Amram took for himself Jochebed, his father's sister, as wife; and she bore him Aaron and Moses. And the years of the life of Amram were 137. The sons of Izhar were Korah, Nepheg, and Zichri. And the sons of Uzziel were Mishael, Elzaphan, and Zithri. Aaron took to himself Elisheba, daughter of Amminadab, sister of Naashon, as wife; and she bore him Nadab, Abihu, Eleazar, and Ithamar. And the sons of Korah were Assir, Elkanah, and Abiasaph. These are the families of the Korahites. Eleazar, Aaron's son, took for himself one of the daughters of Putiel as wife; and she bore him Phinehas. These are the heads of the fathers' houses of the Levites according to their families.

These are the same Aaron and Moses to whom the Lord said, "Bring out the people of Israel from the land of Egypt according to their armies." These are the ones who spoke to Pharaoh king of Egypt, to bring out the people of Israel from Egypt (Exod. 6:14-27).

Lord it was on this day when You spoke to Moses, "I am the Lord. Tell everything I say to you to Pharaoh, king of Egypt."

Moses still maintained, "I am such a poor speaker, Pharaoh will not listen to me."

Lord, just as Moses hesitated to do Your will,
Sometimes I am confused and fearful
To obey You and do what is right.

Forgive my disobedience and use me;
I want to be Your servant.

Amen.

Exodus 7

THE ROD BECOMES A SNAKE

Lord, you said to Moses, "I have put you in My place before Pharaoh.
Aaron, your brother, will be your prophet. You must say everything I command you to say, and Aaron, your brother, will speak
to Pharaoh to tell him to let My people—the people of Israel—
leave this land. But I will harden Pharaoh's heart, even as I
increase the signs and miracles I will do in Egypt. But Pharaoh
will not listen to you. Then I will lay my hand on Egypt and
judge them so I can bring My people of Israel out of Egypt.
Then the Egyptians will know I am the Lord when I stretch out
my hand to bring the people of Israel out of Egypt."

Lord, I feel like Moses, I am so weak to do Your work,
Yet, I yield myself to You,
Fill me with Your power.

If anything happens in my service,
It is because of Your working in my life.

Moses and Aaron went into Pharaoh and did as God commanded.
Aaron threw his rod down in front of Pharaoh, and it turned
into a snake. But Pharaoh called on his magicians and sorcerers
and they also did the same thing using their enchantments. Each
man's rod turned into a snake. Then Aaron's staff swallowed up
theirs. But Pharaoh didn't listen to Moses because God had
hardened his heart.

Lord, I know satan has supernatural power,
But greater is Christ in me
Then satan who is the god of this world.

Exodus 7:14-25

The First Plague—Water Turns to Blood

Lord, You told Moses, "Pharaoh is stubborn; he refuses to let the people of Israel go. Meet Pharaoh in the morning as he goes out to the water. Stand on the riverbank to challenge him with your rod that was turned into a snake."

Lord, You told Moses to tell Pharaoh, "The God of the Hebrews commands you 'to let My people go so they can worship Me in the desert.' Until now you would not listen. This will show you that I speak for the Lord. I will take the staff in my hand and strike the water and it will turn to blood. The fish in the river will die, the river will stink, and the Egyptians will not be able to drink from it."

Lord, You told Moses to have Aaron stretch his staff over the rivers, canals, pools, and reservoirs so that the water in them would turn to blood. There will be blood throughout Egypt, even in wooden vessels and stone pots.

Moses and Aaron did exactly as the Lord commanded. Moses struck the water in sight of Pharaoh and his servants, and all the water in the river turned to blood. The fish died, and the river stank so that the Egyptians couldn't drink its water. There was blood throughout the land. The magicians did the same with their enchantments. So Pharaoh's heart was hardened, and he didn't listen to them. Pharaoh turned and went back into his palace and didn't think about this again.

For the next seven days, the Egyptians dug around the river for water to drink, because they couldn't drink the water of the river.

Lord, the Egyptians worshiped the Nile as a god,
But You were victorious over their god.

Lord, I worship You for Your judgmental power;
Be merciful to me and protect me by Your love.

Amen.

Exodus 8

THE SECOND PLAGUE—FROGS

Lord, You told Moses to go tell Pharaoh, "The Lord said, 'Let My people go so they can worship Me. If you refuse, I will smite all of Egypt with frogs. The river will swarm with frogs. They will enter your palace, your bedroom, and your bed. They will enter the houses of your servants and all Egyptians. They will be in your ovens and food preparation places. The frogs will jump all over you, your people and your servants.'"

Lord, You said to Moses, "Tell Aaron to stretch out his staff over all the rivers, canals, and ponds to bring the frogs out of the waters into all of Egypt." Aaron stretched out his rod over the waters, and frogs overran the land of Egypt.

But the magicians duplicated the feat with their incantations and brought frogs out of the water.

Pharaoh called for Moses and Aaron and told them, "Pray to the Lord to take away the frogs from me and my people, and I will let your people go and sacrifice to the Lord."

Moses answered Pharaoh, "Not only will I pray for the frogs to go away, but you can choose the time when they will leave and stay in the rivers."

Pharaoh said, "Tomorrow."

> *Lord, the world is so quick to seek physical relief from sufferings,*
> *But I am slow to seek relief for spiritual sufferings.*

Lord, teach me to be quick in confessing my sin,
And be just as swift to seek Your presence.

Moses answered, "It will happen at the time you suggested, so you will know that the Lord our God has no equal."

Moses and Aaron left Pharaoh's presence, then Moses cried to the Lord for the frogs to leave.

Lord, You did as Moses prayed, and the frogs died in the houses, courtyards, and fields. The Egyptians gathered them in piles and the land of Egypt stunk. But Pharaoh hardened his heart toward You when he saw relief from the frogs. He would not listen to Moses and Aaron, just as You said.

Exodus 8:16-19

The Third Plague—Lice

Lord, You told Moses to instruct Aaron to reach out his staff to strike the dust of the ground so that it became lice throughout all Egypt. Aaron did as Moses told him, and lice swarmed on the people and animals. Lice came from dust throughout Egypt.

The magicians tried to use the incantations to produce lice, but they couldn't do it. Lice were everywhere, on the people and animals. They told Pharaoh, "This is the finger of God." But Pharaoh hardened his heart toward them, just as the Lord said they would do.

Lord, the work of Your finger is so obviously apparent
That the world realizes that only You do miracles.

Lord, help me clearly see Your work in my life,
And praise You for its power.

Exodus 8:20-32

The Fourth Plague—Insects

The Lord told Moses, "Get up early in the morning to stand before
Pharaoh as he goes to the water and tell him, 'The Lord says to
you, "Let my people go so they can worship Me. If you don't I'll
send swarms of insects on you, your people, your servants, and
into your houses. Your houses will be full of insects, but I will
set aside the land of Goshen where My people live. No swarms
will be there, so you will know I am the Lord as I venerate
Myself in this land. I will separate your people from My people,
and this sign will occur tomorrow."''"

Lord, You did it just as you promised. The following day, terrible
swarms of insects went into Pharaoh's palaces and into the
homes of all the Egyptians. The insects ruined the entire land of
Egypt.

Pharaoh called for Moses and Aaron to tell them, "Go sacrifice to your
God in Egypt."

Moses replied, "We can't sacrifice in Egypt because the animal we sacrifice to God is an abomination to the Egyptians. They would
stone us and kill us if we worship with an animal they consider
abominable. No! We must go three days into the desert to sacrifice as the Lord our God has commanded us to do."

Lord, I thank You that Moses didn't compromise what You
ordered;
May I always worship You in the way You order.

Pharaoh told Moses, "I will allow you to go sacrifice to God in the desert, but don't go very far. When you get there, pray for me."

Moses answered, "I will leave you and intercede to the Lord so that tomorrow the swarms of insects will leave you, your people, and your houses. But don't be deceitful and keep us from going to worship the Lord." Moses left Pharaoh and interceded to the Lord.

Lord, You did what Moses asked and removed the swarms of insects from Pharaoh, his servants, and the Egyptians. Not a single one remained, but Pharaoh again hardened his heart and refused to let Your people go.

Lord, the world only thinks of removal of suffering;
May my motives always be pure in worship,
May I always seek Your glory in my worship.

Amen.

Exodus 9

THE FIFTH PLAGUE—SICKNESS

Lord, You sent Moses to tell Pharaoh what You said, "The God of the Hebrews says for you to let My people go so they can worship Me. If you refuse, My hand will fall on all the livestock—on horses, donkeys, camels, cattle, and flocks. They will catch a serious sickness, and many will die. But I will distinguish between the animals of the Egyptians and the people of Israel. None of Israel's animals will die. Tomorrow I will do this at the same time."

The following day the Lord did it. The livestock of Egypt died, but none of the animals belonging to the people of Israel died. Pharaoh sent and found out none of the animals belonging to the people of Israel died. But still Pharaoh's heart was hard. He wouldn't let the Israelites go.

Lord, I know You allow sickness
To call us to Yourself.

May I always worship You
In my hour of pain.

Exodus 9:8-12

The Sixth Plague—Boils

Lord, You told Moses and Aaron, "Take a handful of ashes from a furnace and throw them into the air in front of Pharaoh. The ashes will become dust that will turn into sores on people and animals throughout Egypt."

So Moses did as You told him and threw the ashes into the air in front of Pharaoh and sores broke out on people and animals. The magicians couldn't even stand before Moses. They had sores just like the other Egyptians. But Pharaoh wouldn't listen to Moses and Aaron because the Lord had hardened his heart, just as the Lord told Moses He would do.

Lord, Your hand of judgment never completely destroys us;
You allow pain to push us to the point of desperation.

Lord, You want to reveal Your glory through our sufferings
Because one utterance of praise while we suffer,

Is greater than a thousand words of praise when we are
well.

Exodus 9:13-35

The Seventh Plague—Hail

Lord, You told Moses to get up early to stand before Pharaoh and tell him, "The Lord says, 'Let My people go so they can worship Me. I am sending plagues on you and Egypt so you will know there is no one like Me on earth. By now I could have stretched out my hand with such severe plagues that you would have been destroyed from off the face of the earth. But I have allowed you to live so you can see My power and My name will be recognized throughout the world.

"Since you are challenging My power, tomorrow at this time I will send a heavy hailstorm unlike anything Egypt has ever experienced. Quickly go and get all your livestock indoors, and everything else you want to preserve, for hail will fall on every animal and human being left outside, and they will die.'"

Those among Pharaoh's servants who feared the Lord escaped because they brought their livestock indoors. They also sought protection from the hail. Those who didn't regard the word of the Lord left their servants and livestock in the field, where they died.

Lord, You told Moses, "Stretch forth your hand toward the sky so hail will fall throughout Egypt, falling on people, animals, and everything growing throughout Egypt."

Moses did what the Lord commanded and the Lord sent rain, thunder, lightning, and hail on the land of Egypt. It was the worst hailstorm in the history of Egypt. The lightning struck throughout Egypt and the hail fell on everything in the field—people, animals, and plants, and broke the trees. But in the land of Goshen where Israel lived, there was no hail.

Pharaoh called for Moses and Aaron and said, "This time I have sinned. The Lord is righteous, I and my people are wrong. Pray to the Lord, we can't take this thunderstorm and hail any longer. I will let you go, you don't have to stay here any longer."

Moses answered, "When I leave to go out into the city, as soon as I spread my hands to the Lord, the thunder and hail will stop. Then you will realize that the Lord owns the earth. But I know you and your servants still won't fear the Lord."

The flax and the barley were destroyed because it was time to harvest them. But the wheat and rye were not hurt because their harvest is much later.

Moses left Pharaoh to raise his hand to Jehovah. The thunderstorm and hail stopped raining. When Pharaoh saw the thunderstorm end, he sinned by hardening his heart again against the Lord and

refused to let the people of Israel go, just as the Lord told Moses
he would do.

Lord, You send rain into our lives to make us appreciate sunny
days;
We consider rain oppressive and restrictive,
But rain gives life to the food we eat.

You send us rain within Your plan and providence;
Help me see Your purpose and submit to Your will.

Amen.

Exodus 10

THE EIGHTH PLAGUE—LOCUSTS

Lord, You said to Moses, "Go tell Pharaoh that I have hardened the hearts of him and his servants to manifest the signs among the Egyptians so you and all Israel can tell your children and grandchildren what I did in Egypt. That way everyone will know that I am the Lord."

Moses and Aaron told Pharaoh, "The Lord wants to know how much longer will you refuse to yield to Him. He wants you to let His people go so they can worship Him. If you refuse to let them go by tomorrow about this time, He will send locusts into Egypt. They will be so thick you won't be able to see the ground. They will eat everything the hail didn't destroy, including the trees. They will fill your houses, plus the houses of your servants and all the Egyptians. This plague of locusts will be worse than anything seen by your fathers and grandfathers. It will be worse than anything seen in Egypt." Then Moses turned and left Pharaoh.

The servants said to Pharaoh, "How much longer will Moses torment us; don't you realize Egypt is being destroyed?"

Lord, help me see that sin destroys the good things of life;
Help me look beyond Your arm of judgment
To see the reason for the bad things that happen.

Moses and Aaron were brought before Pharaoh, who said to them, "Go worship the Lord Your God, but I want to know who is going."

Moses said to Pharaoh, "We will go with our young and old, our sons and daughters, our flocks and our herds, for we will celebrate a feast to our Lord."

Pharaoh answered, "Let the Lord go with you, but I will not let your children go with you. It's clear you are planning evil. Only the men may go to worship the Lord. That's what you want." Then Pharaoh drove them out of his presence.

Lord, You said to Moses, "Stretch forth your hand over Egypt so that locusts may swarm over the land to eat every green leaf the hail hasn't killed." When Moses reached out his rod, an east wind from the Lord blew over Egypt all day and all night. The locusts covered the land of Egypt more severely than it had ever been before. The locusts were so thick the ground looked black. They ate every growing leaf and fruit left from the hail. Nothing remained.

Pharaoh quickly summoned Moses and Aaron, telling them, "I have sinned against the Lord your God and against you. I beg you, intercede to the Lord so He will take away this deadly plague."

Moses left Pharaoh to intercede to the Lord. The Lord answered so that a strong wind blew toward the west, blowing the locusts into the Red Sea. Not one locust remained in Egypt. Even then Pharaoh hardened his heart as God had said, and he wouldn't let the people of Israel go.

Lord, You are the God of the winds,
You allow the winds to blow good things to me;
Thank You, God, for all the blessings of life.

You allow the winds to blow evil across my path;
Help me see Your plan in all things.

Amen.

Exodus 10:21-29

The Ninth Plague—Darkness

Lord, You said to Moses, "Reach your hand to the sky. There will be
thick darkness over the land of Egypt—so thick and black it can
be felt." Moses did as You commanded, and a thick blackness
covered Egypt for three days. No one could see anything, nor
could they travel anywhere. But You, Lord, provided light in the
home of the people of Israel.

Pharaoh called for Moses and told him, "Go worship the Lord, take
your children with you, but leave your flocks and herds behind."

Moses answered, "No, we must have our flocks and herds with us. We
will not leave a hoof behind because to worship properly, we
must have our herds and livestock with us, because we don't
know which one meets the qualification for sacrifices and burnt
offerings."

But Pharaoh hardened his heart as the Lord had said. He would not let
them go. Pharaoh commanded them to leave and said they
would see his face no more, because if they saw his face, they
would die.

Moses answered, "I will do as you say; I will see your face no more."

Lord, there are many people today who are like Pharaoh,
They know the truth of Your word,
But they will not obey You or believe in You.

I pray for those I know who are like Pharaoh;
Convict them of their sin,
And bring them to saving faith.

Amen.

Exodus 5:1–11:10

The Story of Let My People Go

Date: 1491 B.C. ~ Place: Pharaoh's Palace, Egypt

The Egyptian city was bigger than Moses remembered. It had been 40 years since he saw the temples built to the gods of Egypt, but the greatest temple was built to Pharaoh, the one who acted as god to all Egyptians. Pharaoh Thutmosis III was dead, the one who wanted to eliminate Moses as a rival to the throne. No one in Egypt remembered Moses was a murderer; there was no warrant for his arrest.

Amenhotep II was now Pharaoh, a weak man with water in his veins; he couldn't make a decision and stick to it. But weak men are sometimes dangerous when embarrassed; they turn on their enemies with vengeance. There was no way that Moses knew Amenhotep II would be his enemy.

Moses and Aaron stood in line to see Pharaoh in the Great Hall, their voices echoed off its white marble walls. They were waiting for an audience with Pharaoh. Moses wrongly supposed he could demand that the Hebrews be freed—and it would happen. When his time came to speak, Moses told Amenhotep, "God said, 'Let my people go!'"

Amenhotep laughed loud enough for his whole court to hear his mockery; then Pharaoh asked,

"Who is this Lord that I should listen to Him? I don't know this God of yours. I will not let the Hebrews go."

Moses was thrown out of the Great Hall. Moses expected God to motivate Pharaoh to release the Hebrews; but rather than softening Amenhotep's heart, it got harder.

That night Moses tried praying to God, he didn't know what to ask. He was confused. Then God spoke to Moses in the still of the night, telling the 80-year-old shepherd that He had made Pharaoh stubborn so that He would be shown powerful by His miracles. God told Moses that He would send a number of disasters on Pharaoh to humiliate the Egyptian gods and crush the nation. Then God promised,

"I will show the Egyptians my power, convincing them to let my people go. Then they will know I am God."

When next Moses entered the Great Hall for an audience with Pharaoh, Moses told his brother Aaron to throw down his shepherd's stick. It became a serpent in front of Pharaoh and his wise men. Not to be out-done, Pharaoh snapped his fingers; his magicians had power with the dark spirits. They threw down their sticks, and just like Aaron's miracle, their sticks also became serpents. But Aaron's rod that became a snake ate their serpents. Pharaoh's mean eyes were not impressed with the miracle. He surveyed the scene, calling what Moses did magic. Pharaoh left the Great Hall refusing to grant Moses' request to let God's people go.

The following day, Pharaoh's worshiping entourage followed him down the great marble steps leading into the Nile River for his ceremonial purification. This was Pharaoh's way of deifying the river and receiving authority back from it. There were always thousands to watch and cheer Pharaoh's every move. Standing on a distant bank, Moses yelled out to Pharaoh over the quiet waters of the inlet,

"The Lord sent me to tell you to let His people go, but since you refuse, I will strike the water with my rod and the waters of Egypt shall become blood."

Moses raised his rod so Pharaoh and all the officials could see; as he struck the water it slowly became blood. Then, according to the prediction of Moses, all the waters turned to blood—the river, the canals, the reservoirs, and water in the pots in their houses. Amenhotep refused to release the Israelite slaves. It took seven days for fresh water to flow from upstream down the Nile to the place where Pharaoh's palace was located.

Moses was responsible for a number of other miraculous judgments on Egypt just like this one. Frogs came out of the marshes to invade the people's homes, then gnats spread out over Egypt like the dust that blows in their sandstorms. Next insects swarmed into the area, making life miserable.

Each time God sent a plague on the Egyptians, Pharaoh promised to let the Hebrews go into the wilderness to worship their God. But then when the plague was lifted, Pharaoh hardened his heart, refusing to release God's people.

The next plagues didn't affect the Hebrews. God punished only the Egyptians. Moses warned Pharaoh that God would send a deadly disease to kill animals and livestock. Again Pharaoh hardened his heart, and the disease swept across Egypt, but none of the Hebrews' animals died. In the sixth plague, Moses threw soot from a kiln into the air; as the winds carried it over the land, people developed boils wherever the soot touched them. Even Pharaoh's magicians couldn't stand before him because of their boils. Still Pharaoh remained obstinate toward God.

When Moses promised hail would kill the animals, the Hebrews and many officials of Pharaoh's courts ran to get their cattle inside out of danger. Those who refused to believe Moses saw the hail kill their animals, strip the trees of leaves, and destroy their crops in the fields. Pharaoh's heart remained hardened.

Next God sent a strong east wind that brought swarms of locusts that ate everything not destroyed by hail. The ninth plague was three days of thick darkness over all Egypt, except in Goshen where the Hebrews had light. Instead of softening Pharaoh's attitude, each plague made his heart harder; he told Moses this last time,

"You will never see my face again."

My Time to Pray

- Lord, most of the time I don't see the contest between You and satan in this world.

- Give me faith to trust You in good days and bad; give me faith to change the things I can change; give me patience to endure the things I can't change. Amen.

Exodus 11

THE TENTH PLAGUE— DEATH OF THE FIRSTBORN

Lord, You said to Moses, "I will send one more plague on Pharaoh and Egypt; after that he will let you leave. But more than that, Pharaoh will make you leave. Tell the people for every one of them to request gifts (overdue wages) from their neighbors, gold, silver, and jewelry.

The Hebrews were generally liked by the Egyptians. Pharaoh's servants and the Egyptians highly regarded the man Moses.

Moses said to Pharaoh, "The Lord says at midnight I will go throughout Egypt and all the firstborn in Egypt will die, from the firstborn of Pharaoh who sits on the throne to the firstborn of a slave girl doing the most menial task, including the firstborn of the livestock. There will be a terrible wailing throughout Egypt, nothing like anything that's ever been heard before. No one will hate Israel; not even a dog will growl against them. Everyone will realize that the Lord has made a difference between Israel and the children of Egypt. Your servants—those who serve Pharaoh— will come bow before me saying, 'Please leave, you and all the people of Israel.' When Israel leaves, I will go out with them." Then Moses angrily left the presence of Pharaoh.

Lord, You reinforced Moses, "Pharaoh will be stubborn so that more of My power will be shown in the land of Egypt."

Moses and Aaron had done all of these wonders and signs before
Pharaoh, but he wouldn't let the people of Israel go because of
his hardened heart.

Lord, taking the life of the firstborn seems cruel,
But not when I consider the greatness of evil
That pushed You to that judgment.

Lord, You gave the life of Your Firstborn—Jesus Christ;
His suffering seemed so severe for the Sinless One,
But not when I consider the greatness of evil.

Amen.

Exodus 12

THE FIRST PASSOVER

Lord, You told Moses and Aaron that from now on their calendar would begin with this event—the Passover and Israel's deliverance from Egypt. Lord, You told Moses, "On the tenth day of this month, each man must take a lamb for his family—one per household—but if the family is small, a family may share with another family in their neighborhood."

Lord, You described the Passover lamb. "It must be one year old, either a male sheep or goat, with no defects. They must keep it until the fourteenth day of the month, then each family must slaughter its own lamb. They are to take some of its blood and smear it on both sides of the doorposts and on top of the door frame of the house where the lamb will be eaten. The lamb must be roasted in fire with bitter herbs and unleavened bread (matzah). The meat must never be eaten raw or boiled, but roasted in fire. Roast it with its head, legs, and internal organs. Don't let any of it remain till the morning. If it is not entirely eaten, burn it up completely."

Lord, You spoke in pictures through the Passover lamb;
Always help me see the LAMB who takes away my sin.

Lord, when I celebrate the Communion table,
Help me look beyond bread and cup to see Jesus.

Lord, You told them how to eat the Passover, "Eat it with your belt tightened, your shoes on, and your walking stick in your hand as though you're going on a long trip. Eat it hurriedly for it is the Lord's Passover."

Lord, You declared, "That night I will pass through the land of Egypt to execute judgment against the gods of Egypt. I will kill the first-born of all families, both men and animals. I am the Lord. The blood you have smeared on your doors will be a sign. When I see the blood I will pass over you. The plague of death will not touch you."

Lord, You commanded, "From now on you will celebrate this day as a Passover feast to Me. For seven days you must eat only bread made without yeast (matzah, unleavened bead). On the very first day of Passover, remove all yeast from your houses. Anyone who eats bread baked with yeast from the first to the seventh day is cut off from Israel. On the first and seventh day have an assembly set aside to worship Me. Do no work on these days except what must be done, including the preparation of food."

Lord, You wanted Your people to celebrate the feast of Passover to remind them of the power You used to bring Israel out of Egypt. This festival was to be a permanent feast to be celebrated from generation to generation. From the evening of the fourteenth day until the evening of the twenty-first day, they were to eat unleavened bread. During the seven days, no trace of leaven must be found in their homes. This requirement is for both foreigners and those born in their homes. Lord, You emphasized, "I repeat, eat unleavened bread at Passover wherever you live."

Moses gathered the leaders of Israel and told them, "Have each family select a lamb and set it apart. Then slaughter it and drain its blood into a basin. Then take a cluster of leaves and dip it in the blood, and sprinkle it on both sides of the door frame and on its top. No one must go out the door until morning for the Lord will pass through to kill the firstborn in each Egyptian family, but when He sees the blood on your house and over the door, He will not allow the death angel to enter your home.

Lord, those died who were not covered with the blood;
>   *I know my sins are covered by the blood of Christ;*
>   *I pray for those reading this book whose sins are not covered.*

Lord, You told Your people, "Keep these instructions forever. When You come into the land I have promised you, continue to celebrate this feast. When your children ask, 'What does all this mean?' tell them, 'It is the celebration of the Lord's Passover, for when the Lord visited the homes of the Egyptians with death, He passed over our homes. Though God killed the firstborn of the Egyptians, He spared our families.'"

When the people heard the instruction of the Lord, they bowed their heads in worship. Then they did just as Moses had instructed them.

At midnight, the Lord killed the firstborn of all the land, from the firstborn son of Pharaoh who sat on the throne to the firstborn of the prisoner in the dungeon.

Pharaoh and his officials and all the Egyptians awoke during the night when excruciating cries were heard. There wasn't any home without someone dead in it.

Lord, I know You will judge the unsaved in hell;
>   *Help me pray so intensely that I'll shed tears,*
>   *So they won't shed tears throughout eternity.*

Pharaoh sent for Moses and Aaron during the night, "Leave immediately," he demanded, "both you and all your people, go sacrifice to the Lord as you requested. Take your flocks and herds and get out of here." Then Pharaoh had one last request, "But bless me before you go." All the Egyptians urged the Israelites to leave quickly, exclaiming, "Before we're all dead."

Israel took their dough from their mixing bowls before it became leaven, wrapped it in cloth, and carried it with them when they left. The people did as Moses instructed and asked their neighbors for articles of clothing, gold, and silver. This moved the hearts of the Egyptians, and they gave them the equivalent of unpaid wages for all the work Israel did for the nation. So like a victorious army, they plundered the Egyptians.

The people of Israel left Ramases and headed for Succoth. There were about 600,000 men (families) walking on foot, not counting the wives and children. Many people not fully Israelites (Gentiles who married into Israel) went with them, plus flocks and herds. When they stopped to eat, they baked bread from the unleavened dough they brought with them. The Israelites had lived in Egypt 430 years, and they left on the last day of the 430th year. This was the night the Lord set aside to bring His people out of Egypt, so Israel celebrates Passover throughout the generations.

Lord, You gave the commandment that no foreigner may eat the Passover lamb, but any foreigner who is circumcised may eat it. They will be treated as those born in an Israelite family. But no uncircumcised male may ever eat the Passover. The people followed Your instructions and that very day You began leading them out of Egypt, tribe by tribe.

Lord, Your victory always comes;
  Help me to be patient in times of persecution,
  Knowing You will eventually reward Your servants.

Lord, You love to reward Your servants with good things;
  Help me look beyond my difficulties

To see the good days You've prepared for me on earth or in Heaven.

Amen.

Exodus 12

The Story of the First Passover

Date: 1491 B.C. ~ Place: Egypt

Pharaoh said he never wanted to see Moses' face again. After nine miracles, this tenth miracle was enough. It was only the constraining hand of God that kept Pharaoh from killing Moses and Aaron. Or maybe it was his fear of death. Pharaoh had seen the mighty hand of God. He believed in the punishment of God but was not willing to recognize the Lord was the Creator God—Lord over the false gods of Egypt—surely, not Lord of Pharaoh's life.

But God knew what He would do. He told Moses that the tenth plague would be the last and most serious. The last plague would be so devastating that Pharaoh not only would let them go, "Pharaoh will command you to leave."

God promised that a death angel would pass over the land to strike the oldest child in each family. Each family was told to sacrifice a young lamb or goat, then sprinkle its blood over the sides and top of the door. God promised, "When I see the blood protecting your house, the death angel will pass over you."

When the sun went down, a father gathered his Hebrew family around a small, fleecy lamb; it was the only lamb they possessed. But the father wanted to obey God because the plagues were grim reminders that God was serious about their deliverance. The father placed both hands on the head of the lamb, then prayed,

"O God of Abraham, Isaac, and Jacob, we confess our sins...we repent of our sins...we ask for forgiveness for our sins." This prayer was for everyone in his family.

Then the father prayed for each individual in order, confessing the sins of his wife, his sons, then his daughters. When the father placed his hand on the head of the lamb, this was symbolically transferring their sins to the lamb; then the lamb was killed, and its blood was caught in a bowl. The children watched as the father smeared blood on the top and sides of the door of the home. The oldest son nodded his head in approval, believing the death angel would not take his life because the blood was applied. They all believed what God had said,

"When I see the blood, I will pass over you."

When the family went inside the house, Mother instructed the children, "Get dressed for a long journey." Everyone packed their belongings, for they knew their slavery days were over. They were thinking,

Freedom!

The family gathered around the table to eat roasted lamb. The oldest son remarked, "We usually sit down to eat—why are we standing and why are we dressed?" The father answered, "The Lord instructed us that when we eat the Passover meal, be ready to march because the Lord will lead us to freedom." A little one remarked, "The bread tastes funny," referring to the unleavened bread. The mother answered,

"We put yeast in flour to make bread fluffy and tasty. It takes time for yeast to raise the dough. Since God told us to be ready to march at any moment, this bread doesn't have any yeast. God wants us to eat unleavened bread so we will remember to be ready to leave at any time."

"We must not go out of our house during the night," the father warned his children. Fully dressed and with his walking stick in hand, the father and his family waited indoors. This was a night they wouldn't forget.

Then they heard a shriek from one direction, it was a scream they didn't expect. Moans then followed the cry. They heard the wails of death. Just as professional moaners announced to the community the death in a family, these cries drifting through the quiet of night were real—not paid mourners, but the anguished cry that death had visited Egyptian homes to take their firstborn.

Death visited Pharaoh's palace. The only son born to Amenhotep died. The lofty privileges of Pharaoh hadn't spared him the agony of death. Pharaoh bowed his head to hide his face, he wrung his hands. He kept torturing himself, asking,

"The God of the Hebrews sent plagues to tell me to let His people go, but I wouldn't listen. Their God told me He would send an angel of death to strike down the firstborn in every family. Why did I think God would bypass me?"

Pharaoh sent for Moses before the sun was up, demanding he come immediately. There was no arrogance in Amenhotep's face, only the hollow countenance of a beaten foe. With the little authority he had left, Pharaoh commanded,

"Go...." He pointed east toward the Hebrews' Promised Land. "Leave us...take your families and take your possessions...go serve the Lord as you requested!"

As Moses turned to leave the Great Hall, Pharaoh stopped him for one last request. "But give me your blessing as you leave."

Excitement spread from one Hebrew family to another, "Get ready, we're going today." Moses had instructed each family to visit their Egyptian neighbors, for the Egyptians would give treasures for their journey. The Egyptians were glad to give the Hebrews anything to get rid of the Seminites from Asia—the people who looked differently, acted differently, and worshiped only one God, a God different from the Egyptians' gods. The Egyptians with one accord said,

"Leave us before we all die."

The Hebrews gathered at the Great Triumphant Gate to the city—the gate through which victorious Egyptian armies returned from war to display the treasures they won in battle—but the Israelites were leaving through their victory gate, carrying their treasures from the defeated Egyptians. On this day of irony, God's people triumphantly left through Egypt's gate of victory.

The sun shone magnificently as the Hebrews continued to gather at the Triumphant Gate. Hebrew families stretched from one hill to another— far as the eye could see—a thousand times thousands of people ready to march, by count over 600,000 men plus women and children. Then the ram's horn sounded, everyone heard and they all laughed in response. For a lifetime they waited for this moment. A cry of laughter and rejoicing erupted, drowning out the moans in the Egyptian homes grieving for their dead. Moses lifted his shepherd's stick—the rod that turned water to blood—when the people saw the uplifted rod of God and heard the ram's horn, they turned their backs to Pharaoh and Egypt; their faces toward a new life of freedom. The multitude began walking away from their slavery.

> *Lord, freedom is a wonderful experience;*
> *I want to be free from all bondage*
> *In the victory that Jesus gives.*

> *Lord, I know I won't be completely free until Heaven;*
> *Help me see in small victories on this earth*
> *The greatness of freedom I'll see in Heaven.*

> *Amen.*

Exodus 13

REMEMBERING THE PASSOVER

Lord, You said to Moses, "In contrast to the firstborn of Egypt that was killed on Passover night," You said, "Dedicate the firstborn of every Israelite family to Me because they are Mine." You wanted their lives to serve and worship You.

Moses then said to the people, "Also, remember this day that we leave the slavery of Egypt because the Lord by the might of His hand has delivered you from bondage (do not eat any bread with yeast). Also, remember when the Lord brings you into a land flowing with milk and honey that He promised to our ancestors, that day must be celebrated as an anniversary of our exodus. In the month of Abib (March or early April), we will eat only unleavened bread for seven days and on the seventh day, we will celebrate with a great feast to the Lord. During that week we must have no yeast in our houses."

Moses commanded, "On that day each year explain to your children why you celebrate in the way you do. Remind them the Lord delivered us from slavery in Egypt. This visible reminder will be like a sign branded on your hand or between your eyes, so that you keep the Lord's instruction (Torah) in your minds and on your lips.

Lord, I pray for my children and grandchildren
That they may follow Christ in every way;
Help them know You as I know You.

Lord, may my children stand on my shoulders
And reach higher for greater spiritual blessings.

During these celebrations all firstborn sons and firstborn animals must be dedicated to the Lord with the sacrifice of a lamb. As an illustration, you can dedicate a firstborn donkey by sacrificing a lamb in its place. But if you don't do it, you must break the animal's neck.

If during these celebrations, a child asks, "What does this mean?" Remind him that with a mighty hand the Lord redeemed us out of Egypt, out of the bonds of slavery. When Pharaoh refused to let us go, the Lord killed all the firstborn of Egypt, humans and animals. These actions will be the sign that reminds you the Lord delivered us."

After Pharaoh let the people of Israel go, God did not lead them on the king's highway that ran along the sea toward the Promised Land. The war-like Philistines were there and if Israel faced war, they might change their minds and return to Egypt.

Lord, You led Your people to take a right-hand turn into the desert toward the Red Sea. The people of Israel left Egypt like a victorious marching army.

Moses took the bones of Joseph with him because Joseph had made the sons of Israel swear they would take his bones with them when they left Egypt. Joseph knew one day God would lead Israel out of Egypt to the Promised Land.

Israel traveled from Succoth to Ethom and set up camp on the edge of the desert. The Lord guided them by a column of clouds (Shekinah) during the day and a column of fire at night. That way they could travel in the daylight or at night. The Shekinah cloud did not leave their sight.

Lord, just as You led Israel by a Shekinah cloud,
Lead me by the instruction from Scripture.

Protect and guide me on my way.

Amen.

Exodus 13

The Story of Remembering the Passover

Date: 1491 B.C. ~ Place: Leaving Egypt

The mob of celebrating people swaggered away from the city of Raamses—families herding cows, mothers yelling at playful children, young men helping the elderly—they traveled all morning; over two million pilgrims walking away from the Triumphant Gate—laughing, boasting, weeping for joy—an unlikely scene of conquering heroes. By noontime they were out of sight of the city. The ram's horn sounded, slowing the multitude to a stop; it was time to eat. Moses stood upon a high rock, high enough for all to see, and he announced to the great crowd,

"This day we shall remember forever…we shall forever call it *Passover*." Moses told them that from now on, they would re-structure their calendar to begin each new year on *Passover*. This would be the most important day in the year of their new nation. They would celebrate it by eating bread without yeast to remember the great deliverance that God had given to them. Moses reminded the multitude,

"God has promised to us and to our ancestors a land flowing with milk and honey."

The people erupted into a cheer so loud and long that Moses couldn't quiet them until they saw a supernatural phenomenon forming in front of them. Slowly a cloud settled to the ground—not on the distant horizon, but close to them. The cloud was unlike any they had ever seen. It didn't spread out across the sky with the usual white cotton effect, nor was it like the fog that gathered on the river. This cloud was tall like a column of smoke from a great fire; it reached high into the sky, higher than the human eye could see. With thick white smoke on the outside, the cloud was black in its center. Moses announced to the people,

"The Lord will guide us each day by this cloud, this is the Shekinah-cloud—the word *Shekinah* means glory, the cloud of God's glory—for God Himself will lead us, and from the cloud, God will meet with us."

Moses explained that when the cloud lifted up from the earth, it was time for all to follow God's leadership. And when the cloud sat upon the earth, it was time to make camp for that evening. During the dark evenings, every Israelite could see intermittent fire blazing within the cloud. Moses reminded them, "Our God is a consuming fire," a fire to purify, to warm, to guide, to judge.

A mother looked into her food bag and distributed more unleavened bread for her family, it was their noon meal. Since it was still their Passover season, they celebrated their freedom by eating unleavened bread. When the cloud lifted up, the ram's horn sounded; every Israelite prepared to follow the cloud on their afternoon journey. In the heat of the April sun, their celebration was subdued. Everywhere was heard the cow-bells of their animals, lazily following their families.

Suddenly the Shekinah cloud turned right and led them into the hot desert sand.

The cloud did not follow the king's highway out of Egypt toward the land of Canaan. The king's highway had cooling breezes from the Mediterranean Sea and many oasis along the way for clean water. The cloud turned south into the desert, off the beaten path. God's people followed the Shekinah cloud, following the glory cloud because slaves are taught to follow their leader. They headed toward the Red Sea, camping near Baal-Zephon.

God did not lead them straight into the land of Canaan, for they were not ready to fight the mighty armies of the Canaanites. Even though the king's highway was the shortest route to the Promised Land, God told Moses,

"If the people are faced with a fierce battle from a massive army, they will change their minds and return to Egypt."

My Turn to Pray

- Lord, I revel in every victory You've given me. When dark days come, help me remember the victorious days.

- Lord, it was easy to follow a cloud that could be seen up ahead. Today, I can't see a cloud, but I see something better. I see Your direction for my life in Scripture. Help me keep my eyes on Your will for my life.

- Lord, when You unexpectedly turn a right angle in my life, help me accept Your will and follow Your leading.

- Lord, I like it when You lead me on smooth highways. I don't understand why You lead into the desert. Deserts are dangerous, lonely, and I can get lost in the wilderness. Be with me when I walk through the valley of the shadow of death.

Amen.

Exodus 14

Crossing the Red Sea

Lord, You told Moses, "Have the people march toward Pi Hahiroth and set up camp between Migdol (towering rock) and the sea, near Baal-Zephon (Baal, god of typhoons). Pharaoh will think the people of Israel are lost and have been trapped between the sea and the desert. I will harden Pharaoh's heart so that he will chase you with his army. I will glorify Myself at the expense of Pharaoh and his army. Finally, the Egyptians will realize I AM THE LORD."

Pharaoh received word that the Israelites were not planning on returning, Pharaoh had a change of heart toward the Israelites and said, "Why did we let them go, they no longer do our slave work?" So he prepared his 600 best chariots, each with a commander and his soldiers. He chased after the Israelites who had left so boldly. The Egyptians charged after them, the chariots, cavalry, soldiers, and caught up with them as they were camped on the shore of the Red Sea, near Pi Hahiroth and Baal-Zephon.

The people of Israel could see Pharaoh and his army approaching in the distance, and they panicked and cried to the Lord for help. They complained to Moses, "Did you bring us to die in the desert because there were not enough graves in Egypt? Didn't we tell you to let us alone? Wouldn't it have been better to be slaves in Egypt than to die in the desert?"

Moses told the people, "Quit being afraid. Just stand steadfast and watch the Lord deliver you. You see the Egyptians today, but you'll never see them again. The Lord will fight for you. He will deliver you!"

Lord, You said to Moses, "Tell the people not to cry to Me, but go forward. Lift the rod of God out over the sea and divide it in two. A path will open through the sea. Then all the people will walk through it on dry land. I will harden the heart of Pharaoh and the Egyptians this last time. They will follow you, the Israelites, into the sea, where I will be glorified at the expense of his chariots and army. When Pharaoh, the chariots and army are drowned, then all Egypt will know I AM THE LORD."

The angel of the Lord protected Israel. The pillar of clouds moved from in front of the people to the rear, placing itself between the Israelites and the Egyptians. As night approached, the pillar of clouds became a pillar of fire lighting the Israelite camp but became thick blackness so the Egyptians couldn't find the Israelites.

Moses lifted his hand over the sea and a strong east wind (Sahara sandstorm) opened a path through the sea. The east wind blew all night, turning the sea into a path of dry land. So the people of Israel walked through the sea on dry land, a wall of water on each side.

The Egyptians charged into the bottom of the sea—the chariots, horses, and army—following Israel.

Lord, You looked down from the Shekinah cloud early in the morning to see the Egyptians following Israel. You made the Egyptians panic. Their chariots sank in the sand. It was impossible for them to move. The Egyptians shouted, "The Lord is fighting against us. Let's retreat."

Lord, You said to Moses, "Reach your rod over the sea and the waters will return to drown the Egyptians." Moses did as You commanded, and the waters rushed back to their former place. The Egyptians tried to escape, but the Lord swept over them with the sea. Not one Egyptian escaped.

The people of Israel walked on dry land with a wall of water on their right and left side. The Lord saved Israel, and after that, Israel saw the dead bodies of the Egyptians washed up on the shore. Then Israel believed in the Lord when they saw the mighty miracles He did against the Egyptians.

Lord, You lead Your people into danger
So they will trust You for deliverance.

Lead me every day of my life;
I can't ask You not to lead me into danger
Because then I wouldn't experience Your deliverance.

Wherever You lead me I will follow
Teach me to trust You every day of my life.

Amen.

Exodus 14

The Story of Crossing the Red Sea

Date 1491 B.C. ~ Place: The Red Sea

Word reached Pharaoh by his spies that the Israelites had continued marching into the desert wilderness; they were not planning to return to Egypt after they had worshiped their God. Israel was headed farther into the wilderness. Pharaoh was blinded to what the death angel had done a few nights earlier. Pharaoh shouted loudly in the Great Hall,

"What have we done letting our slaves get away!?"

Pharaoh commanded his military leaders to mobilize his army ready for battle. He mounted his chariot to lead the chase after his former slaves. He commanded 600 of his best chariots, along with enough troops to recapture the Israelites. In a forced march, the chariots and troops advanced rapidly out over the desert toward the Red Sea. Pharaoh had been told that Israel was camped at Baal-Zaphon. Soon Pharaoh saw the Jewish multitude in the distance, spreading out on the banks of the Red Sea.

To intimidate his enemy, Pharaoh spread his chariots out across the desert—wheel to wheel—600 chariots wide. Behind the chariots were his armed troops, ready to massacre the defenseless Israelites. At first, Pharaoh's army moved out slowly toward the Israelites, raising a massive dust cloud. As the charging army picked up speed, the dust cloud grew larger, frightening the Israelites. To them, it seemed there were a hundred times more Egyptians than were actually charging toward them. Panic seized the Israelites as they turned against Moses, complaining,

"Why did you bring us into the wilderness to die?" One man shouted out, "Were there not enough graves in Egypt for us?" Another man yelled out,

"Being an Egyptian slave was far better than dying in the desert!"

Faced with a charging army and rebellious Israelites, Moses didn't know what to do. He had seen God turn water to blood and he had seen God send a death angel to pass through Egypt, but Moses didn't know how God would deliver Israel. In the face of death, Moses could do nothing but trust God. He yelled to the people,

"Don't panic...stand where you are and watch the Lord rescue us. We don't have an army, but the Lord will fight for us. We won't have to lift a weapon in our defense."

Then the Shekinah cloud that had been leading Israel lifted up from in front of Israel and moved behind their camp. The Shekinah settled to the ground between the Israelites and the Egyptian soldiers. At first when Pharaoh saw the cloud, he treated it as nothing but a sandstorm. The Egyptian army had experienced a Sahara sandstorm on many occasions, so Pharaoh drove his charging chariots right into the cloud. But the cloud was thick black darkness—so thick every Egyptian became disoriented. They had to retreat, lest they fight among themselves in the thick blackness. The cloud stood between the Egyptian soldiers and Israel. God protected His people with Himself. Then God instructed Moses, "Use the rod of your fathers—point the staff out over the water—a path will open up through the Red Sea for you to walk over on dry land."

God told Moses that He would harden Pharaoh's heart so they would follow Israel into the sea. Once in the sea, God would destroy the army and chariots, then everyone would know that the Lord is God.

In obedience to God and where every eye could see, Moses lifted up the rod of God out over the Red Sea. The sun was sinking over the horizon, and a gentle breeze stirred. Then the skies turned purple, and the darkness of a spring thunderstorm crept over the battlefield. The breeze stiffened into a storm. Soon a howling Sahara sandstorm blew in from the east, a stronger wind than they had ever felt before. Sahara blew all night out over the sea, preparing for Israel's morning escape through the sea. The hurricane force of the wind pushed the waters back into a massive wall on both sides, creating a large valley through the Red Sea from one shore to the other. God had promised they would walk through onto dry land; now the Sahara sandstorm laid down a path of dry sand for Israel to walk on the bottom of the sea.

When the sun rose the next morning, all Israel saw the valley through the sea. The ram's horn sounded, and Moses lifted God's rod, signaling them to march.

With gusts of winds at their back, Israel followed Moses down into the Red Sea, a wall of water on either side of them. Over two million people followed Moses, not understanding what was happening, not recognizing the epic miracle they were experiencing as they walked down into the bottom of the sea on dry ground. Some who feared the walls of water would collapse on them began running. Others refused to look to either side. In fear they walked through, not trusting God. A few rejoiced in the miracle on both sides of them. It took hours for all Israel to cross over the Red Sea—children, elderly, herds of cattle, families—all of them slowly making their way through the dry path at the bottom of the sea to the other side.

The spies reported to Pharaoh, "The sandstorm has pushed the waters of the Red Sea aside. The wind is so forceful that it has blown the waters apart...all of the Hebrews are escaping across the Red Sea." When Pharaoh heard the observation, he climbed to a rocky ledge to observe the phenomenon. Right in front of him he saw for himself what was happening.

Being constantly influenced by magic, this time Pharaoh didn't realize it was the Spirit of God who hardened his heart. The Lord allowed the lustful hatred of Pharaoh to guide him. Pharaoh thought he too could follow the road through the bottom of the Red Sea. Pharaoh turned to his army and yelled, *"CHARIOTS GET READY..."* then Pharaoh, turning to his trumpeter, commanded that he blow, *"CHARGE!"* The 600 chariots rumbled down through the seashore and into the bottom of the Red Sea, following Israel to the other side. The army of soldiers in battle gear followed behind the chariots across the bottom of the sea. The dry sand at the bottom of the sea was dry enough to walk upon but was not firm enough for chariots. The chariot wheels bogged through the sand into the muddy bottom, making it impossible to drive the chariots to the other side. Their commanders began yelling,

"Unhitch the horses," they yelled to the chariot drivers. "We will ride the horses into battle; our horses will stomp down the Hebrews."

Seeing the Egyptians following them into the valley, some Israelites panicked, yelling in fear. They believed the Lord could open up the Red Sea, but they didn't have faith that the Lord could protect them from their enemy. They began running onto the shore on the other side, some trampling those in front of them. Moses waited until all Israel was safe on the other side, then God spoke to him.

"Raise the rod of God out over the sea again."

Moses climbed to the top of a cluster of rocks on the shore, then in sight of all Israel—for their faith needed strengthening—Moses lifted the rod up over the Red Sea. The wind suddenly ceased, and the waters rushed back together like water spilling out of a bucket turned upside down. The terrified Egyptians were covered by the surging currents, drowning all the soldiers, the horses, the entire army of Pharaoh—all were destroyed in the bottom of the Red Sea.

As the bodies of Egyptians floated to the seashore the next day, the Israelites retrieved weapons from the drowned Egyptians; weapons they would need to fight their enemies. Not only had God destroyed the Egyptian foe, God had also provided weapons for Israel's future conquest of the Promised Land.

> *Lord, I know the challenge of danger*
> *Does not build character, it reveals character.*
>
> *Give me character to face the dangers of life with faith*
> *So I can grow in my trust in You.*
>
> *Lord, the people of Israel should have become spiritual giants*
> *Because they walked through the Red Sea*
> *While their enemies, Pharaoh and his army, drowned.*
>
> *But Israel later grumbled in the wilderness and doubted You;*
> *Help me learn from every difficulty and grow*
> *A strong, trusting faith to walk with You.*
>
> *Amen.*

Exodus 15

A Song of Deliverance

Moses and the people of Israel sang a joyful song of victory that praised
    God for triumphing over Pharaoh and the Egyptians.

Lord, I sing with my whole heart to You
    For You triumphed gloriously over Pharaoh;
    You destroy their horses and riders in the sea.

Lord, You are my strength and I sing to You
    For You gave me victory.

Lord, You are my God, I will praise You;
    You are my father's God, I will exalt You.

Lord, You are a warrior;
    Yes, You, Lord, are my defender.

Lord, You have destroyed Pharaoh's chariots and armies
    By covering them with the sea;

Lord, the very best of Pharaoh's officers
    Have been drowned in the sea.

Lord, the deep waters of the Red Sea
    Have covered them as they sank to the bottom.

Lord, Your right hand is sublimely powerful,
    It is glorious in victory.

Lord, Your right hand, O Lord,
    Has smashed the enemy to pieces.

Lord, by Your awesome majesty
    You brought down Your enemies;

Lord, Your anger flashed like fire,
    You burnt them up like stubble.

Lord, Your breath blew like a blast,
    The waters piled up on either side of us;
    The depth of the sea stood straight up like a wall,
    "It stood firm until we passed through."

Lord, the enemy said, "I will chase them and overtake them,
    I will capture them and plunder their goods,
    I will draw my sword and destroy them."

Lord, Your breath blew the water back over them,
    They sank like lead in the angry water.

Lord, what God is mighty like You
    Who is glorious in holiness like You?

Lord, You are awesome in majesty
    As You work miracles for us to see.

Lord, You reached out,
    You swallowed Your enemies.

Lord, with unfailing love You led us,
    You guided us to Your holy presence,
    We are Your people whom You redeemed.

Lord, the gentle nations heard what You did,
    Fear overcame the Philistines;

Lord, the leaders of Edom are terrified,
    All the people of Canaan melted in fear;
    Terror and dread gripped them all.

A Song of Deliverance

Lord, by Your mighty power Your people pass by
    And the nations have nothing to say
    Because the people You redeemed passed them by.

Lord, You will bring them into the Promised Land,
    You will plant them on their own mountains.
    The place You choose as their home.

Lord, the Promised Land will also be Your home,
    The place where You will plant Your sanctuary.

Lord, You will reign forever and ever
    Because Pharaoh's horses, chariots, and soldiers
    Rushed into the bottom of the sea.

Lord, You brought the waters crashing down on them
    But we—Your people—walked through on dry land.

Miriam, the prophetess, Aaron's sister, danced with a tambourine, leading all the women in dancing. She led them saying, "Sing joyfully to the Lord, for He triumphed mightily, He threw both rider and the horse into the sea."

Moses led the people of Israel away from the Red Sea into the Sinai Desert. For three days they didn't find water. When they got to the oasis at Marah (bitter), they couldn't drink the water because it was alkaline water. The people grumbled against Moses demanding, "We need water to drink!"

Moses cried to You for an answer. Lord, You showed Moses a small tree. When Moses threw it into the water, it became good to drink.

Lord, You tested their faithfulness at Marah, then You told the people, "If you will listen intently to My voice and do My commands and directions, you will not suffer the diseases of the Egyptians. I am Jehovah-Rapha, the God who heals you."

When the people of Israel left Marah, they came to Elim where there were 12 springs and 70 palm trees.

The Shekinah halted and they camped there beside the spring.

Amen.

Exodus 15

The Story of a Song and a Complaint

Date 1491 B.C. ~ Place: Marah, in the Wilderness

For the next three days Israel marched into the seething desert, a desert hotter and more cruel than they experienced in Egypt. Each family filled their leather bottles with water, each family bringing as much water as possible, but their water lasted only three days.

Moses knew this desert; he had spent 40 years leading sheep in this area. He knew that if each person brought enough water for three days, they could make it to Marah, a solitary pool of water surrounded by a few trees at the foot of a mountain. But when the Hebrews arrived at Marah, they couldn't drink the water; it was poisoned with alkali and very bitter. The site of Marah seems clearly to have been at `Ain Chawarah (the white chalk spring), named from the chalky mound beside it.

Moses gathered his people together to explain this was extremely unusual, but their thirst turned them as bitter as the water they couldn't drink. One man yelled,

"You told us there would be water at Marah...you lied!"

"Give us something to drink!" the multitude chanted. Another yelled, "Did you bring us into the desert to die of thirst?"

Moses retreated into God's presence to cry to Him, as the people cried in unbelief. Three days earlier they experienced the deliverance of God through the Red Sea, now they doubted God's ability to satisfy their thirst. Moses cried out to the Lord for an answer. The Lord told him to cut down a tree and throw it into the water. When he obeyed, the water became sweet; the people drank.

They stayed at Marah for a few days as Moses began teaching the people how they needed to live with one another as a great nation. He taught them that many of the sexual practices of the Egyptians led to disease and sickness. Moses told the people,

"Listen to the voice of the Lord, separate yourselves to God; and obey His commands and laws." Moses then said, "God has promised that we will not have the diseases of Egypt when we obey Him. His name is Jehovah-Rapha, the Lord Who Heals."

My Time to Pray

- Lord, why is it we forget the miracles you do for us and complain and doubt You? Teach me to trust You when all my needs are met as well as times when my pocketbook is empty.

- Lord, why do so many Christians only see one day at a time? Give me faith for the long haul.

- Lord when times are difficult, teach me to go to You in prayer, just as Moses prayed when there was no water.

Amen.

Exodus 16

Bread From Heaven

All the people of Israel left Elim and traveled into the Sin Desert toward
Sinai and arrived on the fifteenth day of the second month (one
month after leaving Egypt). The people grumbled against Moses
and Aaron, "We wish we were back in Egypt, where we had pots
of meat boiling and plenty to eat. Why didn't God kill us there?
Now we will starve to death in this desert."

Lord, may I ever feel Your Spirit work in my heart,
And never lust after the satisfaction of the world.

Lord, You said to Moses, "I will rain down bread from Heaven for you.
The people are to go out each morning to gather as much as
they need for that day. I will test them to see whether or not
they will obey My Word. Tell them to gather twice as much on
the sixth day of each week so they will have food on the
Sabbath."

Moses and Aaron gathered the people and said, "Now you will realize
the Lord who brought you out of Egypt can provide for you. In
the morning you will see the Lord's glory. The Lord has heard
your grumblings against Him. Your complaints are not against
us, but against Him. What I am telling you will happen this
evening. The Lord will give you meat this evening and bread
tomorrow morning."

Moses said to the entire community of Israel, "Here is the Lord's reply
to your complaints." As Aaron was speaking, the people looked
toward the desert and the glory of the Lord appeared in a cloud

101

and the Lord said to Moses, "I have heard your grumblings. At dusk you will have meat and in the morning you will have bread. Then you will realize I am the Lord."

Lord, You were gracious to give Israel food to eat
After they wanted the fleshpots of Egypt.

Lord, You've been good to me,
Even when I'm unappreciative of Your goodness;
Thank You for grace and not judgment.

Quail covered the camp that evening, and the next morning the desert was wet with dew. When the dew disappeared, a fine flake of something like frost covered the ground. When the people saw it, they ask, *"Man ha?"* which is interpreted, "What is it?" and pronounced manna. Moses answered, "This is bread which the Lord has given you to eat. The Lord has commanded each person to gather according to what he can eat. Gather two quarts for each person." The people did this; some gathered more, some gathered less. But when they got back to their tents, those who gathered much had none left over, and those who gathered too little had enough. Each family had what they needed.

Moses told the people, "Don't keep any of it until the next day." But some didn't listen, they did it anyway. But what they kept had a terrible smell and was filled with maggots.

Lord, the bread I need today is not physical bread;
I need spiritual strength to overcome my stubborn will.

Lord, strengthen me by the Holy Spirit
To grow strong in the inner person.

I need daily strength for each day.
I trust You to supply all my needs.

The people gathered manna each morning according to God's command; day by day, each family gathered according to its need. As the sun became hot, the manna melted and disappeared. On the sixth day, they gathered twice as much as on other days—four quarts per person.

When the leaders of the people came to Moses, he said, "The Lord has set aside the sixth day to provide for the Sabbath. You are to consecrate that day unto the Lord. Bake some of it or broil some of it for the Sabbath, because you won't find manna in the fields on the Sabbath." Even then, some people went out to look for manna, but it was not there.

The Lord said to Moses, "How long will these people doubt me and refuse to do what I have told them to do? Do they not realize I have given them the seventh day to rest? That is why I have given them twice as much manna on the 6th day so there will be food on the Sabbath. On the Sabbath you must rest and stay in your tent. Do not try to pick up manna on that day." So the people rested on the Sabbath.

The people began calling it manna. It was like a white coriander seed and tasted like honey.

The Lord told Moses, "Take two quarts of manna and keep it for generation to generation so they can see the bread that I fed my people in the wilderness when I brought them out of Egypt."

Moses told Aaron, "Get a container and pour two quarts of manna into it and store it in a sacred place to be a lesson to future generations. Aaron did exactly what the Lord commanded (eventually it was kept in the Ark of the Covenant). The people of Israel ate manna for 40 years until they came to the land of Canaan, where they were able to eat the crops of that land.

Lord, thank You for daily feeding my soul on Scripture
  Like You daily fed Your people with manna in the wilder-
  ness.

I need Your daily strength from the Bible
  Just like Israel needed daily physical strength from
  manna.

Teach me again that I can't live on yesterday's blessings,
  Just as Israel couldn't keep manna from one day until the
  next.

Yet every day You give me what I need for that day,
  Just as each Israelite had all they needed each day.

Amen.

Exodus 16

The Story of the Bread From Heaven

Date: One Month Later ~ Place: Between the Red Sea and Mount Sinai

After a month out of Egypt, the unleavened bread ran out, and the people began to panic when their rations ran low. Some families brought more food than others, a few shared with those who were needy. But eventually, two million people began to get hungry. When Moses brought them together to teach them about God, they didn't want to listen to him. The people began to complain about no food.

"We had the fleshpots to eat every evening in Egypt." They accused Moses of bringing them into the desert to starve them to death. After seeing past miracles, they had difficulty trusting God for His future care. Apparently they had more faith in Pharaoh's provision in Egypt than they had for

God's supply in the wilderness. When Moses cried to God with the problem, the Lord told him,

"I am going to rain food down from Heaven for the people. They can go out each morning to pick up as much food as they need to satisfy their appetite for that day. But I will only give them bread each day for that day; I will test them to see if they can obey My instructions."

God told Moses that they would find bread on the ground each morning; each person was to gather one small pot of food for the day. If they gathered more than one pot of food for the day, it would spoil by evening time. God promised,

"Each family will have just the amount of bread they need."

God told Moses that each family should gather twice as much bread on the day before the Sabbath. It would not spoil overnight. They were to celebrate the Sabbath to God. Even though every Israelite could see the guiding cloud each day and the pillar of fire each evening, some still had difficulty trusting God to take care of all their needs, even though He told them,

"When you find bread on the ground, then you will know that I am your Lord."

That evening Israel went to sleep with the instructions that God would rain bread on them the following morning.

Early the next morning a family left their tent to walk out to the desert, finding it was wet with dew, but as the dew disappeared in the warm morning sunlight, thin, white flakes like icy frost covered the ground. Everywhere they saw thin, white frosty flakes of food. A little boy asked his father, "What is it?" The question, "What is it?" is pronounced in the Hebrew language *manna*, so the people called the white flakes *manna*. It looked white like a coriander seed and to the taste, it was like honey cakes. By midmorning, the manna had evaporated in the hot midday sun.

The family went out with pots, each family member gathering up white flakes of manna until a pot was filled. Like flour from which bread was baked, the mother could ground the manna into flour, making bread for the family. Another woman added water, boiling manna in a pot over the fire, making porridge for the children. By gathering a pot full per person, everyone had their bread for that day.

Not all Israelites obeyed God. "Get six pots full," the father told the children. They filled several extra pots with the manna. It was not that they disbelieved God; they just wanted to make sure that they had extra food for the future. But that evening maggots filled their pots of manna and the next morning a terrible stench from the extra pots of manna filled their tent.

Another family sneaked out on the Sabbath day. They had forgotten to pick up extra on the day before their rest day. There was no manna for them.

But the Israelites needed more than bread to eat. They needed protein that came from meat. God told Moses that each evening, flocks of quail would fly low over the desert. The Israelites were to go out in the twilight— between the light of day and the darkness of night—then use their shepherd sticks to knock the quail out of the air. The quail would provide their meat.

My Time to Pray

- Lord, give me daily food, just as You gave Israel manna each day.

- Lord, teach me gratitude for all You give me. May I not grumble over Your provisions, as Israel grumbled in the wilderness.

- Lord, manna was very simple, yet it provided strength for Israelites to do their daily work. Help me be grateful for simple food You provide for my strength.

Amen.

Exodus 17

THE BATTLE OVER WATER

The whole multitude of the people of Israel left the Desert of Sin and
followed the Shekinah cloud to the oasis at Rephedim and
camped there. But the oasis was dry; there was no water. The
people grumbled, demanding of Moses, "Get water for us!"
Moses answered them, "Why are you fussing at me? You are
doubting the Lord who promised to provide for us."

The people grew thirstier, so they grumbled again to Moses, "Why have
you led us into the desert from Egypt so that we will die in the
desert for lack of water, along with our children and livestock?"

Lord, You had miraculously led Israel through the Red Sea and
You had miraculously provided water at Marah;
Why couldn't they trust You to do the miraculous again?

Lord, sometimes I'm just like the people of Israel in the desert;
I doubt Your leading even when You've provided in the past,
I believe; help Thou my unbelief. Give me more faith.

Lord, Moses cried to You, saying, "What shall I do? The people want to
stone me?" You answered him, "Go stand before the people and
take with you the leaders of every tribe. Also take your rod, the
one you used to divide the waters of the Red Sea."

Lord, You told Moses, "I will stand with you before the people of Israel
upon the great rock at Horeb. Strike the rock with the rod and
water will gush out of it for the people to drink."

Moses did as the Lord commanded, and water gushed out of the rock. After that Moses called the rock Massah (burden) and Meribah (contention) because the people of Israel doubted You, the Lord, saying, "Is the Lord with us or not?"

Lord, it's amazing how unbelievers turn against You
And refuse to follow Your servants.

Keep my ear tuned to Your voice so I'll obey
Both You and the leaders You put over me.

Amalek, a fierce warring tribe, came to attack Israel over water rights. There was no contention until Israel found water.

Moses told Joshua to enlist able-bodied men to fight Amalek. Moses said, "I will intercede for you with the rod of God in my hand on the top of the hill." So Joshua gathered his army and Moses went to pray at the top of the hill, with Aaron and Hur.

When Moses lifted his arms in intercession, then Israel prevailed in battle. But when Moses' arms got tired, he dropped them, and Amalek prevailed. So Aaron and Hur sat Moses on a stone and held his hands up in prayer, one on one side and the other on the other side. They continued until the sun went down, and Israel prevailed.

Lord, You told Moses, "Write this in a book and read it constantly to remind Israel of the hatred of Amalek for Israel. They will continually battle Israel and Me from generation to generation."

Moses built a monument to remind the people of Israel of their victory over Amalek and named it Jehovah-Nissi (the Lord our Banner).

Lord, Your banner is waving over me
In all my trials and tribulations that declares,

"There is victory" to those who trust in You;
I will rally to Your banner when difficulties come.

Amen.

Exodus 17

The Story of the Battle Over Water

Date: Three Months After Leaving Egypt ~ Place: Rephidim in the Wilderness

"Mother, I am thirsty," the little girl said, wiping her mouth. The people of Israel had walked several days from Marah, the last oasis. Before leaving the pool of water, everyone filled all their containers with water, but after one week in the desert, now the bottles were empty. The little girl asked the question that everyone feared to ask, "When are we going to find water?"

"We will find water in Rephidim," Moses announced to the multitude. The news spread out over the crowd. Everyone's spirit perked up, saying,

"Water is just ahead at Rephidim..."

"I watered my sheep on many occasions at Rephidim," Moses announced to the multitude. Even though many felt faint, the promise of water motivated them to struggle through the heat of late spring. When children couldn't walk any farther, parents carried them. They could almost smell water in their nostrils, so everyone reached deep within to keep going.

A young man came running over the horizon toward them, one of the young men who scouted out the territory. Everyone saw panic in his face; they knew he must have bad news. The young man spoke privately to Moses,

"There is no water at Rephidim...the oasis is dry."

Quickly the word spread throughout the multitude, and within a short period of time, almost all of the two million people heard there was no water at Rephidim. People congregated around Moses shouting,

"WE MUST HAVE WATER!"

One voice rang out over all the rest,

"Why did you take us out of Egypt...why did you bring us here to die in the wilderness?"

The people had forgotten that a week ago Moses had thrown a tree into the poisoned water to give them good water. Rather than trusting God, bitter criticism infected the multitude.

Not knowing what to do, Moses retreated to a private place and there fell upon his knees, praying to the Lord.

"Why did You lead me here? The people are about to stone me." Israel had not learned that God led them into difficulties to teach them to trust Him. The multitude yelling at Moses couldn't look beyond their thirst to see that God was their source of provision. Even Moses reflected his doubts by asking questions, but the audible voice of God said to him,

"Take your rod—the one that turned water into blood—and strike the rock. Water will come pouring out of the rock so My people will have water."

It took a great display of faith for Moses to walk back among the complaining people with determination on his face. As he did on other occasions, he held his rod high before them. Etched in the rod was the signet of Abraham, Isaac, Jacob. The God of their fathers wanted to be their God.

Moses walked straight to the massive rock in front of them. Because God had told him to strike the rock, Moses was prepared to hit it hard. He would obey. Because God told him that water would come out of the rock, Moses knew the people would have water to drink. Moses waited for the crowd to gather. Then, standing where all could see him, he raised his shepherd's rod high into the sky and yelled to the crowd,

"Can the Lord not take care of us?" then Moses struck the rock with his staff. Immediately, water gushed from the rock.

"O-o-o-o-h-h-h..." the crowd marveled as they saw a stream of fresh water pouring out of the rock. As water began filling the empty pond, the thirsting people ran quickly with pots to catch the water, almost fearful the parched, dry sand would soak up their pleasure. Then Moses announced over the happy, babbling crowd,

"This place will be called *Massah* in the future, a word that means testing. This was the place God tested us and we failed the test." Then Moses also announced, "This place will also be called *Meribah*, a word that means strife because it was a place where we argued with God."

The people of Israel rested at Rephidim because there was water there. The Shekinah cloud did not lift to lead the people farther into the desert, so the weary travelers rested and repaired their broken luggage and repacked their possessions.

Soon a warring tribe of Amalekites gathered on the top of a small hill on the horizon, overlooking the camp of Israel. They formed a battle line, their way of scaring an enemy. Amalek had heard of the water at Rephidim; they had come to claim the well, for water was as precious as gold in the desert; no one can drink gold when thirsting to death.

The Amalekites sent word to Moses to leave Rephidim because that was their territory. They claimed the well, the oasis, and the rock that gave water. They didn't care that God had miraculously given the Israelites the water from the rock; the territory was theirs.

Moses stood before his multitude and told the people of Israel that they might have to fight Amalek. He announced, "This territory does not belong to them; this is barren land that belongs to anybody who sets up his tent for the night. This water belongs to any traveler who is thirsty."

Moses turned to one of his most trusted staff members—Joshua, a gifted organizer. Moses instructed young Joshua to distribute weapons to men of fighting age; the weapons they had found from the bodies of the Egyptian soldiers on the beaches of the Red Sea. Then Moses instructed,

"As you go into battle, I will go to the top of this hill to pray for you." Moses also told the elders of each family, "As I hold up this rod—with signets of our fathers—God will give us victory."

Early the next morning Moses climbed to a place on top of the mountain. He was ready to lift his rod and pray as Joshua and his untested Israelite soldiers formed a long battle line against the Amalekite warriors. Moses lifted his staff to God, asking for victory in battle.

When Amalek attacked the Israelite line of defense, God gave them courage and strength to repel their first attack. But the heathen were not easily beaten; they formed a counterattack, ready to charge wildly into the Israelite defense line. Because Moses' arms had become tired during the long first attack of Amalek, he was not able to hold up the rod of God during the second attack. He lowered his hands as the charging Amalek army broke through the Israelite line, and the Hebrew soldiers retreated.

Quickly Aaron and Hur (brother-in-law, for he married Miriam) ran up the hill to tell Moses that he must keep the rod held high so the Israelite army could stand against the enemy. But Moses was over 80 years old, while strong enough to lift his rod to the sky for God's work, he was not strong enough to keep it there for a long period of time. Aaron and Hur instantly saw the developing crisis; they knew Moses' arms must be held up for a victory. Aaron commanded his friend,

"You hold up one arm, I'll hold up the other," and they held up Moses' arms as he prayed for God's victory. The next charge of Amalek was repelled and Amalek retreated. Every soldier cheered wildly, knowing God gave them the victory as Moses held his hands up in prayer.

Shortly, the aged Moses was no longer able to stand. Aaron directed him to sit on a nearby rock. As Moses sat upon the rock, Aaron and Hur continued holding up his hands to God.

There were several more attacks by the soldiers of Amalek, charging the line of Israel; but the only time they prevailed was when Moses' arms were not held up in prayer. Finally Joshua felt it was time for Israel to mount a charge against Amalek. During the lull of the battle, Joshua told his soldiers to prepare to charge the enemy. He could see determination in their eyes. He knew that they were ready to charge the enemy; their confidence was in God who gave them victory. Then Joshua with a sword held high, yelled to his soldiers,

"CHARGE!"

"THE BATTLE IS THE LORD'S!" the Israeli soldiers yelled as they charged Amalek. Their fierce determination scared Amalek's army so that they turned to run. Most of the enemy retreated to the rear. Those who tried to retrieve their goods were slaughtered by Israel. Those who escaped into the desert would not be an immediate threat to Israel because they were without their goods, camels, or any assurance that they could defeat God and His warriors.

My Time to Pray

- Lord, I'm in constant spiritual warfare; help me keep my hands held high in prayer.

- Lord, thank You for friends who pray with me, teach us to be faithful as were Aaron and Hur (see Matt. 18:19).

- Lord, You are the Rock who was smitten for me; thank You for living water.

Amen.

Exodus 18

A LESSON IN LEADERSHIP

Jethro came to meet Moses and the people of Israel after they arrived at
Mount Sinai. Jethro—Moses' father-in-law—had heard about all
the miracles that the Lord had done for Israel in delivering them
from Egypt. Moses had left Zipporah and their children with
Jethro when he confronted Pharaoh. Moses named his first son
Gershom (I have been an alien in a strange land) and the second Eliezer (God is my help), because God had delivered Moses
from the death warrant of Pharaoh.

Moses went out to greet his father-in-law and bowed before him, then
they embraced and asked each other about their welfare. Then
they went into a tent.

Jethro said, "I have brought your wife and two sons to you."

Moses rehearsed for Jethro all the miracles and plagues that the Lord
did against Pharaoh and Egyptians to deliver Israel. Then Moses
told Jethro about the problems of the people of Israel after they
left Egypt.

Jethro rejoiced in all the Lord had done for Israel. He said, "Blessed be
the Lord who has delivered you out from the hand of the
Egyptians and from Pharaoh. Now I know the Lord is greater
than the gods of Egypt, for He was victorious over them." Then
Jethro sacrificed a burnt offering to the Lord. Next, Aaron and
the elders came for a big banquet with Jethro.

Lord, remind me there is a demonic spirit behind idols,
And the plagues were a battle between You and satan.

I trust in You and will not fear demons because "Greater is He who is in me, than he who is in the world."

Moses sat the next morning as judge for the people to arbitrate their problematic issues. He was hearing different cases from early morning until the evening.

Jethro saw all that Moses did, he then asked Moses, "Why are you the only one who arbitrates these cases? The people are standing in line from morning till evening."

Moses answered, "Because I know the laws of God and can talk to God about these matters. They come to me when they have a disagreement, and I tell them what God says."

Jethro said, "What you're doing is not good. You will eventually break down, both you and the people who wait for you. You can't do this thing alone."

Lord, keep me from being so egotistical
That I think I'm the only one who can solve problems.

Teach me the wisdom of delegation to those better qualified than I. May I do diligently what only I can do.

May I delegate to others who do it better than I.

Jethro then told Moses what to do, "Teach the leaders and the people the commandments of God and explain to them how to live and how to serve God. Then choose the best qualified men to counsel the people about their problems. Choose men who fear God, live by the truth, and are not greedy. Moses, you spend your time talking to God and serving Him and intercede to God about the people's problems. Then delegate qualified men over groups of thousands, hundreds, and tens. Let them solve all the cases. They can take care of small matters and you take care of the big problems. That way, they can help bear the burden of leadership.

Jethro concluded, "If you'll delegate your responsibility, you won't wear out, and the people will be happier."

Moses did what his father-in-law suggested. He chose qualified men and made them heads over thousands and hundreds and tens. They arbitrated the problems but brought the difficult ones to Moses. Then Jethro left and returned to his own land of the Midianites.

Lord, I don't need a Bible verse to solve some problems;
I should just do the common sense thing.

Help me be wise enough to know when to look in the Bible and
when to use my good judgment to solve the issues of life.

Amen.

Exodus 18

The Story of A Lesson in Leadership

Date: About Three Months After Leaving Egypt ~ Place: Desert of Send

Israel—the plodding multitude—moved out across the desert heading toward Sinai. All the nomadic tribes in the area knew this massive nation was moving into their territory. Outlying shepherds saw the migration of thousands of people and rushed back to their nomadic tribes to tell them an unbelievable story. People were coming...but not an army...a group of many thousands of migrating people looking for a place to live.

Israel was invading an area sacred to most of the nomadic tribes. They had heard how the Amalekites were defeated, and they feared the God of the

Israelites. Each nomadic tribe picked up tents, children, herds, and moved out of the way of the Israelites. That is, all of the nomadic tribes ran away except one. When Jethro, the father-in-law of Moses, heard that his son-in-law was returning with thousands of people, he announced to his tribe,

"We must go see Moses…"

When Jethro arrived at the camp of the Israelites, he was ushered right to the center where Moses lived. "Where's Moses?" he asked. They told Jethro,

"Moses is taking care of business."

Moses was busy that day hearing disputes among the Israelites. Obviously when two million people are amassed together in one concentration of humanity, all types of disputes break out. Some accused others of stealing their flock; another had an unruly son, another wanted to divorce his wife, and another just wanted advice from Moses if he should marry a certain girl. Each person who had to see Moses lined up along a row of tents, waiting patiently in the hot sun for their moment to get a decision from Moses. Each wanted to talk with Moses because Moses talked with God; one woman said,

"Moses will tell us what God wants us to do."

Moses arrived at the family tent after dark, warmly greeting his father-in-law. Jethro asked,

"Where have you been so long?"

"Doing the business of leadership."

The next day Jethro went with Moses, because he wanted to see his son-in-law "do the business of leadership." Even before Moses heard the first dispute, there was a long line of people reaching out into the desert, twice as long as the day before. When the people were marching, there were few disputes; but when they camped for two or three days, this is when their disputes broke out. Idleness provoked controversy.

Jethro carefully watched Moses as he listened to the first dispute. To Jethro, the two argumentative men had a trivial problem; one man's camel had been startled by the other man's dog. The camel then ran through the other man's tent, tearing up his possessions. To Jethro this was a trivial issue, one he would not have even bothered with in his tribe. Jethro would have allowed a family elder to resolve the dispute. But here was Moses—a leader of two million people—listening carefully to trivial problems. Not trivial to the people involved, but the problems were small when compared to the demands of leading two million people.

All that morning, Moses listened to one issue after another as Jethro patiently waited for an opportunity to talk with his son-in-law. During the noon meal, Jethro and Moses retreated out of the sun inside the tent. It was here when Jethro asked with a sharp barb,

"What are you doing?" Jethro's question was condemning. Then a father-in-law corrected his younger family member; Jethro chided Moses, "Answering every question, this is not right...you'll wear yourself out...you must save your energy for important decisions influencing millions...you must give time to your family...you must give more time to pray to God."

Moses was stunned at Jethro's reaction. The son-in-law respected Jethro's leadership of a nomadic tribe, even though much smaller than Israel's multitude, but still Jethro understood how to delegate responsibility to family heads. Moses tried to answer him,

"But I must hear the people..." Moses pleaded. "The people come to me for wisdom...the people know that I talk to God...the people listen to me because God talks to me."

Jethro had sized up Moses' problem, and he had some advice for him, "Let me tell you how to better lead these people...you are God's leader for almost two million people." Jethro knew that the fate of God's people depended upon him; Moses shouldn't wear himself out with individuals, nor should he tire himself out with incidental problems. Jethro said to him,

"You should go to God and let Him give you the directions how these people can become a great nation. Then you should tell the people the answers God has given you. You must teach them the laws of God and how to apply them to their lives. If you can give them principles how to solve their problems, they won't need to come to you."

But that was not the end to Jethro's advice. Even though Jethro wanted Moses to teach God's principles to the people, still many people would have questions. Jethro said,

"Find wise men who are honest and trustworthy...especially those who won't take bribes...appoint them to judge the people. Put one person over a thousand, another person over a hundred and another person over ten."

Jethro explained that these judges could resolve most of the ordinary problems of the people. He went on to explain that important problems or difficult problems could be brought to him. He explained,

"Let these judges help you carry the leadership load, you will live longer and more people will be involved in leading the nation."

Shortly after Jethro gave his advice to Moses, he said goodbye to his son-in-law and returned to the land of the Midianites. Even though he stayed only a short time, Jethro's wisdom helped Moses solve a problem that would have crippled the young nation. But God had used Jethro in another way; as Israel left Rephidim, they pushed on toward Sinai—the mountain of God. On that mountain God would speak to Moses to give the people divine laws and principles for the nation. God had used Jethro to prepare Moses to receive the Ten Commandments.

My Time to Pray

- Lord, sometimes You speak through older, wiser counselors. Help me listen and learn Your principles from them. Lord, You used Jethro to give some common sense to a younger family member. Help me use the wisdom You've given me when I give counsel to younger people.

- Lord, help me see what You're doing in my life today so I'll understand what You're preparing me to do.

Amen.

Exodus 19

God Visits His People

Date: 1490 B.C., Three Months After Leaving Egypt ~ Place: Mount Sinai

The people of Israel arrived in the desert at the foot of Mount Sinai three months after leaving Egypt. They camped at the foot of Sinai.

Moses went up into the mountain to meet God. It was there the Lord met him and said, "Go tell the descendents of Jacob, 'Remember what I said to the Egyptians and how I carried you on eagles' wings to bring you out of Egypt. Now therefore, remember the earth is mine. If you will obey My voice and keep My commandments you will be a unique people that I will treasure more than all other people. You will be a kingdom of priests and a holy nation.'"

Lord, today I can be what You promised Israel;
I want to be a priest who intercedes to You,
I want to be holy as a sacrifice to You.

Lord, You want Your people to be different from the world;
I will live a separated life from the world,
I will live a separated life to You.

Moses came down and called the elderly leaders of the tribes together and told them what God had said.

The people answered, "We will do everything the Lord tells us to do."

Moses went back up the mountain to tell God what the people said.

The Lord said to Moses, "I came to you in a thick black cloud so the people can hear when I speak and believe in Me. Go tell the people to sanctify themselves today and tomorrow. Tell them to wash their clothes because on the third day I will come down to Mount Sinai so they can see Me. Put 'no trespassing' signs around the mountain. Anyone who goes onto the mountain or touches it will die. If they barely touch it with a hand, stone them, whether the violator is a person or an animal. Tell them to come to the foot of the mountain only when they hear the sound of the trumpet."

Lord, I expect smoke when You appear
Because the Bible says You are a consuming fire.

I will never see You with my eyes;
Help me see You in my heart.

Moses went down to tell the people to get ready by sanctifying themselves and washing their clothes. He told them not to have sex with their wives until after the third day.

On the third day in the morning a thick black cloud descended on the mountain with thunder and lightning and a trumpet sound so loud that it scared the people so they shook with fear. Moses led the people to the backside of the mountain to meet God. Sinai was covered with smoke because the Lord descended there, and the smoke arose in a giant column into Heaven as it came from a giant fire. The mountain shook with an earthquake. The trumpet got louder and louder. Then God called Moses to come up into the mount.

God said, "Go, command the people not to come up here or try to see Me, because they will die if they try. Tell the priests to sanctify themselves lest they die when they sacrifice to Me. Go down to the people, but make sure neither they nor the priest try to come up onto the mountains, for they will die if they do it."

Moses went down to tell the people what God said.

Lord, You want those who come to worship You
  To be clean on the inside and outside.

I ask You to cleanse my heart by the blood of Christ;
  I will clean up my speech, thoughts, and life,
  I will also clean up my outward person.

Amen.

Exodus 20

THE TEN COMMANDMENTS

God gave these commandments to Moses saying, "I am the Lord your God and have brought you from bondage in Egypt.

"You shall not have any of the world's gods before Me.

"You shall not make any carved images or likenesses to represent Me—not anything in heaven, not anything on earth, nor anything under the water. You shall not bow down to any images or sacrifice to them. For I am a jealous God and will judge people to the third and fourth generation of those who hate Me. But I will show mercy to those who love Me and unto thousands and beyond.

"You shall not wrongly use My name, because those who speak My name falsely will be guilty of sin.

"You shall observe the Sabbath as a holy day because it was then when I, the Lord God, rested. You shall do all your work in six days, but the seventh day is a day of rest. You shall not work on the Sabbath, neither shall your son, daughter, including men servants or women servants who work for you, plus your animals. For in six days, I the Lord created the heavens, earth, sea, and everything in it. Then I rested on the seventh day and blessed it and made it holy.

"You shall honor your father and mother so you'll live a long time.

"You shall not kill individuals.

"You shall not have sex with anyone who is not your spouse.

"You shall not steal.

"You shall not lie to another, or about another.

"You shall not be greedy. You should not lust after your neighbor's house, his wife, his servants, his animals, nor anything that is your neighbors.'"

> *Lord, help me keep all Your commandments*
> *And please You in all I do.*

> *Your commandments show Your desire for holiness;*
> *I cannot be holy in myself.*

> *I need imputed righteousness to be holy;*
> *I can only be perfect in Christ's righteousness.*

Response

The people were frightened by the thunder, lightning, smoke, and loud trumpet blast, so they moved away from Mount Sinai and stood a long distance away. They said to Moses, "Speak to the Lord for us and we will listen to you, but we will die if God speaks directly to us."

Moses said to the people, "Don't be afraid. God came down to Sinai to test you to see if you would fear Him, and separate yourself from sin." Then Moses came close to the thick clouds of Sinai where God was.

The Lord said to Moses, "The people know that I have talked with you, so tell them not to make gods of gold or silver. They shall sacrifice to Me on an altar that sits flat on the ground made of regular field stones. Don't use your tools to carve any special stones for an altar. Your altar should not be on a pedestal."

Lord, I know I can't see Your face and live;
All I can see are the clouds of glory.

Lord, when I see the glory of Your majesty,
I bow my heart to worship You.

Amen.

Exodus 20

The Story of the Ten Commandments

Date: 1490 B.C. ~ Place: Foot of Mount Sinai

Everyone felt in their bones the cloud would lift shortly and they would leave Rephidim. Families filled their water bottles, packed their tents, and they watched the Shekinah cloud to see what God would do. When it lifted, the ram's horn sounded, Moses lifted his rod, and the people began the trek across the desert to Sinai.

Mount Sinai rises 7,550 feet off the desert floor, it was the appointed place that Moses knew well because there Moses met God at the burning bush; there he was commanded to go to Egypt to free the Israelites.

The morning after arriving at Sinai, each family went out early to gather manna—white flakes on the desert floor—enough to eat for that day. As a mother and children were filling their pots, the young son pointed to Sinai, asking,

"Mother...why is Moses climbing the mountain?"

They squinted through the rising sun to see Moses slowly making his way up through the rocks; Joshua his assistant was with him. Quickly the mother snatched up her children to return to the safety of her tent door. Everyone in the camp knew that Moses had met God at the burning bush, and now they knew he was going back to find God's presence, it was scary to imagine what might happen.

The Shekinah glory cloud lifted up from the front of the multitude to cover the top of Sinai, like a driving storm cloud heavy with black rain and thunder with lightning moving into the area; except the cloud hunkered down on Sinai. As Moses approached the edge of the cloud, he was fearful to enter the moist atmosphere, not knowing what would happen in the presence of God. Then from out of the cloud, the audible voice of God spoke to him.

"Give the following instructions to the people of Israel. Remind them that they have seen what I did to the Egyptians and how I lifted up Israel on eagle's wings and brought them to Myself. Now, therefore, if you will obey My voice and keep My covenant, then You shall be a unique treasure to Me above all the people of the earth. You will be a kingdom of priests to Me and a holy nation."

Later that afternoon, all the people saw Moses coming down the mountain. Again parents stood in the tent doors holding their breath, fearful as the old man descended the mountain, he could fall and hurt himself. They had seen him disappear into the clouds; now he was returning. Each family was anxious to know what God had said to their leader.

When Moses arrived in the camp, he assembled the elders—the head of each family—to gather immediately at his tent. He told them what God had said to him. In turn, each family head went to gather his tribe about him, rehearsing what God had told Moses. God wanted to know if they would worship Him and obey Him. Then as one man, the family heads of Israel said, "We will do all that the Lord has said to us."

The following day Moses ascended the mountain again, going back into the presence of God. It was there that Moses told the Lord that the people wanted to obey Him.

"All right..." the Lord said to Moses, "in three days return to Me, and I will give you the laws by which you shall live...these laws will be My laws...and Israel shall be My people."

Moses returned to tell the people how to prepare themselves for God. "First..." Moses told them, "wash your clothes...for you cannot appear before the Lord in dirty clothes."

Next Moses set boundary lines at the foot of Mount Sinai so the people could not come near the mountain. He instructed them, "Be careful that you do not go onto the mountain, nor even touch the edge of the boundaries because those who do will surely die." He told them that any animal that strayed onto the mountain would have to be killed. Concerning their private lives, Moses instructed them, "Do not have sexual relations for the next three days."

On the third day, there was a powerful display of thunder and lightning in the thick black storm cloud that covered the top of Sinai. Then everyone heard the signal—a long, loud blast from the ram's horn—and all the people fell to their faces to worship God. They remembered the destructive power of God in Egypt when the firstborn died. They remembered God pushing back the walls of the Red Sea. The thundering presence of God on Sinai was not a cheerful thing but a scary experience.

Inside the thick darkness, they saw fire burning and smoke billowed up into the clear desert sky like smoke from a massive furnace. The whole mountain shook with a violent earthquake, rocks crashed down the mountainside toward the desert floor. The ram's horn grew louder and louder until they heard the voice of God,

"Moses...come up into the top of the mountain..."

Moses obeyed God, climbing the heights into the presence of God. It was there the Lord gave Moses the Ten Commandments. The finger of God etched in stone ten laws that were to become the basis of all their living.

1. *Do not worship any other gods in place of Me.*

2. *Do not make any idols of any kind for any reason. Do not bow to them nor worship them for I, the Lord your God, am a jealous God.*

3. *Do not take My name—the name of the Lord your God—in vain, for you will not go unpunished if you misuse My name.*

4. *Remember to observe the Sabbath day to keep it holy.*

5. *Honor your father and mother so that you will have a long life in the land that I, the Lord your God, will give you.*

6. *Do not commit murder.*

7. *Do not have sex with anyone who is not your spouse.*

8. *Do not steal.*

9. *Do not lie or testify falsely against anyone.*

10. *Do not covet your neighbor's house, wife, servants, animals, or anything that your neighbor owns.*

My Time to Pray

- Lord, I will not come lightly or jokingly into Your presence, but I will fear You and worship You.

- Lord, no one has seen Your presence and lived, yet I have Your presence in my heart. Thank you for giving me eternal life.

- Lord, if You had not told me how to live in the Ten Commandments, I would have lived a self-centered life to please myself. Now, I will put You first in my life.

- Lord, Your Ten Commandments tell me to be holy and separate myself to You. I yield myself to You at this moment.

Amen.

Exodus 21

Consequences of Actions

Lord, You told Your people how to treat their servants. "If you buy a
Hebrew servant, that servant must serve you for six years.
However, that servant must be released on the seventh year and
be free. If you received that servant as an unmarried man, then
he must leave you by himself. If you received him as a married
man, then his wife will leave with him. But if you gave him a
wife and she gave birth to sons and daughters, then the wife and
children belong to you, and the man must leave by himself. But
if the servant says, 'I love my master, my wife, and my children—
I don't want to be free,' then you must certify this by a local
judge, then take him to the door post of your house and pierce
the servant's ear with an awl, and that servant will serve you the
rest of his life.

Lord, You are the source of all true justice.
When I appear before a local judge,
Remind me that true justice comes from You.

Lord, just as piercing an ear lobe was a sign of submission,
Remind me of my submission to You.
I love You and want to be Your slave.

Lord, You said, "When someone hits another so that he kills someone,
the offender must be put to death. But if that person did not
intend to kill and it was an accident, there will be a place to
which he can run for safety. However, if someone cleverly plots
to kill another, do not recognize his place of safety. If he has run
to the altar for safety, take him away and execute him. If anyone

hits his father or mother, he must be put to death. If anyone kidnaps another, whether to sell them or hold them captive, then the kidnapper must be put to death. The one who curses his father or mother must be executed. If two men get into an argument and one hits the other with a rock or his fist, but does not kill him, though the wounded man is incapacitated, the man who hit him will not be executed but must pay for losses until the wounded man is fully recovered. If a man hits a male or female servant with a stick and the slave dies, then he must be punished. But if the slave lives, then he will not be punished because the slave is his property."

Lord, because You value life, those who kill another
Must be punished according to Your word.

Because You value obedience in the home, the disobedient
Child must be dealt with severely
Lord, make me obedient to You, to parents, and to my
employers.

Lord, if two fight and they hurt a pregnant woman, causing her to have a miscarriage, but there is no additional injury, then the one hurting the woman must pay the damages that are demanded by the woman's husband. However, if there was further injury, then the penalty is "a life for a life, an eye for an eye, a tooth for a tooth." If you put out the eye of your male or female slave, then you must let that slave go free. If you knock out the tooth of a male or female slave, you must let that slave go free.

Lord, Your law protects the life and property of individuals;
Thank You for guidance how I should treat others,
And how they must treat me.

May I learn to live within the constraints of law,
And may I serve You within that freedom.

Lord, if a bull gores a man or woman to death, then the bull must be stoned. The owner of the bull will not be held responsible unless the bull had a habit of attacking people and the owner had been warned but the owner did not keep the bull penned up. If the bull kills someone, then stone the bull to death and also execute the owner. However, the owner can redeem his life by paying what is demanded of him. If a bull gores a male or female slave, then the owner must give 30 shekels of silver to the owner of the slave, and the bull must be stoned to death.

Lord, you teach I'm responsible for the consequences of my actions;
Help me be a good steward of all that I have.

Lord, when a man digs a hole in the ground and leaves it uncovered, if a donkey or bull falls into it, then the man must pay damages to the owner of the animal. The man must pay for the animal but the carcass belongs to him. If a man's bull hurts another man's animals, the bull must be sold and the money divided. If it is common knowledge that a bull was dangerous—had a habit of goring—the owner must pay the full price of damages.

Lord, I am responsible for whatever belongs to me;
Keep me from hurting another with my possessions.

Amen.

Exodus 22

PROTECTION OF PROPERTY

Lord, You said, "If a man steals a bull or a sheep and kills it or sells it, then he must pay the owner back—five cattle for one bull, or four flock animals for one sheep. If he does not have anything, then he must be sold into slavery to pay for his robbery. If the stolen animal is found alive in his possession, whether it is a bull, a donkey, or a sheep, then he must pay back double. If the robber is caught while breaking and entering in the dark, and he is hit so hard that he dies, the owner is not guilty if he acted in self-defense in darkness. Then no murder charges may be made. However, if this break-in occurred during the daytime, then the owner may be charged with murder."

> *Lord, teach me to be satisfied with my possessions,*
> *Then I won't covet the possessions of others*
> *And I will never become a thief.*

Lord, You said, "If a man allows his field or vineyard to be overgrazed, or 'burned' and if he allows his animal to run free and graze in another man's field, then he must pay back what is lost from his good field or vineyard. If a fire breaks out and spreads into another man's field, in such a way that the sheaves of grain or the standing grain or the field itself is completely destroyed, then the one who started the fire must pay for the whole thing."

Lord, You said, "If a man delivers money or goods to his neighbor to hold for him, and it is stolen from the second man's house, then if the robber is caught, the robber must pay back double. If the robber is not caught, then the owner of the house must approach the local judges to decide whether the one holding the property was the one who stole his property or not. For every case of illegal possession, whether it is for a bull, a donkey, a sheep, clothes, or any other lost property that one claims is his, the case for both parties must come before the local judges. The one whom the judges find guilty will pay back double to his neighbor."

Lord, You said, "If a man delivers a donkey, a bull, a sheep, or any animal to his neighbor to hold for him, and the animal dies, gets hurt, or is taken without anyone seeing it, then the second man must take an oath by the Lord to verify that he did not steal his neighbor's goods. The owner of the animal must accept this oath, and the second man will not have to pay anything. If the animal was torn to pieces by a wild animal, let the second man bring the carcass as evidence. He will not have to pay for what was torn apart. If a man borrows an animal from his neighbor and it gets hurt or dies while its owner is not present with it, then the borrower must surely pay in full. But if its owner is present, then the borrower does not have to pay. If the animal was rented, then the money paid for it covers the loss.

Lord, You said, "If a man seduces a virgin girl who is not engaged and goes to bed with her, then he must certainly pay a dowry for her to be his wife. However, if her father absolutely refuses to give her to him, then he must pay the usual bride-price for virgins."

Lord, You said, "You must not allow a sorceress to live among you. Whoever has sex with an animal must certainly be put to death."

Lord, You said, "The person who sacrifices to any god must be completely destroyed. Sacrifices can only be made to You."

Lord, help me fully obey every command You give;
  May I not compromise or dabble with sin.

Because there are many consequences to sin,
  You give us commands to protect us.

Lord, I will keep Your commandments;
  Please keep me and protect me from harm.

Lord, You said, "You must not do wrong to a foreigner or persecute him, because you also were once foreigners in the land of Egypt. You must not take advantage of any widow or orphan. If you give them any trouble at all and they cry out to Me in any way, then I will surely hear their cry for help. I will become very angry and arrange for your death. Your wives will become widows, and your children will have no father. If you lend money to any of My people who are poor among you, then you must not act like a creditor to that person. You must not charge him interest. If you ever take your neighbor's robe as a guarantee, then you must restore it to him before the sun goes down, because that is the only covering he has for his body. What else will he sleep in? Whenever that person cries out to Me, I will hear it, because I am merciful."

Lord, You said, "You must not blaspheme God or curse a ruler of your people. You must not delay giving an offering to Me from your harvest or from the overflow of your vats. You must dedicate your firstborn sons to Me. You must do the same with your bulls and with your flock animals. The animal that is born first must stay with its mother for one week. On the eighth day, you must give it to Me. You must be holy to Me. Therefore, you must not eat any meat that was torn in pieces by wild animals in the field. Throw it to the dogs."

Lord, this chapter teaches me much about personal property;
Thank You for allowing me to own things.

Lord, I dedicate all my "things" to You;
I don't want "things" owning me.

Amen.

Exodus 23

JUSTICE

Lord, You said, "You must not spread a false report. Do not help an evil person by giving false testimony. You must not follow a mob to do evil. When you give testimony in a lawsuit, do not twist justice by trying to be on the side of the crowd. You must not give any special favors to a poor man in his lawsuit. If you happen to meet your enemy's bull or his donkey as it wanders around, then you must certainly return it to him. If you see the donkey of the one who hates you lying helpless under its load, then don't leave it. You must certainly help it get up. You must not twist what you say in a lawsuit. Keep away from a false charge. Do not put an innocent man or an honest person to death. I will hold the guilty party personally responsible. You must never take a bribe. Bribes have a way of causing people to look the other way. They twist the words of righteous people. You must not persecute a foreigner, because you know what it feels like to be a foreigner. You were once foreigners in the land of Egypt."

Lord, truth is important, it's the way things are;
Keep me from lies, and help me tell the truth
So I can honestly serve Jesus the truth.

Lord, You said, "You are allowed to plant seed in your field for six years and gather its harvest. However, on the seventh year, you must let your land rest and remain unplanted, so the poor may glean your field in the sabbatical year so they have something to eat. Whatever they leave can be eaten by the wild animals. You must do the same thing for your vineyard and olive trees."

Lord, You said, "You will do your work for six days, but you must rest on the seventh day, so that your bull and your donkey can rest. The son of your slave-woman and the resident foreigner need to get their rest, too.

Lord, You said, "Be careful about everything that I have told you. Don't even mention the name of other gods. Don't let their names be heard from your mouth!"

Lord, You said, "Each year, you must celebrate the following three festivals to Me: (Passover, Pentecost, and Tabernacles). Observe the Feast of Unleavened Bread—Passover—for seven days as I have commanded you. Observe it in the month of Abib, the month when you came out of Egypt. During the month of Abib you must eat bread that does not contain any yeast. No one will be allowed to appear in My presence empty-handed, but you must bring a gift. And you must observe the Feast of Spring Harvest—Pentecost. And at the end of the fall harvest, you must observe the Feast of Ingathering, also called the Feast of Tabernacles. Celebrate it from the fifteenth through the twenty-second day of the seventh month (usually about mid-September to mid-October) after you gather in the autumn crop of your labors from the field. All of your males must appear in My presence these three times each year."

Lord, there were special days to worship You
In the Old Testament;

I will worship You every day in the New Testament,
But especially on Sunday.

Lord, You said, "You must not offer the blood of the Passover lamb with yeast. The part of the Pascal Lamb that is not eaten must not remain overnight until morning."

Lord, You said, "You must first bring into Me the very best of what your land produces. You must not cook or boil a young goat in its mother's milk.

Lord, mother's milk was intended for life, not death;
You did not want Your people to be heartless.

Help me understand the difference between what is sin,
What is unhealthy, and what is inappropriate,
Such as boiling a young goat in its mother's milk.

Lord, You said, "Listen, I am sending an Angel ahead of you to protect you along the way. He will bring you to the place that I have prepared. Pay attention to him and listen to what he says. Do not rebel against him, because he will not forgive your violations, since My name is in him. However, if you will truly listen to what he says, and you do everything that I say, then I will be an enemy to your enemies, and I will oppose those who oppose you. My Angel will go ahead of you and bring you into the land of your people."

Lord, You said, "You must *not* bow down to their gods, or worship them, or act like these heathen people. Instead, you must completely destroy them and smash their so-called 'sacred' posts in pieces! Instead, you must worship Me, your God. I will bless your bread and your water. I will take away sickness from among you. In your new land, your women will not be sterile or have miscarriages. I will help you live out your full lifetimes. I will send My terror ahead of you. I will throw all those people whom you meet into confusion. I will cause all of your enemies to run in retreat from you. I will send the wasp ahead of you to drive out the Hivites, the Canaanites, and the Hittites from your path. I will not drive them out all at once. If I did, the land would become too empty, and the wild animals would outnumber you. I will drive them away from your path little by little until you are strong enough in number and you can inherit the land. I will set your borders from the Red Sea all the way to the Philistine Sea and from the Arabian Desert to the Euphrates River. I will put those who live in that land under your control. You will drive them out of your way. You must *never* make any covenant with them or with their gods. They must *not* live in your land. If they do, they will cause you to sin against Me. If you worship their gods, it will certainly be a trap for you."

Lord, You wanted Your people to separate themselves
From the sins and evil of worldly people.

That is still Your standard for me today;
I will live among evil people, but I'll not live
Like heathen people, nor worship their gods.

Amen.

Exodus 24

Moses and the Elders Worship God

Lord, You told Moses, "Come up in the mountain to Me. Bring with you
Aaron, Nadab, Abihu, and 70 of the leaders. Don't let them
come too close to Me. You, however, may approach by yourself.
Let the others worship at a distance. The people of Israel are not
to set foot on the mountain."

Moses told the people all the commands the Lord had given him. The
people answered, "We will do everything the Lord commands."
Moses carefully wrote down all the words You gave him.

He woke up early in the morning and set up an altar at the foot of the
mountain. Then he set in place 12 large stones to represent the
12 tribes of Israel. He sent some young men to sacrifice burnt
offerings and peace offerings to You. He sprinkled half the blood
on the altar, and the other half he put in basins to sanctify the
people. Then he read to the people out of the book of the
covenant.

The people responded, "We will do everything the Lord has spoken."

> Lord, the shed blood is always the beginning place,
> > I again ask You to forgive me by the blood of Christ.
>
> I praise You for the blood of Jesus shed for me,
> > From it I get cleansing, strength, power, and life.

Moses, Aaron, Nadab, Alihu, and the 70 leaders went up to the mountain. They saw the glory of God manifested, and underneath
there seemed to be a pavement of sapphire as clear as the sky.

Even though they saw God's glory, He did not destroy them. They even ate a meal together in the presence of God.

The Lord said to Moses, "Come up into the mountain where I will give you stone tablets inscribed with the Ten Commandments. From these you can teach the people."

Moses and Joshua climbed the mountain of God. Before he left he said to Aaron and Hur, "Stay here to wait for us, take care of any problems while I am gone." Moses went into the cloud that covered the mountain. The cloud was the Shekinah glory of the Lord that covered Sinai. The people of Israel at the foot of the mountain saw the awesome sight that looked like a burning fire. Moses climbed higher and stayed there 40 days and nights.

Amen.

Exodus 25

FURNITURE IN THE TABERNACLE

The Lord told Moses how to prepare a sanctuary for the people of
Israel to worship Him. He said, "Here are the things the people
may bring to Me; gold, silver, bronze, blue, purple and red yarn,
fine cotton linen, goat's hair to make into cloth, leather that is
tanned, and acacia wood. They should give olive oil for lamps,
spices for anointing, and fragrant incenses. Also they should give
onyx and other precious stones to be set in the priest's vest."

The Lord said, "I want the people of Israel to make a tent so I can dwell
among them. This tent of meeting will be called a Tabernacle.
You are to furnish it according to the design I will show you. It
will reflect the plan of the heavenly sanctuary.

The Lord said, "Make an ark (box) of acacia wood—the most sacred
piece of furniture. It will be 3 feet long, 2¼ feet wide, and 2¼
feet tall. Cover it with pure gold inside and out, then put a solid
gold crown around the outside top. Cast four gold rings and
attach them to the four feet of the box. Make two poles of acacia
wood and overlay them with gold. These are the carrying poles.
Place them in the rings and leave them there permanently. When
you are finished, put the stone tablet inscribed with the Ten
Commandments into the box."

Lord, you want the best—pure gold—for Your seat on earth;
  This means I must give my best to You,
  Every day, everything, I give You all that I have.

Lord, only pure gold is good enough for You,
Not 14-karat, or even 22-karat, but pure gold.

May I never offer you second best or half-hearted service;
I give the best of all I have to You.

The Lord said, "Make a top for the box of pure gold. It will be the place of atonement. I will come sit there among My people, it will be called the Mercy Seat or the Seat of Atonement. It must be 3¾ feet long and 2½ feet wide."

Lord, this is the most holy place in all Israel,
For the Shekinah glory cloud will sit here;
This is where your presence sits among Your people.

Lord, I come symbolically to the Holy of Holies
To bow in Your presence and worship Your majesty.

The Lord said, "Sculpture two cherubim (angels) and place them at each end of the Seat of Atonement. Hammer them out of one piece of gold making it one piece. The cherubim are to face each other with bowed heads, looking down on the mercy seat. Their wings will spread out above the ark. Place inside the ark the two stone tablets inscribed with the Ten Commandments. Then put the cover—the mercy seat—on the ark. I will meet with you there above the Commandments I have given."

Lord, the two cherubim are the two closest to You on earth;
They are made of pure gold to represent purity,
May I live a pure life, so I can be close to You.

The two cherubim are sculpted from beaten gold;
Blows from hammers made them what they are.

Lord, You, the Divine Sculptor, have used hammers on me
To fashion in me discipline and character.

May I learn from trials and tribulation in this life
So I can draw near to You as the cherubim.

The Lord told Moses, "You are to make a table of acacia wood, 3 feet
long, 19 inches wide, and 18 inches high. Cover it with pure
gold, and place a pure gold crown around the top. Make four
gold rings and attach them to the four corners by the four legs.
Make two poles of acacia wood, cover them with gold, and use
them to carry the table. Also make bowls and pitchers. Put the
Bread of My presence on the table in My presence. It is to be
there always."

Lord, bread stands for strength, growth, energy, and life;
Thank You for daily bread that gives me all of the above.

The bread was symbolic of your presence;
I draw strength from You.

The Lord told Moses, "Make a candlestick (Menorah) and sculpture it by
hammering all of it out of one piece of pure gold—its base,
shaft, and legs to hold the light. It will have six branches; these
will come out of each side of the center shaft. The light for each
of the six branches will have a cup shaped like an almond blos-
som, with both buds and petals. The light for the center shaft
will be decorated with four almond blossoms with buds and
petals. Everything must be of one piece of pure gold that is hammered into shape. Make seven lamps for the one candlestick
(Menorah) and set them so light is reflected toward the front.
The tongs and trays also must be made from pure gold. It will
take 66 pounds of gold to make the Menorah. Do it according
to the heavenly pattern I showed you here on Mount Sinai."

Lord, You didn't ask us to worship You in the dark,
But You put light in the Tabernacle for sight.

In the same way You never ask us to worship You in ignorance,
You have shown us how to believe, live, and worship;
I worship You according to Your light.

Lord, there were three lights on each side,
And one light on the center pole
Making seven lights that gave one illumination.

Lord, I am just one light among many lights,
Teach me harmony, to shine with other lights,
So we can worship You and be a testimony to the world.

Amen.

Exodus 26

Preparing the Tabernacle

The Lord instructed Moses, "Make an inside ceiling for the Tabernacle roof with ten sections of finely woven sheets of linen. Embroidery representations of cherubim from blue, purple, and red yarn on the ceiling. Each section of cloth must be the same size, 42 feet long and 6 feet wide. Attach five sections together for one side of the Tabernacle and five sections for the other side. Put loops of blue yarn on the edge of the outside section. Fifty loops on the edge of one section of cloth will match the 50 loops of the other section. Then make 50 gold clasps to fasten the two sections together, making it a single unit."

The Lord instructed, "Make a covering for the outside roof of the Tabernacle tent. Make heavy sheets from goat's hair. There must be eleven sections, each 45 feet long and 6 feet wide. All eleven sections must be the same size. Join five sections together to make one set and the other six to make the other section. The sixth section of the longer section will double over the front opening. Attach 50 loops together with 50 gold clips as before, to fasten the two together. Because the outer coverings are bigger than the inner more beautiful cloth, the edge will hang over to protect it from the elements. Then cover it with tanned ram skin and on top of that, a covering of goatskin leather. These four coverings are the roof of the Tabernacle."

The Lord instructed Moses to make a frame using posts from acacia wood for the Tabernacle. "Each post is to be 15 feet high with a 2-foot connector. There will be two places on each post to connect it to the other posts. Twenty posts will support the south side, and 20 posts will support the north side. Make 40 silver braces—two for each post to tie them together. There will be six posts on the rear of the Tabernacle—the west side. There will be special posts for each corner. These are double posts held together by gold rings. There will be boards on the ground for all the posts to set on. The boards will have silver sockets to hold the boards in place. Make crossbars of acacia wood to run across the five crossbars for the north and five for the south. Also make five crossbars for the rear or west side of the Tabernacle. Overlay the posts and the crossbars with gold. Always set up this Tabernacle according to the heavenly plan I have shown you."

The Lord instructed Moses to hang a special curtain (the veil) on the inside to separate the Holy of Holies. They were to skillfully embroider into the cloth the representation of the cherubim using blue, purple, and red yarn. The veil was to be hung on gold hooks and to be held up with four poles made from acacia wood, covered with gold. The posts were to fit into silver sockets on boards. This curtain was to separate the most Holy of Holies from the Holy Room.

The Lord said, "Place the Ark of the Covenant behind the veil. Then place the mercy seat on top of the Ark of the Covenant behind the veil. Place the Table of Showbread of My presence and the Golden Candlestick (Menorah) outside the veil in the Holy Room across from each other. The Menorah must be on the south side and the table on the north side. Make another curtain of fine linen at the entrance into the Holy Room. Embroider it with blue, purple, and red. Hang this curtain from the five posts at the entrance."

Lord, You consented to come dwell among Your people;
  You didn't dwell among the world,
    Nor did the world recognize Your condescension.

Thank You for coming to live in my heart;
    May I carefully prepare a place for You
    As the Israelites carefully prepared the Tabernacle.

Amen.

Exodus 27

THE BRAZEN ALTAR AND COURTYARD

The Lord told Moses, "Make an altar where you can sacrifice to Me.
Make it 7½ feet long, 7½ feet wide, and 4½ feet high. Put horns
on the four corners so you can tie the animals to it. Cover it
with bronze. Make utensils out of bronze to service the sacrifices; meat hooks, fire pans, pots to remove ashes, and shovels.
Make a bronze grate netting with bronze hooks on the four corners. Hook it halfway under the top of the altar. Make two acacia wood carrying poles and cover them with bronze. Put the
poles in the rings on the four corners to carry the altar. The altar
will have a large open space for the sacrifices. Make the altar
just like the heavenly pattern I showed you."

Lord, You had the Israelites take an altar with them
Because they sinned daily,
And needed a place of cleansing daily.

Lord, I am no different than the Israelites;
I sin daily and need daily cleaning.

As I walk in the light, may the blood of Jesus Christ
Cleanse me from every sin.

The Lord told Moses how to lay out the courtyard for the Tabernacle
and enclose it with curtains 150 feet long, 75 feet wide, and 7½
feet high. The Lord said, "Prepare sections of fine cloth 150 feet
long. They will be hung from 20 bronze posts that are set into
20 bronze bases. The curtains will be draped from a silver curtain rod, attached by silver hooks. Both sides will be identical—

150 feet. The west end will be 75 feet long with ten posts; the curtains will be supported just like the others. The entrance (door) will be on the east with two sections of cloth on either side of the door—22½ feet on the right side and the same for the left entrance. The entrance (door) will be made from fine linen cloth 30 feet long, embroidered in blue, purple, and red yarn. It will be hung from a silver curtain rod attached to four bronze posts."

The Lord commanded, "Make all the tent pegs of bronze that are used to support the courtyard curtains and Tabernacle."

The Lord told Moses, "Tell the people to bring pure olive oil for the candlestick (Menorah) so it will be kept burning continually. The Menorah will be outside the veil in the Holy Room. Aaron and his sons—all the priests—must keep it burning in My presence day and night. This is a requirement for future generations."

Lord, the Menorah is seven lights that make up "one" light,
I will add my testimony to other believers
So we can be "one" light to unsaved people.

Lord, just as the Menorah was kept burning constantly,
May I be a continuous testimony burning constantly to You.

Amen.

Exodus 28

CLOTHES FOR THE PRIESTS

The Lord said to Moses, "Invite your brother Aaron to separate himself
to you from among the sons of Israel, along with his sons—
Nadab, Abihu, Eleazar, and Ithamar—so that they may serve Me
as priests. Make special holy clothes for your brother Aaron that
are beautiful and glorious. Tell all those to whom I have given
skills to make clothes, that they must make clothes for Aaron to
set him apart so that he may serve Me as the High Priest. These
are the clothes they are to make: a vest with a pocket, a robe, a
woven coat, a turban, and a belt. They must make holy clothes
for both your brother Aaron and his sons, so that they may
serve Me as priests. Have them use gold thread, and blue, purple, and red yarn, as well as fine-spun cotton. They are to make
the vest with gold thread, plus blue, purple, and red yarn of fine-
spun cotton. The vest must have two shoulder straps attached to
two of its corners, so that it may be joined together. The vest's
waistband must be sewn just like it—all one piece and sewn
with gold thread, and with blue, purple, and red yarn from fine-
spun cotton."

Lord, You said, "Take two onyx stones and engrave upon them the
names of the twelve sons of Israel in the order of their birth—six
of their names on one stone and the remaining six names on the
other stone. Engrave the names of the sons of Israel on the two
stones in the same way that a jewel-cutter engraves a seal. Then
mount the stones in delicate gold settings and put a stone on
each shoulder strap of the vest as jewelry, so Aaron will carry
their names into My presence. Make delicate gold settings for

the stones, then make two pure gold, braided chains like a rope, and attach them to the settings."

Lord, Aaron carried the names of his brethren into Your presence
Just as I must carry others to You in prayer;
Make me an effective intercessor.

Lord, You told Moses, "You must also make a chest pocket for the vest. It is from this chest pocket you will understand My plan. Let the skilled craftsman make it like the vest—use gold, blue, purple, and red yarn, and make it from fine-spun cotton. It must be square—9 inches long and 9 inches wide and folded double, forming a pocket for the Urim and Thummim. Then you must mount stone settings on it, four rows of jewels: the first row will be a topaz, ruby, and a beryl. The second row will be a turquoise, and a sapphire, and an emerald. The third row will be a ligure, a jacinth, and an amethyst. The fourth row will be a chrysolite, an onyx, and a jasper. Mount them in delicate, gold settings. There are to be twelve jewels, one for each of the names of the sons of Israel. Each jewel will be engraved like a seal-ring with the name of one of the twelve tribes."

The Lord said, "Braid pure gold chains like a rope for the chest-pocket. Make two gold rings for it and attach them to the two corners of the chest pocket. Join the two gold chains to the two rings which are at the corners of the chest pocket. Attach them to the shoulder straps of the vest at the front."

The Lord said, "Make two more gold rings and attach them to the bottom of the shoulder straps of the vest. This is near the seam, which is just above the elaborate waistband of the vest. Let them tie the rings of the chest pocket to the rings of the vest with a blue cord, connecting it to the waistband, so that the chest pocket cannot separate from the vest."

The Lord said, "Whenever Aaron goes into the Holy Place, he will be carrying the names of the sons of Israel over his heart on the chest-pocket. This will be a constant reminder of My presence. Put the Urim and the Thummim in the chest pocket. These will be used to determine My will. They will also be over Aaron's heart when he goes into My presence. In this way, Aaron will always be carrying the instrument for Israel to understand My will."

The Lord said, "Make the robe all blue. It will have an opening in the center. Sew a reinforced hem around the collar so that it will not get torn. Around the lower hem of the robe, embroider pomegranates from blue, purple, and red yarn, with golden bells between them all around. There should be a golden bell interspersed by a pomegranate all the way around the lower hem of the robe. Whenever Aaron is serving as the High Priest, he must wear this robe. When Aaron goes into My presence in the Holy of Holies, the sound of the bells will be heard, so you will know he is alive and has not died."

The Lord said, "Make a crown of pure gold and engrave this phrase upon it as on a seal: 'HOLINESS TO YAHWEH.' Attach it to a blue cord and put it on the front of the turban. Aaron must wear this crown, which represents his responsibility for the holy things of worship. This crown will always be worn by Aaron so that I can always accept your gifts."

The Lord said, "Weave the blue coat from fine-spun cotton, symbolizing purity. Make a turban out of the same material. The sash must be made by a needle-worker. Make the coats, belts, and turbans beautiful and glorious for Aaron's sons. Put these clothes upon your brother Aaron and his sons. Ordain them and make them holy by anointing them with oil, so that they may serve Me as priests. Make cotton shorts reaching from the waist to the thighs to cover their nakedness. Aaron and his sons must wear them when they go into the Tent of Meeting or when they approach the Altar to serve in the Holy Place so that they may not incur My wrath and be killed. All priests must continually do this.

Lord, I'm amazed how carefully You planned the clothes
Of those priests who came into Your presence.

Cover me with a robe or righteousness when I enter Your Presence
to worship or intercede for others; Without the
righteousness of Jesus Christ, I can't enter Your presence.

Amen.

Exodus 28:30

The Story of the Urim and Thummin

Date: 1492 B.C. ~ Place: Foot of Mount Sinai

The High Priest's garments were all laid out on the table in front of Moses and Aaron. The tailors had made everything exactly as commanded by God. They had woven the cloth and measured two times before cutting. That's the source of the old Jewish saying, "Measure twice, cut once." The tailors kept saying, "Exactly according to the commandment of God."

Moses picked up each piece of clothing that the High Priest would wear when standing before God for the people. Moses told his brother, "You will be the first High Priest and your sons will follow you in this ministry." Then, Moses explained,

"After you die, it will be called the Aaronic priesthood, so you must lay the foundation and do everything exactly as commanded by God." Then Moses told his brother,

"Not only must you do everything exactly as God commands you, but you must also dress exactly as God commands."

Aaron picked up each piece of clothing to finger the texture. He understood what each piece of clothing was for, and he understood the symbolism behind each item of clothing. But one perplexed him. "What's the purpose of this pocket?" Aaron held up the vest and pointed to the pocket.

"This pocket is close to your heart," Moses answered, "That's where the urim and thummin are kept."

"What's that?" the brother asked Moses.

"The urim and thummin are two precious jewels, one white and one black. They are perfectly round, both exactly the same, so that when you reach into the pocket for one, you'll not know which is in your hand." Moses explained to his brother that the chest pocket was called "the breastplate of judgment," for out of that vest God guided His people.

"When someone comes to you for a decision, you must pray to God for an answer. Then reach into the pocket and pull out one of the jewels. If you bring out a white jewel, the answer is yes. If you bring out a dark jewel, the answer is no."

Moses explained the chest pocket was made of four layers of cloth. The urim and thummin were kept between two layers of cloth in the pocket.

"When someone shall stand before Eleazer—your son—who shall ask directions from the Lord, the precious stones will tell them the direction the Lord wants them to go." *All the people of Israel will follow the direction of God* (Num. 27:21, expanded).

"What do these words mean?" The words *urim* and *thummin* were new words to Aaron. Moses gave his brother a Hebrew lesson. "Even though you will have only one jewel for an *urim*, the word is plural and *urim* means 'lights.'" Moses explained God will give His people light in contrast to the heathen who live in darkness. "Sometimes the jewel will glow like it has fire within the stone. The word *urim* also means fire."

"The word *thummin* means 'perfection' or 'truth.'" Moses explained Israel could find out truth by the urim and thummin. He said if hidden sin was done by someone in one of the twelve tribes, the urim and thummin would tell the truth and point out the guilty person. Each tribal head would come before the High Priest and the urim and thummin would tell which tribe was guilty. Then the families of each tribe will pass before the High Priest to locate the guilty one. Finally, individuals would pass before Aaron to determine who is guilty.

Moses explained, "We will not know everything. We are human; we will only know in part" (1 Cor. 13:12, expanded).

Aaron began to understand the awesome responsibility he had as High Priest to reveal hidden things to God's people. Yet Moses explained what God had told him on the mount, "The secret things belong to the Lord our God, but those things that are revealed belong to us and our children to do them" (Deut. 29:29).

"Remember," Moses continued, "it is presumptuous to pry into those things that belong to God."

My Time to Pray

- Lord, I don't use precious stones to find Your will, I will go to the Word of God to find Your will.

- Lord, I don't go to an earthly High Priest for guidance, I will go to Jesus Christ who is my High Priest; He stands in Your presence interceding for me.

- Lord, I don't have to wait in line to get Your direction; instantly and at all times, You guide me into truth by Your indwelling Holy Spirit who leads me to do Your will.

- Lord, I will take advantage of all You've given me; I will walk joyfully in Your will for my life.

Amen.

Exodus 29

DEDICATION OF AARON AND HIS SONS

Then the Lord said to Moses, "Now this is what you must do to Aaron
and his sons so that they may serve Me as priests: Take one
young bull and two rams that have no defects, bread that contains no yeast, and cakes mixed with oil and wafers brushed
with oil; all unleavened. You must make them out of fine wheat
flour. Put them in a basket and present them to Me along with
the bull and the two rams. Then bring Aaron and his sons to the
doorway of the Tent of Meeting and wash them with water in
the Laver. Dress Aaron with the priestly clothes and put on him
the coat and the vest and the chest pocket. Wrap the waistband
around his waist. Place the turban upon his head, and put the
holy crown on top of the turban. Then take the special anointing
oil and anoint his head."

Lord, the word "anointed" means "Christ," this is why
The High Priest is a type of Jesus Christ.

Jesus fulfilled the three-fold anointed office.
Jesus was anointed to High Priestly intercession.
Jesus was anointed as King to rule our lives.
Jesus was anointed as prophet to deliver Your message to
me.

Lord, thank You for Jesus, "the Anointed One," who is the Christ;
Anoint me to be holy and to serve You continually.

Lord, You said, "After this, bring the sons of Aaron and put caps upon
them. Then you must bring a bull to the front of the Tent of

161

Meeting. Aaron and his sons will place their hands upon the bull's head and kill the bull in My presence, at the doorway of the Tent of Meeting."

Lord, when anyone laid their hands on the head of an animal to Confess their sins, they were transferring their guilt onto the animal.

When the animal was put to death, that was a symbolic act That their sins were judged instead of them.

Lord, I know my sins were transferred to Jesus Christ, And He died for forgiveness of my sins.

"Take some of the bull's blood and put it upon the horns of the Brazen Altar with your finger. Then pour out all the rest of the blood at the base of the Altar. Take all the fat that covers the internal parts, the best part of the liver, and the two kidneys, with the fat that is on them, and burn them upon the Brazen Altar as an offering to Me. But you must completely burn its hide and its waste outside the camp. It is a sin-offering."

The Lord said, "Also, take one ram and have Aaron and his sons place their hands upon its head. Then you will kill the ram, take some of its blood, and sprinkle it around the Brazen Altar. Then you must cut up the ram into pieces and wash its internal parts and legs. Burn them with its head and other pieces upon the Brazen Altar. It is a burnt offering to Me. I will accept it as a sweet aroma. Then you must take the other ram and have Aaron and his sons place their hands upon its head. Kill the ram, take some of its blood, and put it upon the right ear lobe of Aaron and the right ear lobes of his sons, upon the thumbs of their right hands, and upon the big toes of their right feet. Sprinkle the rest of the blood around on the Altar. Take some of the blood that is on the Brazen Altar and some of the special anointing oil and sprinkle it upon Aaron and upon his sons. So, Aaron and his sons will be consecrated to Me. Also, take some of the ram's fat, the tail, the fat that covers the internal parts, the best part of the liver, the two kidneys, its right thigh, also one loaf of bread, one cake of bread with oil, and one wafer from the basket of unleavened bread and put the whole thing in the hands of Aaron and his sons. Wave them as a wave-offering in My presence. After they wave them before Me, then take them and burn them upon the Altar, along with the burnt offering, for a sweet aroma in My presence.

Lord, just as the priests waved their offerings in Your presence,
Symbolic of giving it to you,

So I offer to You my whole body, including my hands,
Feet, eyes, ears, mouth, and nose;
Accept them and use me.

The Lord said, "After you wave the breast of the ram for Aaron's ordaining, it will be your share, set aside as the priest's portion, so their family may eat it. That food will belong to Aaron and his sons as their regular share."

The Lord said, "Aaron's holy clothes will belong to his sons who follow him, who will be anointed in them and to be ordained in them. The son who takes Aaron's place as High Priest will wear them for seven days, whenever he goes into the Tent of Meeting to serve in the Holy Place. Remove the ram of ordination and cook its meat in a separate place. The replacement will eat the ram's meat and the bread that is in the basket at the doorway of the Tent of Meeting. In this way, they eat those things that cover sins when they are ordained. However, no outsider is allowed to eat from it, because that food is holy! If any of the meat from the ordination or any of the bread remains until morning, then you must burn the leftovers. It must not be eaten, because it is holy!"

The Lord said, "Ordain Aaron and his sons, according to everything I have commanded you. During a period of seven days, each day offer a bull as a sin-offering to cover sins. Also, you must purify the Altar, making it holy. Then the Altar will be holy. Whatever touches the Altar will be holy."

The Lord said, "Now offer a two-year-old lamb upon the Altar each and every day. Offer one lamb in the morning, and offer the other lamb at twilight. With the first lamb offer one-tenth of a bushel of fine flour mixed with one quart of crushed oil, and one quart of sweet wine for a drink-offering.

"Offer the other lamb at twilight. Offer it according to the grain-offering and drink-offering of the morning as a sweet aroma to me. It shall be a continual burnt-offering throughout your generations at the doorway of the Tent of Meeting in My presence. I will meet with you and speak with you there. I will also meet with the sons of Israel there. The Tent of Meeting will be made holy by My glory and presence. Then, I will live among the sons of Israel, and I will be their God, and they will know that I am their God. I brought them out of the land of Egypt, so that I could live among them and be their God."

Lord, Your presence comes to dwell with us only after the blood
Cleanses us from sin and makes us holy in Your sight.

Thank You for the inestimable privilege of knowing You
And having Your protective presence in my life.

Amen.

Exodus 30

THE ALTAR FOR BURNING INCENSE

The Lord said to Moses, "You must also make the Altar for Burning Incense to represent continued prayers coming up to Me. Make it from acacia wood. It will be 1½ feet long and 1½ feet wide (18 inches square). It will be 3 feet high. The horns on its four corners will be made from one piece of pure gold. Also, put a crown around the top of it. Below the molding, make two gold rings. Attach them to its two opposite sides. Make two carrying poles from acacia wood and cover them with gold. They will go through the rings to carry the Altar of Burning Incense. Put this altar in front of the curtain that hides the Ark of the Covenant in the Holy of Holies. Aaron must burn incense of sweet-smelling spices upon this altar every morning when he trims the lamps. Again when Aaron prepares the lamps each evening, he will burn incense as a symbol of My continual presence throughout your generations. Offer no unholy incense, burnt offering, or grain-offering upon that altar. Also do not pour any drink-offering upon it.

The Lord said, "Aaron is to make atonement upon its horns once a year throughout your generations. Offer the blood of the sin-offering on the Day of Atonement once a year."

Lord, I didn't know You had a sense of smell.
　　May my prayers please You,
　　Just as sweet incense pleases a person's smell.

Lord, the Altar of Burning Incense stands for our prayers
　　That must continually be offered to You.

You said the sweet-smelling incense will please You.
May my prayers be precious to You.

The Lord said to Moses, "When you take a census of the sons of Israel, each one must pay a gift for his life. This will prevent a disaster from happening when they are counted. Each one who crossed over the Red Sea must give a half-shekel. This includes everyone who is 20 years or older. The rich people will not give more than a half-shekel, and the poor people will not give less, when they give an offering to Me. This represents an atonement for their sins. Take the atonement money and set it aside for the maintenance of the Tent of Meeting."

The Lord said to Moses, "You must also make a reflective Laver as well as its bronze stand. Place it between the Tent of Meeting and the Brazen Altar, and fill it with water. Aaron and his sons will wash their hands and feet before they sacrifice to Me so they will not die. Also, whenever they approach the Brazen Altar to burn an offering by fire to Me, they must wash their hands and feet so that they will not die."

Lord, the Laver was made from the women's mirrors,
Just as a woman uses a mirror to prepare herself,
May I be cleansed and see myself pure and holy for You.

Then, the Lord said to Moses, "Take 15 pounds of fine spices: of free-flowing myrrh, 7½ pounds of sweet-smelling cinnamon, and again 7½ pounds of cassia and one quart olive oil. Mix these into a very special holy anointing oil, a fragrant blend that is the work of a perfumer. This is the sacred anointing oil used to anoint the Tent of Meeting and the Ark of the Covenant, the Table of Showbread of My presence, the (Menorah) Golden Lampstand, the Altar of Burning Incense, the Brazen Altar of Burnt offering, and the Laver and its stand. Anointing consecrates them in such a way that they are holy, and whoever touches them will become holy.

"Anoint Aaron and his sons and make them holy, so that they may serve Me as priests. Tell the sons of Israel, 'This will be My holy anointing oil throughout your generations. It will not anoint the bodies of ordinary men. You must never make anything like it for yourselves. It is holy and you must treat it holy. Whoever mixes anything like it or anoints an outsider will be cut off from his people!'"

Then the Lord said to Moses, "Take these sweet-smelling spices—stacte, onycha, and galbanum and pure frankincense all in equal amounts—and make a fragrant blend of incense. It is to be salted; pure and sacred. Grind some of it into powder and place it in the Altar of Burning Incense in the Tent of Meeting where I will meet with you. It will be holy to you. Do not use this formula to make any incense for yourselves. It will be holy to Me. Whoever makes anything like this sweet smell will be cut off from his people!"

Amen.

Exodus 31

WORKERS CHOSEN TO MAKE THE TABERNACLE

Then the Lord said to Moses, "I have chosen Bezalel from the tribe of Judah to be the general foreman. He is the son of Uri and the grandson of Hur. The Spirit of God has filled him with talent, understanding, and knowledge. He has special skills in making artistic designs for work in gold, silver, and bronze, in cutting and setting jewels, in carving wood, and in doing all kinds of craftsmanship. Along with Bezalel, I have also selected Aholiab, the son of Ahisamach, from the tribe of Dan. He will work with Bezalel. I have prepared the hearts of all those who have the same ability, so that they may make everything that I have commanded you: the Tent of Meeting, the Ark of the Covenant, and the Mercy Seat, all the equipment of the Tent, the Table of Showbread of My presence with its tools, the Golden Lampstand (Menorah) with all of its tools, the Altar of Burning Incense, the Brazen Altar of Burnt offering with all of its tools, the Laver and its stand, the finely woven clothes for Aaron and the clothes of his sons, so they can serve as priests, the special anointing oil, and the incense of sweet-smelling spices for the Holy Place. They must make everything exactly as I told you to make it."

Then the Lord said to Moses, "Also, tell the sons of Israel to truly observe My Sabbaths, because this is a sign between Me and Israel throughout your generations. This is how you will demonstrate that I am the Lord who makes you holy. Therefore, you must keep the Sabbath, because it is holy. Everyone who pro-

fanes it will certainly be put to death! Anyone who does any
type of work on the Sabbath will be cut off from among his people! Work for six days of the week, but the seventh day is a
Sabbath rest. It is holy to Me. Whoever does any kind of work
on the Sabbath day will certainly be put to death! Therefore,
Israel must keep the Sabbath day, observing the Sabbath
throughout their generations as a permanent covenant with Me.
I created the universe in six days, but I ceased working on the
seventh day. And I was refreshed."

After God finished talking with Moses upon Mount Sinai, He gave
Moses the two tables of stone that were written by the finger of
God!

Lord, You gave the Sabbath to Israel as a gift of rest
And as a covenant between You and them.

When they broke the Sabbath, they disobeyed You;
Jesus came and kept the Law with His perfect life.

In His death He fulfilled the Law and
Justified every law breaker who repented and believed in
Him.

Lord, I believe in Your Son and trust Him for salvation;
Now I will live holy to please You and serve You.

Amen.

Exodus 32

THE GOLDEN CALF

The Israelites were troubled because Moses had been on the mountain for such a long time. They gathered to Aaron and said, "We don't know what happened to the man—Moses—who brought us out of Egypt. Get busy to make us some gods to lead us to the Promised Land."

Aaron said to the people, "Have your wives, daughters, and sons strip off their gold earrings and bring them to me." The people did as he commanded. Aaron received their earrings and melted them down and molded it into the shape of a calf. They said, "Here is your god who brought you out of the land of Egypt."

Aaron built an altar for sacrifice in front of the golden calf and announced, "Tomorrow we will have a feast to the Lord." Early the next morning the people got up and offered burnt offerings and peace offerings. Then the people celebrated with eating and drinking. Then they indulged their lust in heathen revelry.

The Lord said to Moses, "Get up quick. Hurry down to the camp. Your people that you led from Egypt are corrupting themselves. They have already backslidden from the way I told them to live and worship. They have made a golden calf, worshiped it, and sacrificed to it. They have said, 'Here is our god who brought us up out of Egypt.'"

The Lord continued to speak to Moses, "I have seen that they are a stubborn and rebellious people. Now leave me alone so I can burn

my judgment against them. Then I will make out of you—
Moses—a great nation to take their place."

Moses pleaded with God, "Why are You going to destroy the people You
brought out of Egypt with miracles by Your hand? If You do
that, the Egyptians will say, 'God was evil to bring His people
out of Egypt to slaughter them in the desert and wipe them off
the face of the earth.' Remember Your promise to Your servants
Abraham, Isaac, and Israel. You swore by Yourself that You
would give them as many descendants as the stars of the heavens. You also promised that they would inherit the land to possess it forever." So the Lord didn't carry out His threat against
the people.

Moses left the presence of God to go down the mountain. He held the
two stone tablets where the Ten Commandments were inscribed
by the hand of God. They were inscribed on the front and back
by God Himself.

Joshua heard the people shouting in the camp and said, "It sounds like
soldiers fighting in the camp."

Moses replied, "It is not the shout of victory, or the cry of defeat. I hear
people celebrating." As Moses got near the camp he saw the
golden calf and dancing. Moses erupted in anger. He threw
down the two stone tablets, shattering them on the ground. He
took the calf and melted it in fire, then ground the gold into fine
powder and spread it on the water and made the people drink.

Moses demanded of Aaron, "How did these people make you commit
such a terrible sin?"

Aaron replied, "Don't get mad at me, you're my master. You know these
people are hardheaded and are committed to sin. The people
were afraid because you stayed such a long time on the mountain. They didn't know if you were alive. So they asked me,

'Make us gods to lead us.' I asked that anyone with gold strip it off and give it to me. I threw it into the fire and out came this golden calf."

Moses saw that the people were completely out of control, because Aaron had allowed them to dance without inhibition—to the laughter of their enemies—then Moses stood to shout, *"WHOEVER IS ON THE LORD'S SIDE, COME STAND BY ME."* All of the descendants of Levi rallied to Moses. He told them, "This is what the Lord wants you to do: strap on your sword, go throughout the camp killing everyone who is in obvious sin associated with the golden calf. You must kill your friends, kinsman, and neighbors." That day 3,000 died.

Moses told the Levites, "You have separated yourselves to the Lord this day, because you have stood with God against your friends, kinsman, and neighbors. Because of your faithfulness, God will now ordain you into His priesthood."

Moses said to the people the next day, "You have done a terrible sin. I will go back to intercede for you on the mountain. Perhaps God will forgive you."

Moses said to the Lord, "Please forgive their sins, these people have committed a terrible sin. They made a god out of gold. Now please forgive their sin—if You won't, then blot me out of Your book."

Lord, You replied, "I will blot out only those who sinned against Me. Now go lead these people into the Promised Land. My angel will lead you. The time will come when I will punish these people for their sin." A plague struck the people because they worshiped the golden calf.

Lord, I can't imagine anyone worshiping a golden calf;
But I wasn't raised a heathen; they will do anything
To satisfy their lustful imaginations.

I will not worship any gods or have them in my life;
I worship You, the only living and true God.

Amen.

Exodus 32

The Story of the Golden Calf

Date: 1492 B.C. ~ Place: Foot of Sinai

When Moses came down from Sinai, the people were shouting so loudly Joshua mistakenly thought there was a battle. But Israel had lost its moral war; they were defeated by their lust. The people were dancing naked, some were bowing before a golden bull to worship it. While Moses spent 40 days in the presence of God, the people had turned their backs on his leadership and repudiated the God they promised to obey and worship.

The anger of Moses burned white hot; he threw down the two stone tables on which God wrote the Ten Commandments, breaking them to small pieces. He called for repentance and asked who would stand with him. It was the Levites—the physical brothers of Moses—who stood with him. At the command of Moses, they took their swords to kill the rebellious leaders, those who abandoned God to worship an idol and fulfill the lust of the flesh. *Where will the slaughter stop? everyone thought. Would the Levites kill all their families, their tribes, all twelve tribes? If the Levites didn't kill them, would God do it?*

Moses ran as fast as his old legs would carry him toward the tent where intercession was made. He was going to meet God. He was going to intercede for the people. He yelled to the crowd as he scurried toward the center of the camp,

"You have sinned a great sin!"

Everyone knew it; Moses didn't need to remind them. Even though winded, Moses continued to yell as he ran,

"I will make intercession for you...." He quickly added, "Perhaps God will not destroy us all." Moses rushed boldly into the presence of God to intercede for the nation Israel. He spread himself out before God on his face, and with tears wetting his long, stringy beard, Moses begged God,

"Oh these people have sinned a great sin..." His voice trembled with strain. "Forgive their sins."

Moses pleaded many times until God interrupted him,

"Let Me alone," God angrily told Moses. "These people are stiff-necked and rebellious; my anger burns against them for making a golden calf as an idol."

Moses wept at the words of God, "Please forgive them," he continued to beg. But God was determined to destroy Israel. The Lord's voice could be heard throughout the tent—the large tent—where God met Moses.

"I will blot out these people," God announced his judgment to Moses. "I will begin a new nation through you."

"No!" Moses responded. He didn't want to be the Father of a new nation. Abraham was the Father of Israel. Israel had a wonderful heritage of Isaac, Jacob, Joseph, and the elders in Egypt. Moses prayed to God,

"These people are your people...You have delivered them from Egypt...." Moses reminded God of the miracles that delivered Israel out of bondage.

"Remember Abraham, Isaac, and Israel your servants," Moses reminded God of His promises to them.

"The Egyptians will laugh at You if you bring Your people into the wilderness to destroy them."

Each family head stood in the door to his tent to watch the black cloud of the presence of God hunkering down over the tent. The presence of God filled the tent to listen to the prayers of His servant Moses. They talked for a long time; finally Moses put his whole life on the line for Israel. Moses told God,

"Please forgive their sins..." then Moses paused to think about how he would phrase his words. He blurted out,

"If You can't forgive their sins...blot me out of Your book."

The heart of God is broken over the sin of His people, but more than that, the heart of God responds to the earnest intercession of His servants. In tenderness, God told Moses,

"I will forgive their sins..."

Moses had prevailed, and God had forgiven their sins. Israel would not die. But because of their transgression, God added a condition to His blessing them. God told Moses to lead the people to the Promised Land, but things would not be the same in the future as they had been in the past. God told Moses that He would not go with them, but,

"I will send the Angel of the Lord to lead you..."

God told Moses that the Shekinah glory cloud would not lead them into the Promised Land.

"My Angel will go before you!"

My Time to Pray

- Lord, give me a holy fear of sinning against You; I see what the sin of Israel did to them.

- Lord, you punished Israel for her sin, so I know You will punish me. Forgive me of all my sin—ignorant or presumptuous sin—cleanse me with the blood of Christ.

- Lord, Moses was an effective intercessor for those who sinned against You. Help me be an effective intercessor who prays for my family and lost friends.

Amen.

Exodus 33

MOSES ASKS TO SEE GOD

The Lord said to Moses, "You have delivered the people from Egypt. Now go from here toward the land I promised to give to Abraham, Isaac, and Jacob and to their descendants. I will send an Angel before you to drive out the Canaanites, Amorites, Hittites, Perizzites, Hivites, and Jebusites. It is a land flowing with milk and honey. I will not go with you because of your stubbornness. If I went with you, I'd probably destroy you on the way."

The people mourned when they heard these harsh words, and no one wore ornaments. The Lord had previously told Moses, "Tell the people to remove your ornaments until I decide what to do." So from Mount Sinai on, the Israelites didn't wear jewelry.

Moses pitched a tent outside the camp where people who wanted to pray to the Lord would go. It was called the Tent of Meeting, where God met His people. When Moses went to the Tent of Meeting, the glory cloud would descend on the entrance of the tent. Each man would prostrate himself in prayer at the entrance of his tent. The Lord would speak with Moses face to face as a man speaks to his friend. Afterward, Moses would return to his tent, but his young assistant, Joshua the son of Nun, remained in the Tent of Meeting.

Moses said to the Lord, "You have told me to take these people to the Promised Land, but you haven't told me who You will send with me. You have said, 'I know you by name' and You said, 'I have found favor in your sight.' If this is so then tell me what You intend to do, so I can follow You. But don't forget, these are Your people."

The Lord answered, "I will go before you. You will find your rest and peace."

Moses answered, "If Your presence doesn't go with us, do not let us go into the Promised Land. There is no other way for us—I and Your people—to know that we've found favor in Your sight than for You to go with us. Your presence is the difference between us and other people on earth."

The Lord answered, "I will do what you ask me to do, because you have found favor in My sight. You are My friend."

Lord, I want to be Your friend.
Please find me favorable in Your sight.

I know I am not perfect, and I fall short;
Forgive my sin and I'll be perfect in Jesus Christ;
Thank You for being my friend.

Moses requested, "Please let me see Your glory!"

The Lord answered, "I will let My goodness pass before you, and I will say My name in your presence, but you can't see My face, because no human can see Me and live. I will show favor on whom I will and show mercy on whom I will. Here is a place; stand on this rock. When My glory passes by, I will put you in the crevice of the rock, and when I pass by, I will protect you with My hand. Then I will remove My hand and you will see My backside, but you can't see My face."

Lord, I'm like Moses. I want to see Your glory;
Manifest Yourself to my heart
So I can know You better.

Lord, I want to see You glorified in my life;
Manifest Yourself in my life for others to see You.

Amen.

Exodus 33

The Story of Seeing the Face of God

Date: 1492 B.C. ~ Place: Mount Sinai

Yesterday, the smell of death infused the camp. Many had died because they rebelled against God. Now the thought of death permeated their thinking; they heard that the presence of God would not go before them to the Promised Land. A depressing atmosphere drifted over the tents.

Today Moses was climbing to the top of Sinai again to meet God. Today was a new day.

The mountain was steep—the paths were treacherous with lurking serpents and dangerous cliffs. Moses faced physical barriers; he was old—over 80 years old. Some thought he was too frail to make it to the top again and return. As he began his journey to the top of Sinai, a pessimistic voice yelled from the multitude,

"Moses...you will die on Mount Sinai!"

The voice didn't frighten Moses; it was the people who faced danger. The smell of gloom drifted over the entire camp of Israel. Those rebellious Jews were dead who polluted themselves by dancing naked before the idolatrous golden bull...was God's judgment finished?

"Whew." Moses paused to catch his breath. The path was steep, and his old legs were tired. He stumbled to a rock and sat down.

After a few minutes of rest, he continued his slow climb because his muscles had weakened over the years. He pulled hard on his staff each time he climbed over a large stone. He pushed himself over the rocks with his shepherd's staff, the one he called "the rod of God."

Again Moses stopped to rest and think. He remembered when he lifted the rod, the Red Sea parted; he remembered when hitting the rock, out came water.

No miracles today, Moses said to himself, thinking he needed divine help to get up to the top of the mountain.

Yesterday had been a tough day. Yesterday Moses had to deal with the sin of Israel. Yesterday was the worst day in the history of Israel.

Moses was still resting, thinking about yesterday—his intercession before God. He looked down the mountain, seeing the tents of Israel all in rows.

A heavy wet cloud drifted toward Moses, almost immediately enveloping him. He could no longer see down the mountain to the tents of Israel on the desert floor. He couldn't look up to see the top of Sinai. The cloud cover got thicker, Moses couldn't see the path. Then he realized this was not an average cloud because he felt something different; he felt the presence of God. This was the thick cloud in which God dwelt.

Moses dropped to his knees and waited a moment. He was listening for the voice of God. All he could hear was the slight breeze of the wind through the underbrush. There were no trees at this height on Sinai. When Moses felt the presence of God, he spread his robe on the ground before Him. Then Moses knelt on his robe, bowing his face to pray.

"Lord God, You have let me bring these people out of Egypt..." he looked for words to say what he felt, "but You have said You will not go with us."

Moses wanted more than an angel to guide him to the Promised Land.

"Lord God, You know my name," Moses prayed, "you know I am unfit to be a leader of Your people." Because Moses wanted God to go with him, he continued praying,

"If I have found grace in your sight...You must go with us." Then Moses' voice broke with tears of regret. He prayed, "Because these are Your people...go with us."

Moses knew God heard him because he felt the presence of God in that cloud. He knew God heard prayers no matter where they were made, because God is everywhere. Moses knew that Sinai was special to God. It was on this mountain that Moses saw the burning bush that didn't burn up. It was on this mountain Moses received the Ten Commandments. Because Moses had previously felt the presence of God on this mountain, he prayed,

"If I have found grace in Your sight...go with us. If you consider this people Your nation...go with us!" This time Moses added, "If your presence goes not with me, don't carry us to the Promised Land."

God answered from the dark cloud, "I will go with you."

Moses wanted to shout! God had heard the request. God had forgiven his people. God had restored His people to their favored position.

Most would have thought that Moses' answer was enough. Moses just got the greatest answer to prayer in his life. God had previously said He wouldn't go with the people of Israel. However, because of the intercession of Moses, God listened and said He would go with His people. For most people, that would have been enough, but Moses was ready to ask for something greater. Moses asked for something he didn't need, but he wanted. Moses prayed,

"Show me your glory."

Moses' face was bowed to the ground. Even if God had instantly flashed His glory to show Himself, Moses would have missed it because his face was buried in the dirt.

"No man can see God and live."

The midday was midnight; the top of Sinai was covered with a black cloud, darker than any thundercloud Moses had ever experienced. Moses in the presence of God could see nothing. The cloud was thick black smoke...as thick as the blackest night...as thick as blood...as thick as death itself.

Moses was not afraid to ask to see God because he had been moved beyond fear. He had confronted the thieves and wild beasts of his shepherd days and had lived. He had confronted Pharaoh, the most powerful man on earth, and lived. Moses had faced death many times and lived. Now Moses was in the presence of God—talking to him, listening to Him, waiting for Him. If he should die in the presence of God, it was nothing because in facing death, he had died many times before. Now Moses wanted to see God.

"Show me Yourself," again Moses prayed.

"You cannot live if you look upon God," was the answer he heard.

Still Moses wanted to see the God he served. Moses remembered when he saw a bush burning with fire but didn't burn up. He went closer to investigate the fire. It stood for the fire of God—for God is a consuming fire that judges sin and rebellion.

"I saw the fire..." Moses prayed, "now I want to see God."

Moses would not dare lift his head. In humility, he bowed to the ground. He remembered seeing the finger of God that wrote the Ten Commandments on tablets of stone. Right before his eyes, Moses saw God write the Ten Commandments.

"I saw the finger of God..." Moses paused in his prayer, "now I want to see God."

Moses remembered the power of God. He was there when the wind pushed back the Red Sea. He felt the dry sand crunch under his sandals as he walked across the bottom of the seabed. He saw the power of God in Egypt with the frogs, lice, darkness, and water turned to blood.

"I've seen Your power..." Moses continued his prayers, "now I want to see You, my God."

One last thing Moses remembered as he bowed on his face before God. Moses remembered the Passover. He remembered that God instructed him to kill the lamb and anoint the doors with blood. Moses remembered the death angel passed through Egypt to kill the firstborn.

"I have seen death..." Moses prayed, "I've seen the destruction of the death angel that killed the firstborn...but I want to see the glory of God...I want to see You, my God."

"No one can see My face and live," God told Moses. "You cannot see My face."

Then God told Moses what He would do. "I will make My goodness pass before you," God explained to Moses. "I will proclaim My name before you, because when you know My name, you know Me."

God told Moses that He would be gracious to whom He would be gracious, and He would show mercy on whom He chose. Then God included Moses, "I will show mercy to you," God told Moses. "Come, there is a place where you can see My glory."

God led Moses to the top of Sinai, to the very top. The cloud was thick, Moses couldn't see the path as he walked, trusting the leadership of God to guide him to the top.

God took Moses to a great rock, a rock taller than a house, wider than a clump of bay trees that spreads its branches. At the very top of Sinai was a split rock, just like a knife splits a loaf of bread. The split from the top of the rock to the bottom was just large enough to hide a man.

"There..." God instructed Moses. "Hide in the crevice of the rock."

A sense of dread overcame Moses as death sat on his shoulder laughing at him. Death was almost better than a full-view of God, for finite human flesh cannot reside in the presence of an infinite God. If not alive, then dead you stand in the presence of a pure God.

"I'll die!" Moses finally screamed.

"No!" God assured. "My presence will pass before you, but you'll not die."

The God of Heaven prepared to pass in review before the top of Sinai. The God of light who lives in a cloud of thick blackness was poised to do what He said. As Sinai was covered with night, down on the desert floor the Israelites saw the display of a ferocious lightning storm on Sinai. All the families of Israel retreated into their tents—flaps were secured. Families huddled in fear.

The presence of God moved toward the split rock where Moses was hiding. Then in an act of mercy, God reached out His hand to cover the crevice in the rock. The glory of God did not consume Moses. The hand of God protected Moses' life. The glory of God roared by as a tornado in its path, only more powerful. The glory of God flowed by silently as a great river, only more forcefully. The glory of God was felt, as a mother's tenderness influences everything in a room. The majesty of God was on parade, and as the king passes by, observers see nothing else but the sovereign awesomeness of the king. Nothing else mattered but God.

Moses huddled in the cleft of the rock. He cared not how the rock was split, but only that he felt safety inside the huge pierced area. He was hidden behind the hand of God, as the God of glory passed by. Then Moses heard God's powerful voice.

"The Lord...the Lord God—merciful, gracious, longsuffering, abundant in goodness and truth. The Lord shows mercy to thousands—forgiving iniquity—but the Lord will visit the iniquity of the unrepentant father, and on His children unto the third and fourth generation."

The loud voice of the Lord grew silent, as one hears a voice gently fading as the speaker walks away, singing as he goes. As the voice got fainter, the distance grew greater.

Then God removed His hand, and Moses saw it. He saw the backside of God in the thick, black cloud moving down the valley. Moses experienced the intimate presence of God, even though it was receding. Then straining his eyes to see, Moses could barely make out a form in the thick cloud. Moses strained to see, pondering what he was seeing. What was it?

Moses saw the backside of God.

My Time to Pray

- Lord, Your glory is awesome. I worship Your majesty.

- Lord, I worship You, a holy God who is powerful to do all You want to do.

- Lord, Moses saw Your glory in a cloud on Mount Sinai; I see Your glory in Jesus Christ in the pages of the New Testament.

- Lord, I have met You in the secret place, now help me tell others about Your saving grace.

- Lord, thank You for protecting Moses in the cleft of the rock. I too hide for protection in the cleft of the Rock, who is Jesus Christ.

Amen.

Exodus 34

MOSES' FACE SHINING

The Lord said, "You must celebrate the Feast of Unleavened Bread
(Passover) for seven days, at the appointed time each year in the
early spring. That symbolizes your coming out of Egypt."

The Lord then said, "Everything that comes first from the womb is
mine. Set aside the firstborn males of the cattle and flocks.
Redeem the firstborn donkey with a lamb. If you won't do it,
then break its neck. Do the same with your firstborn son,
redeem him with a lamb."

The Lord said, "Celebrate the Feast of the first Harvest (*sharuot*) with
the first gathering of grain and celebrate the Feast of the Final
Harvest at the end of harvest."

The Lord said, "Three times a year all males will appear before me. I am
going to drive out your enemies. No one will attack you or harm
you when you come up to worship Me. They will not covet your
land if you come up three times a year to appear before Me."

The Lord said, "Do not offer leavened bread when you sacrifice to Me.
Eat all the sacrifice lamb; do not leave any until the morning.
Bring the best of your harvest to sacrifice to Me."

Lord, I will give You the best of my time, energy, and thoughts;
I will give You the best of everything.

It is a privilege to worship You;
I will give You nothing less than my best today.

The Lord said to Moses, "Write all these commandments, for they represent the covenant I make with Israel." Moses was on the Mount 40 days and nights, and he fasted, neither eating nor drinking. Then Moses engraved the Ten Commandments on two stone tablets.

When Moses came down the mountain with the two tablets engraved by his hand, he didn't realize his face was radiating because he had been in the presence of God. When Aaron and the people saw Moses' face, they were afraid to come near him and ran away. Moses called to them and Aaron and the leaders returned, where they talked together.

Lord, may my life shine with Your radiance
　　When I've spent time talking to You in Your presence.

May others see Jesus in my life
　　And may they want to worship You, as I worship You.

Moses then gave the people the instruction that You, Lord, gave him on the mountain. When Moses finished speaking, he put a veil on his face because of the people. When Moses went into the tent to worship You, he took off the veil until he came out. Then Moses would tell the people what You, Lord, told him. The people would see his face aglow. So he would put the veil back on until he returned to speak with You.

Moses cut two tablets from stone, just as the Lord told him. They were just like the first one. The Lord said, "I will write on them the same Ten Commandments that were on the ones you broke. Climb up the mountain (Sinai) in the morning and appear before Me on the top of the mountain. Don't bring anyone with you, and no one can come near the mountain, not even the flocks or herds to graze there."

Moses cut two stones like the first ones and got up early and climbed
the mountain as the Lord told him to do. He took the two
stones with him.

Lord, You came down on the mountain in a cloud and called out Your
name, "The LORD." You passed before Moses to proclaim, "I am
the Lord, I am the Lord, the merciful and gracious God, slow to
anger, rich in love and truth, showing grace to thousands of generations, and forgiving every kind of sin and rebellion. But I will
not overlook rebellious sin, but will punish children for the sins
of their parents to the third and fourth generations."

Moses bowed his head to the ground, laying flat before You, saying, "If I
have found favor in Your sight, Lord, please go with us to the
Promised Land, even though the people are rebellious and hardheaded. Forgive their sin. Make us Your own special people."

Lord, the prayer of Moses is my prayer for grace,
Forgive my sin, both willful and ignorant;
Meet with me daily, lead me to do Your will.

Lord, You said, "I will make a covenant in front of Your people. I will do
miracles for them, such as have not been seen by any other people or nation. All the nations will see these miracles, which will
be awesome. Here are the commands you must do. I will drive
out the Canaanites, Hittites, Perizzites, Hivites, and Jebusites.
Do not make covenants (treaties) with those who live in the land
where I am leading you. That way they won't be a snare when
you possess the Promised Land. You must destroy their pagan
altars, smash their religious pillars, and cut down their sacred
poles (trees). Don't bow down to any idol, since Adonai (My
very name stands for jealousy) is a jealous God.

"Do not make any covenant (treaty) with those who live in the
Promised Land, because it will make you wander from Me to go

after their idol gods and sacrifice to them. If you make a covenant with them, they will invite you to eat their sacrifices. Then you will take their daughters as wives for your sons; their daughters will prostrate themselves to their idols, and your sons will commit spiritual adultery against Me."

Lord, I want to live separate from sin
So I can be holy and acceptable to You.

Forgive my sin and make me perfectly whole.
Accept me into Your presence.

Amen.

Exodus 34

The Story of Moses' Face Shining

Date: 1492 B.C. ~ Place: Foot of Mount Sinai

Moses stayed on Sinai for 40 days—a second 40 days talking to God. He fasted in the presence of God. Just as a person loses his appetite in an emergency, Moses didn't eat, nor was he hungry. He fed on the presence of God. Moses was hungering and thirsting after God's righteousness.

God again gave Moses the Ten Commandments. The first time God wrote the Ten Commandments with His finger. This time God spoke, and Moses chiseled them on stone tablets.

Moses talked to God; God talked to Moses.

After 40 days, Moses slowly began his descent down the mountain. His walk was more difficult than ever before. Not only was Moses old, his 80-

year-old knees also didn't have the strength of his youth. But Moses had fasted for 40 days; he had lost weight and lost strength. His legs were weak; he rested often. Then too, the stone commandments were heavy. After a torturous trip down the mountain, Moses saw the tents of Israel between two small hills,

Not much farther, Moses thought, *I'll be home soon.*

The path between the two hills was tedious, and the two stones were getting progressively heavier as he got closer to home. The lack of food affected his sight. His feet slipped often on the sandy path.

As Moses appeared between the two hills, the watch spotted him. Aaron, Moses' brother, had posted men to watch for Moses. While Moses was enveloped in the thick cloud at the top of Sinai, all Israel had prayed. Most of them stayed in their tents, leaving only for essential requirements. Everyone felt the threat of death about the camp. Each wondered where judgment would next strike. Many thought Moses died on the mountain. To them the thick cloud resembled a fierce thunderstorm. They were sure that the frail old man would perish in the elements. Without Moses to lead them, a few wanted to break camp to head back to Egypt. When the watchers saw Moses descending the mountain, they yelled out toward the camp,

"MOSES...MOSES IS COMING!"

Aaron was relieved when he heard the good news that his brother was coming. He was not sure how long he could keep the camp of Israel together without Moses' leadership.

"MOSES IS COMING..." people yelled as they rushed to the doors of their tents, repeating the glad news. "Moses is coming down the mountain!" The news spread through the camp; people were ecstatic. Moses was not dead. They almost spoke as one,

"MOSES IS COMING."

Then they saw it—almost everyone saw it at once. Suddenly their voices chilled the name "Moses" stuck in their throats. The yells turned to silence.

A threatening silence.

What was wrong? No one had to explain, they all saw it, even from afar.

The face of Moses was shining.

It was daylight, but his face glowed like a candle held close to a face at night. Even in the daylight, his face shone like sunlight glistening off a lake.

"What's wrong with him?" a voice broke the paralyzing silence.

The hushed crowd stood silently, gawking, doubting. Some mothers rounded up their children and herded them into their tents. They couldn't be too careful. They had never seen a man's face shine.

"Is it the death angel coming to slaughter us?" someone asked.

"No...it's Moses."

"Why is his face shining?"

Moses didn't know his face glistened. When someone stands in the light, they forget the experience of darkness. Moses had been in the presence of God, the glory of God passed in front of Moses, only he had not seen the face of God. God shielded Moses with His hand. Moses saw only the backside of God—just a rear view—and his face shone.

Aaron and the other leaders backed away as Moses approached them. They covered their faces with upheld arms.

"WHAT'S WRONG?" Moses yelled out to them.

"Your face..." Aaron didn't know how to explain it but told Moses his face shone like the sun.

Taking a scarf, Moses hid his face from the people. Then the people cautiously approached their leader. Fear of the unknown makes people shun even those they love.

For the next 40 days Moses' face shone—for the same length of time he fasted in God's presence—Moses kept a veil over his face. When he went into the tent to pray, Moses removed the veil to talk with God but put it back on when talking to the people.

My Time to Pray

- Lord, I'm changed when I enter Your presence; may others see the change You make in me.

- Lord, when I fast, I hunger and thirst for Your righteousness; may I feed on Your presence.

- Lord, there is an appropriate time to leave Your presence and go live my life in the world. Go with me and help others see Your glory in my life.

Amen.

Exodus 35

GATHERING MATERIALS
TO CONSTRUCT THE TABERNACLE

Moses gathered all the people of Israel and told them, "Work for six days but the Sabbath is a holy day to the Lord. You must rest unto the Lord. Whoever does any work on the Sabbath will be put to death. That means don't kindle any fires in your dwellings."

Moses told the gathering a second thing. "Take up an offering for the Lord from those who have a willing heart to give Him gold, silver, and bronze. This offering includes fine linen that is blue, purple, and red; goats' hair, tanned hides of rams and fine leather. Also bring acacia wood, oil for light, spices for anointing oil, and sweet incense. Don't forget onyx stones and other jewel stones for the priest's vest."

Moses continued telling the people, "Let all the gifted craftsmen come to fashion everything the Lord commanded—the tent for the Tabernacle, its covering for inclement weather, fasteners, planks, curtain rods, poles, and footings; plus the utensils for the table for showbread, plus the candlesticks, Menorah with cups for light, and oil for light. Also, we must construct the altar for burning incense, that has the anointing oil and fragrant incense, and we must construct the curtains for the entrance into the larger room. We must construct the Brazen Altar for burnt sacrifices, its utensils and basin. We must make the curtains for the outside walls of the Tabernacle courtyard, including poles, pegs, ropes, and curtain rods.

Moses added to his instruction, noting, "We must make the garments for ministering in this holy place, the holy garment for Aaron—the High Priest—and garments for his sons to wear as they minister for us.

The whole congregation of Israel left to go to their tents. Then those hearts that were stirred and willing returned with gifts to build the Tabernacle and to make the holy garments for the priest. Both men and women brought jewelry, belts, and gold as offerings to the Lord. Some brought fine linen, blue, purple, and red yarn, and tanned leather. Some brought acacia wood. Women who could spin yarn into cloth brought fine linen. Others used their skill to spin goats' hair into coverings. The leaders brought the onyx stones, plus spices for fragrance and oil to make light.

The people of Israel brought a free-will offering to the Lord, and all those who had a willing heart brought their gifts.

Moses told the people, "God has called Bezalel to be our workman. Bezalel is filled with the Spirit of God, is wise, and has a lot of knowledge and has skilled talents. He can design the gold, silver, bronze, plus he can carve jewels and wood for us. Also, Aholiab has the same skills."

Moses challenged the people, "God has filled them with the ability to guide all our work. He can lead the designers, tapestry makers, and the weavers of blue, purple, and red thread into fine linen."

Lord, You give different talents—spiritual gifts—to different people;
Thank You for the gifts you've given me.

I yield them to You just as those who constructed the Tabernacle;
Use me to glorify Yourself, as You used them.

Amen.

Exodus 35

The Story of the Tabernacle

Date: 1490 B.C. ~ Place: Foot of Mount Sinai

There was not a cloud in the sky as Moses and Aaron walked the broad passageway between the tents where the people lived. Moses pointed down the straight road noting,

"These are our city streets in the desert." Each of the twelve tribes were camped together—but not helter-skelter like the Bedouins—Israel's tents were pitched in a straight line, the tent of the eldest first, followed in descending order by the younger families. There were narrow streets within the tribes and broad streets between the tribes. Various herds of animals were corralled on the outer edges of the camp; even the animals were divided by tribes and families. And out behind the bushes and rocks were allotted places for bathrooms, divided by sexes; everything was laid out by the pattern that God gave Moses on the Mount.

Moses and Aaron saw a long red pennant with a lion, blowing softly in the desert breeze. It was the flag of Judah; the tribe camped next to the Tabernacle. Each of the twelve tribes had its own flag hoisted high for all to see—especially children. The flags helped the little ones find their way back home.

"LOOK..." Moses shouted, "the fence is up." There in the very middle of the camp was a large 7½-foot-tall cloth fence, woven from fine linen. It was the fence surrounding the Tabernacle. The cloth fence was 150 feet long and 75 feet wide; bronze posts and silver hooks held the curtains in place.

"We'll see if anyone tries to get through the fence," Moses laughed with the enthusiasm of a builder, for the cloth fence was the last thing the infant nation had constructed. "God will live inside that fence," Moses told his brother. "We'll build a large tabernacle—a big tent—it will be God's dwelling place.

"The Shekinah cloud will be poured out of Heaven, right into that Tabernacle, there'll be a seat in that tent—a Mercy Seat—where God can sit when He visits us."

Moses described to his brother how the cloud would leave the top of Mount Sinai to settle down over the camp of Israel. Like a funnel, the Shekinah cloud would pour the presence of God right into the Tabernacle. God would descend in that cloud—the people could come to worship God in His tent.

"God told me there could be only one entrance," Moses explained as the brothers walked through the gate of the Tabernacle and looked into the yard they had just discussed. "One gate will remind everyone there is only one way of salvation to God."

Moses and Aaron walked into the clearing at the center of the cloth fence, and piles of goods were everywhere—gold utensils, silver, exquisite acacia wood, tapestry. The people brought their gifts for the workmen to construct a Tabernacle where they could worship God. The workmen—Bezalel and Aholiab—were busy fashioning the tent and its furniture into a worship center.

Now, the curtain fence stretched all the way around the giant yard, and the sacred area where people would worship God was finally enclosed. "Why such a big yard?" Aaron asked his brother.

"So many people can gather with their priest to worship God at the same time." There were more than two million Israelites following the Shekinah cloud to the Promised Land. They wouldn't all want to worship at the same time, but there would be hundreds upon hundreds assembling at any one time.

"Follow me," Moses told his brother Aaron. "I want to walk you through the Tabernacle area where a worshiper will approach God."

Moses explained that the pattern God had given him on Mount Sinai was the same path an Israelite would follow to approach the Lord. Every piece of furniture in the Tabernacle had a meaning; Aaron and his sons would have to explain to the people what each piece of furniture meant. As the two walked to the north end of the giant courtyard Moses explained,

"Just as there is only one door into the Tabernacle—that means there is only one way to God." There was only one entrance where they would come to make a sacrifice for their sins. There the priest sacrificed blood to atone for the sins of the people.

As Moses and Aaron walked through the courtyard to see some workmen sewing skin and fabric for the tent, other workmen were melting women's jewelry into blocks of solid gold, and others were melting silver. Still other workmen were beating the gold blocks into furniture for the Tabernacle.

Moses pointed to a large bronze grate on top of a huge metal box, called the brazen altar. It was there animals would be sacrificed to God. Moses explained, "After the blood is spilt and the animal is killed, the body will be burnt on the top grate."

Then Moses pointed inside the bronze box, 5 feet square, explaining fire would always be burning, showing that God was always ready to accept their worship and offering. A hole would be dug into the earth under the brazen altar to catch the embers and coals.

Next they saw the giant bowl called the Laver—7 feet across and 5 feet deep; it would hold hundreds of gallons of water. The golden bowl was crafted from the inside with women's brass mirrors. As people looked into the Laver, they would see their reflections in the water, then peering deeper, they would see a second reflection of themselves in the golden mirrors. Moses explained,

"The water in the Laver is for ceremonial cleaning. When you see a double reflection of yourself, you are reminded to look deeper than your surface appearance. You must search deep within your heart for deceptive sin that keeps a person from becoming more godly."

Moses and Aaron watched the workmen sew the covering for the big tent where God would dwell. The outside covering was dark brown badger skin; the thick hide protected the interior from rain, sun, and extreme weather. Outside, the tent was not beautiful, but an inside layer was the Tabernacle ceiling. A beautiful embroidered tapestry of angels, created by bright reds, greens, and blues brightened the tent within.

Moses and Aaron entered the first room of the Tabernacle, called the Holy Room. It contained the furniture where priests prayed to God.

The two brothers both saw it at the same time—a beautiful golden candlestick—as tall as a woman. Over 60 pounds of pure gold was used to mold the giant candlestick that would give light to the priest entering the Tabernacle. This Menorah had seven branches, each with a light to remind the people that even though there are many who shine for God, together they give off one massive light to heathen darkness.

The Table of Showbread was also located in the Tabernacle. Priests would bake unleavened bread every day to place it on the table to remind Israel that God feeds them and provides for their needs. It was the bread of God's presence. It reminded Israel that God satisfied their hunger and God gave them strength.

Then right in front of the veil was the Altar of Burning Incense. The priest would burn incense as a symbol of prayers going up to God. Just as an Israelite didn't like the sour, musty smell of a tent, but enjoyed the smell and sweet fragrance, so God enjoys the prayers of His people, as if they are perfume offered to Him.

My Time to Pray

- Lord, may my life be a sweet-smelling fragrance to You; be pleased with the offerings I give You.

- Lord, help me learn from the Tabernacle how to properly approach You.

- Lord, may I serve You with the spiritual gifts You've given me, just as Bezalel and Aholiab used their abilities to build the Tabernacle.

Amen.

Exodus 36

BEGINNING CONSTRUCTION OF THE TABERNACLE

The Lord commanded, "Bezalel and Aholiab are to do the work exactly as I command. Every competent person to whom I have given talent should work with them to accomplish the work of constructing the Sanctuary."

Moses called for Bezalel, Aholiab, and every talented individual whose heart the Lord had stirred to come do the work. Moses gave these persons all the gifts of money and supplies that the people brought to accomplish the construction of the Sanctuary. The people continued to bring more and more free-will offerings to Moses every morning. All of the talented men who were working on the Sanctuary left their jobs to go tell Moses, "The people are bringing too much to do what the Lord told us to do!"

Moses gave an order, and it was spread around through the camp, "No one should bring any more contributions for the Sanctuary!" What they already had brought was plenty; it was more than enough to accomplish the work.

The talented persons doing the work made ten curtains. They were made of fine-spun cotton with blue, purple, and red yarn. Angel-like figures were embroidered on them for the ceiling of the tent. Each curtain was 42 feet long and 6 feet wide. All the curtains were the same size. Bezalel joined five curtains to one another and then joined the second five curtains to each other. He put blue loops upon the edge of the outside curtain of the first and second sets. He made 50 loops in the first curtain and 50 loops on the edge of the second curtain. The loops were opposite one another. He made 50 gold clips to join the curtains to each other, so that the Holy Tent was a complete unit. Bezalel also made eleven curtains of goats' hair for an outer layer to go over the blue curtains. Each curtain was 45 feet long and 6 feet wide. The eleven curtains were all the same size. He joined five curtains by themselves and the other six curtains by themselves. He also made 50 loops on the edge of the outside curtain in the first set and 50 loops on the edge of the outside curtain in the second set. He made 50 bronze clips for joining the covering together, so that it would be a complete unit.

Next Bezalel made an outside covering of goat's hair to go over the blue linen ceiling, then he covered it with the tanned hides of rams.

Bezalel made the upright frames for the Holy Tent out of acacia wood. Each frame was 15 feet long and 2¼ feet wide. Each frame had two joints for attaching itself to the other frames. This is what he did for all the frames of the Holy Tent. He made 20 frames for the southern side of the Tent, plus 40 silver bases to go under the 20 frames—two bases under each frame for its two joints. Then, for the northern side of the Tent, he made 20 frames and 40 silver bases. For the back side of the Tent toward the west, he made six frames. He also made two frames for the corners of the Holy Tent on the back side. There were eight frames with their silver bases, sixteen bases with two bases under each frame. Then Bezalel made cross-bars out of acacia wood: five cross-bars for the frames on one side of the Holy Tent, and five cross-bars for the frames of the other side of the Tent, and five cross-bars for the frames of the back side of the Tent, toward the west. He also constructed the middle cross-bar to pass through in the center of the frames from one end to the other. He covered the frames with gold and made gold rings for them as holders for the poles. He also covered over the cross-bars with gold.

Bezalel also made the curtain out of blue, purple, and red yarn and fine-spun cotton. Skillful workmen embroidered it with angel-like figures. He made four posts of acacia wood and covered them with gold. Their hooks were made out of gold, and he cast four silver bases for them. A needle-worker made a flap for the doorway of the tent out of blue, purple, and red yarn and fine-spun cotton. The flap was hung on five posts and hooks. Bezalel covered their tops and bands with gold, but their five bases were made out of bronze.

Amen.

Exodus 37

Constructing the Ark of the Covenant

Bezalel made the Ark (box) of the Covenant out of acacia wood. It was 3¾ feet long, 2¼ feet wide, and 2¼ feet high. He covered it over with pure gold, inside and out. And he put a gold crown around the top. He cast four rings of gold, two rings on one side, and two rings for the other. He made poles out of acacia wood and covered them with gold. He put the poles through the rings on the sides of the Ark of the Covenant to carry it. He also made the Mercy-Seat—lid—out of pure gold. It was 3¾ feet long and 2¼ feet wide. He made two gold angel-like figures— cherubs. He sculptured them out of hammered gold, to be placed at both ends of the Mercy Seat. One cherub was on one end, and the other was on the other end. These cherubs had their wings spread toward God who would sit on the Mercy Seat. And their wings covered the Mercy Seat. Their wings and their faces were toward each other. The faces of these cherubs were downward, in the direction of the Mercy Seat.

Bezalel also made the Table of Showbread of His presence out of acacia wood. It was 3 feet long, 1½ feet wide, and 2¼ feet high. He covered it over with pure gold and put a gold crown around the top. He made a rim of about 9 inches all around it and made a gold molding for it too. Next he cast four gold rings and put the rings through the four corners which were on its four legs. The rings were put close to the rim to hold the poles that were used to carry the Table of Showbread. He made the poles for carrying the Table out of acacia wood. Then he covered them with gold.

The utensils for the Table of Showbread (dishes, pans, bowls, and jars for pouring out drink-offerings) belonged on top of the Table. He made them out of pure gold.

Bezalel also made the Golden Lampstand out of pure gold that was hammered. Its stand, its shaft, its cups, its buds, and its flowers were all sculptured from one piece of gold. There were six branches projecting from its sides: three branches of the Golden Lampstand out of its one side, and three branches to its other side. Three cups were made like almond blossoms on one branch—one bud and one flower—and three cups. The same was made for all six branches that projected from the Golden Lampstand. On the Golden Lampstand itself, there were four cups shaped like almond blossoms with their buds and flowers. Their buds and their branches were all sculptured from one piece of gold. The entire Menorah was hammered from one piece of pure gold. Bezalel made its seven lamps, along with its wick-trimmers and its trays, out of pure gold. He made it and all of its utensils from one talent of pure gold.

Bezalel made the Altar of Burning Incense from acacia wood. It was square—1½ feet long and 1½ feet wide. It was 3 feet tall. The horns were made of one piece of gold. He covered the top, surrounding sides, and the horns of the Altar of Burning Incense with pure gold. He also made a gold molding for it all around. He put two gold rings for it under its molding, upon its two sides, two rings on opposite sides. The rings were holders for the poles to carry it. He made the carrying poles out of acacia wood and covered them with gold. A perfumer also made the holy anointing oil and the pure incense of sweet-smelling spices.

Amen.

Exodus 38

CONSTRUCTING THE BRAZEN ALTAR

Bezalel made the Brazen Altar of Burnt offering from acacia wood. It was square—7½ feet long and 7½ feet wide. It was 4½ feet tall. He put horns upon its four corners; they were all constructed of one piece of bronze. He covered the Altar with bronze. Then he made all of the utensils for the Altar—the buckets, the shovels, the pans, the meat-hooks, and the fire-pans—out of bronze. He made a grill out of bronze for the Altar beneath, under the ledge that was located halfway up. He cast four rings on the four ends of the bronze grill as holders for poles. He made the carrying poles out of acacia wood and covered them with bronze. He put the poles through the rings on the sides of the Altar to carry it.

Bezalel also made the Laver and its stand out of bronze. The bronze came from the metal mirrors of the women who helped to serve at the doorway of the Tent of Meeting.

Bezalel also made the courtyard. For the southern side of the courtyard the curtains were long, made of fine-spun cotton. There were 20 posts and 20 bases made out of bronze. But the hooks of the posts and their bands were made out of silver. And for the northern side, the curtains were 150 feet long, made of fine-spun cotton. There were 20 posts and 20 bases that were made out of bronze. The hooks of the posts and their bands were made out of silver. For the west side, the curtains were 75 feet long, along with ten posts and ten bases, but the hooks of the posts and their bands were made out of silver. Finally for the eastern side, the curtains were 75 feet long. The curtains for one side of the entrance were 22½ feet wide, along with their three posts and three bases.

It was the same for the other side. Next to the entrance to the courtyard there was a 22½ foot long curtain, along with their three posts and three bases. All the curtains of the courtyard were made of fine-spun cotton. The bases for the posts were made out of bronze, but the hooks of the posts and their bands were made out of silver. The tops of them were plated with silver. All the posts of the courtyard were also banded with silver. The flap for the doorway of the courtyard was made by a needleworker, of blue, purple, and red yarn, as well as fine-spun cotton. It was 30 feet long and 7½ feet high, the same height as the curtains of the courtyard. Their four posts and four bases were all made out of bronze, but their hooks were made out of silver. The tops of them and their bands were plated with silver. All the tent pegs for the Holy Tent and for the surrounding courtyard were made out of bronze.

The following are the amounts of metal used for constructing the Holy Tent which Moses ordered to be counted by the Levites under the direction of Ithamar, the son of Aaron, the High Priest. Bezalel, from the tribe of Judah, made everything that the Lord had commanded Moses. He was the son of Uri and the grandson of Hur. Aholiab, from the tribe of Dan, helped Bezalel. Aholiab was the son of Ahisamach. He was a craftsman and a designer. He was also a needleworker in blue, purple, and red yarn, and in fine-spun cotton.

The total amount of the gold that was used for the work of constructing the Sanctuary was a little more than one ton. The total amount of the silver received from all those in the congregation was 3¾ tons. These gifts were received from each one who was 20 years old or more and who crossed over the Red Sea—603,550 men. The 3¾ tons of silver were used for casting the bases of the

Sanctuary and the bases of the curtain. There were 82¼ pounds for each base.

Bezalel made hooks for the posts from the shekels he received. He plated the tops of them with silver, and he made bands for them. The total amount of the bronze from the contribution was 603,250 pounds. Bezalel used that to make the bases of the doorway to the Tent of Meeting, the Bronze Altar with its bronze grill and all of its utensils. The bases of the surrounding courtyard, the bases of the entrance to the courtyard, all of the tent pegs of the Holy Tent, and all of the tent pegs of the surrounding courtyard.

Amen.

Exodus 39

MAKING THE PRIESTS' CLOTHES

The workers made finely woven clothes from blue, purple, and red yarn for serving in the Holy Place. They also made holy clothes for Aaron, just as the Lord commanded Moses. Bezalel made the vest with gold thread from blue, purple, and red yarn, and from fine-spun cotton.

Then skillful workmen hammered out the gold into thin plates and cut it into threads to be woven into the blue, purple, and red yarn, and into the fine-spun cotton. They made shoulder straps for the vest, joined together at the upper ends. They made a skillfully woven waistband with gold thread of one piece with the ephod. It was made of blue, purple, and red yarn and from fine-spun cotton, just as the Lord had commanded Moses. They mounted the onyx stones in delicate, gold settings, engraving them like a seal with the names of the sons of Israel. Bezalel put the jewels on the shoulder straps of the vest to remind everyone about the sons of Israel, just as the Lord had commanded Moses.

Bezalel made the chest pocket with the same skillful craftsmanship as the vest. It was made of gold thread, blue, purple, and red yarn, and fine-spun cotton. When doubled, it was square—1 span or 9 inches. They set four rows of jewels in it: in the first row there was a ruby, a topaz, and a beryl. The second row had a turquoise, a sapphire, and an emerald. The third row had a ligure, a jacinth, and an amethyst. The fourth row had a chrysolite, an onyx, and a jasper. They were mounted in delicate settings. There were 12 stones, one for each of the names of the sons of Israel. Each one was engraved like a seal with the name of one of the 12 tribes. On the chest pocket they put braided chains of pure gold, like ropes. They made two delicate gold settings and two gold rings. And they attached the two rings to two of the corners of the chest pocket. They attached the other two ends of the two braided chains, attaching them in front to the shoulder straps of the vest. Then they made two gold rings and attached them to the two corners of the chest pocket on its inside edge, next to the vest. Then they made two gold rings and attached them in front to the bottom of the shoulder straps of the vest, next to the seam, just above the skillfully woven waistband of the vest. They tied the chest pocket by its rings of the vest with a blue cord so that it connected with the skillfully woven waistband of the vest, so that the chest pocket would not come loose from the vest, just as the Lord had commanded Moses.

Bezalel also made the robe for the High Priest completely of woven blue cloth. It had an opening in its center, like a reinforced collar. A band was around this opening so that it would not get torn, and embroidered pomegranates designed of blue, purple, and red yarn was around the hem of the robe. They also made bells of pure gold and put them between the pomegranate designs all around the hem. Each bell was followed by a pomegranate design all the way around the hem of the robe. It was worn when serving as High Priest, just as the Lord had commanded Moses. They also made finely woven coats of cotton for Aaron and his sons, a fine cotton turban, cotton-decorated caps, cotton underwear from fine-spun cotton, and a belt made from fine-spun cotton, and blue, purple, and red yarn, the result of a needleworker, just as the Lord had commanded Moses. They made the plate for the holy crown from pure gold and they wrote an inscription upon it like the one on a seal: "HOLINESS TO YAHWEH." Then they tied a blue cord to the crown to hold it tightly to the turban, just as the Lord had commanded Moses.

This is how all the work of the Holy Tent of Meeting was finished. The sons of Israel did everything exactly as the Lord had commanded Moses. Then they brought the Holy Tent to Moses: The Tent with all of its furniture, clips, frames, cross-bars, posts, bases; the covering of the tanned hides of rams, the covering of dolphin skins, the covering of the flap, the Holy Ark of the Covenant with its carrying poles and the Mercy Seat, the Table of Showbread, with all its utensils and the holy loaves of bread (the bread of the presence), the Golden Lampstand with its lamps all set in order, all of its utensils, and the oil for light; the Golden Burning Altar for Incense, the special anointing oil; the sweet-smelling incense; the flap for the doorway of the tent; the Brazen Altar with its bronze grating, its carrying poles, and all of its utensils; the Laver with its stand; the curtains for the court-yard with their posts and bases; the flap for the entrance of the courtyard with its ropes, tent pegs, and all of the tools for the maintenance of the Holy Tent; the finely woven clothes for those serving in the Holy Place, the holy clothes for Aaron the High Priest, and the clothes of his sons for serving as priests.

The workmen did all the work exactly as the Lord had commanded Moses. Moses examined all the work. When he saw that they had done it exactly as the Lord had commanded, he blessed them.

Amen.

Exodus 40

Putting the Tabernacle Together

The Lord told Moses, "Get the Tabernacle ready by the first day of the new year—Passover—when you will remember your delivering from Egypt. Place the Ark of the Covenant in the Holy of Holies behind the veil. Then place in the Holy Room the Table of the Bread of My presence. Next bring in the Menorah and light the lamps. Then place the Altar of Burning Incense at the center of the veil in the Holy Room. Then hang the curtain that is the entrance into the tent.

Then the Lord told Moses, "Hang the curtain that surrounds the court-yard. Next place the Brazen Altar at the entrance into the Tabernacle so that all who enter will make a blood sacrifice to Me. Set the Laver between the Brazen Altar and the tent, and fill it with water."

Then the Lord told Moses, "Anoint the tent and all its furnishings to separate them to Me. They must be absolutely holy."

Then the Lord told Moses, "Bring Aaron and his sons to the front of the tent. They must be washed with water to symbolize their cleans-ing. Cover Aaron in sacred clothes, then anoint him, symboliz-ing he is separated as my priest. Do the same with his sons. Present them in their tunics and anoint them as their father was anointed. They and their sons will serve me forever as priests, from generation to generation.

Just as the Lord commanded, Moses set up the Tabernacle for celebrat-ing the Passover.

Just as the Lord commanded, Moses set the foundational boards in place, attached the sockets, inserted the poles, and attached the cross-bars. Then he spread the various coverings over the frame of the Tent.

Just as the Lord commanded, Moses placed the two stone tablets inscribed with the Ten Commandments into the Ark of the Covenant. He placed the lid—the Mercy Seat—on top of it. He inserted the carrying poles in place and hung the veil so the people couldn't see in.

Just as the Lord commanded, Moses placed the Table of Showbread on the north side of the Holy Room, and then he arranged the Bread of God's presence on the Table.

Just as the Lord commanded, Moses hung the entrance curtain over the way into the Tent. Moses then brought in the Menorah and set it across from the Table of Showbread. Then he lit the lamps in the Lord's presence. Next Moses brought in the Altar of Burning Incense and placed it in front of the veil. Then he burned incense, symbolic of prayer, going up to God.

Just as the Lord commanded, Moses placed the Laver between the Tent and the Brazen Altar. He filled it with water so the priests could wash themselves before the sacrifice and the Brazen Altar at the entrance of the Tabernacle.

Just as the Lord commanded, Moses hung the curtain around the courtyard that surrounded the Tabernacle and the altar. Then he hung the curtain that was the entrance into the courtyard. So, finally, Moses completed the task, just as the Lord commanded him to do.

Then the Shekinah glory cloud settled over the Tabernacle, and the glory of the Lord filled the place. Moses couldn't go into the Tabernacle because God's glory filled the Tabernacle.

From then on, when the cloud lifted from over the Tabernacle, the people prepared to march. Wherever the cloud led them, the people followed. When the cloud did not lift up from the Tabernacle, the people remained where they were. The cloud surrounded the Tabernacle; at night a burning fire was seen in the cloud.

Lord, Your presence filled the Tabernacle because Moses obeyed;
  May I be just as obedient to prepare my life,
  May I be filled with Your glory, as You filled the
  Tabernacle.

Lord, You settled among Your people and You led Your people;
  Come settle in my life with Your presence;
  Come lead me daily as You led Israel.

Amen.

Exodus 40

The Story of Putting the Tabernacle Together

Date: 1490 B.C. ~ Place: Foot of Mount Sinai

Several large tents sat silently, empty. No one was there; no one was working there any longer. All the projects were finished. A few days ago they bristled with noise and activity. Now, silence.

These were the manufacturing tents where craftsmen had crafted furniture for the Tabernacle. Each piece of furniture was made in a different tent.

Four men walked from one tent to the other, inspecting each piece of furniture. "Is this table the exact length?" Moses asked as he rubbed his fingers over the smooth acacia wood. Moses and his brother, Aaron, were inspecting the furniture for the Tabernacle with the two who supervised the work.

"Exactly," was all Bezalel said to Moses. He was the chief supervisor for making everything.

Then Moses turned to Aholiab, the other supervisor who helped Bezalel, "Is this table the exact measurement?"

"Exactly," Aholiab answered.

God had told Moses on the Mount that truth was established at the mouth of two witnesses. So Moses was satisfied when Bezalel and Aholiab agreed. He didn't have to measure the table. Moses had told them to follow God's blueprint exactly, no exceptions. If everything were not perfect, God's presence wouldn't come live there in the Tabernacle.

A huge crowd stood at a distance watching the four men on final inspection. They had waited a long time for the erection of their house of worship. Their faces showed stress and worry; they wanted to obey God exactly as much as Moses.

"Do you want to inspect the curtains and roof coverings?" Bezalel asked.

"Are they the exact measurement?"

"Yes."

"Was the cloth and goat's hair perfectly woven?"

"Yes."

"Have you done everything perfectly as God commanded?"

Bezalel and Aholiab answered together, "Yes."

Then Moses turned and yelled to a work crew standing by, *"BEGIN CONSTRUCTION!"* The large crowd standing at a distance shouted, "Hallelujah" and "Amen!" Many others just cheered.

The workmen put the foot sockets in place, they stood the poles upright, and those first poles, pointing toward the sky, told the people construction was actually begun. The workmen giving orders to one another could hardly be heard because of the crowd cheering. The poles were put in the foot sockets forming the large tent that was the Tabernacle itself. Finally the people saw the framework of a tent begin to unfold before their eyes.

"It's small," a woman shouted. A man answered, "A woman always thinks the family tent is small until she has to clean it." Some laughed.

When the framing poles were in place, then the long, flowing, beautiful cloth of red, purple, and blue with cherubim embroidered on it was draped over the building. Then the goat's hair covering for protection, and finally, the skins sewn together held everything in place, beautiful on the inside with a rugged exterior.

Moses waited until all the bronze tent pegs were driven into the ground and guide ropes held everything secure. He would not allow any of the furniture to be moved into the Tabernacle until everything was perfect.

If a slight wind blew down a wall into the Tabernacle—and people saw into the Holy of Holies—they might die.

When the four men were satisfied, Moses came out the entrance to motion to the workmen.

The priest brought the Ark of the Covenant into the Holy of Holies. The poles were in place to carry the Ark. Then Moses approached the small box (the word *ark* means box) and looked inside. Nothing was there, not even sawdust. Moses put there the two stone tablets carved with the Ten Commandments.

Then he covered the box with its lid, the Mercy Seat. It was solid gold; God would sit on that box—the Mercy Seat on top of the Ark of the Covenant—when His presence visited Israel.

The veil was hung in place between the Holy of Holies and the outer room called the Holy Room. Next, the table was brought in that would hold the showbread, the Bread of His presence. It was placed near the veil on the north side of the room. Moses arranged the bread then prayed, "This bread is Your presence."

The Menorah was next brought into the room, and placed on the other side across from the Table of Showbread. Moses carefully lit each of the seven lights. Again Moses prayed, "This light is symbolic of Your illumination to Your people."

The Altar of Burning Incense was next placed front and center of the veil. Moses burned incense on the altar as a small puff of smoke arose off the altar, "That's symbolic of my prayers to You," Moses told God.

The Brazen Altar where sacrifices would be offered to God was next brought into place—right in front of the entrance into the Tabernacle. No one could approach God without first offering a blood sacrifice. Immediately Moses offered a burnt offering to God, an offering of worship and thanksgiving. Then Moses offered a meal sacrifice, an offering of fellowship with God.

Finally, the Laver—the huge basin where Aaron and the priests would ceremoniously wash their hands and feet to be clean while ministering for the people—was brought in.

Then the workmen began setting each pole in place around the courtyard. Then they hung the curtains. Moses walked through the entrance into the courtyard. The crowd could no longer see them. The cloth fence was 7½ feet tall. With Aaron, Bezalel, and Aholiab, Moses walked around the inside cloth fence of the courtyard, inspecting every socket, pole, and curtain rod. Everything had to be secure and perfect. Moses remarked, "It must be perfect as God commanded."

Bezalel and Aholiab left Moses and Aaron alone at the entrance of the Tabernacle. They joined the crowd. What would happen now? No one knew, for man had never built a sanctuary for Jehovah. Man had always worshiped God in the open field. Sacrifices had always been offered on field stones laid on the ground. Would God honor sacrifices offered on an altar? Would God occupy a tent?

Everyone thought, "Will God come?" Then they asked themselves, "How will He come?"

Moses prayed inwardly, *God, we have done exactly what You command-ed....* He let his thoughts trail off. He didn't now what to do next.

Then it happened. Moses and Aaron didn't see it first. Some in the crowd were not looking at the Tabernacle. They stared at the top of Sinai. It's hard to tell when clouds travel, for they are always moving.

"LOOK!" a cry came from the crowd. "He's coming!" All eyes focused on the Shekinah cloud on top of Sinai; it was moving. The cloud moved toward them and toward the Tabernacle. It remained high in the sky until it got immediately above the Tabernacle. Then the Shekinah cloud dipped toward the Tabernacle. Slowly. Finally, the cloud descended into the Holy of Holies.

God came to sit on His Mercy Seat, which was the lid of the box. God did not choose to sit on a golden throne encrusted with jewels, as heathen dictators show their power and ego. No! God sat on a simple box in a tent. God sat on the Mercy Seat because only in His mercy could His people live when He came to live with them.

Moses left the Tabernacle to stand with his people. The cloud was too awesome. It filled the courtyard and covered the tent. God was now among His people.

At night the Shekinah cloud was a black cloud filled with burning fire. During the day, the Shekinah looked like a column of smoke descending from Heaven. People say the Shekinah ascended into Heaven, reaching all the way to God's throne in the Temple of Heaven. They say God has a train—a long flowing cape worn by royalty—and that train is God's Shekinah column of smoke that flows from the throne of Heaven to the simple box in the Tabernacle. Beholding it was glory.

EPILOGUE

The Academy Award winning movie Exodus tells of Jewish people's struggle to find a homeland in Palestine after the Holocaust and Hitler's prison camps in World War II. It was so named because the movie reflected the struggles of the people of God to throw off the shackles of slavery in Egypt. And still today the struggle continues between Israel and the surrounding Arab nations.

Why has Israel had so many persecutions throughout history? It's because of unseen spiritual warfare. Israel is the "apple of God's eye." He chose Abraham and promised to bless his descendents (see Gen. 12:2-3). Satan knows God's ultimate plan is with the Jews, so satan will do everything possible to eliminate the Jewish people.

The Book of Exodus is that window in history when God wins, because He delivers His people from slavery and begins preparing them to live in the Promised Land.

PRAYERS FROM LEVITICUS
TO HEAR GOD'S VOICE

Preface

THE STORY OF WRITING LEVITICUS

The noon sun blistered the tents of Israel. Very few people were stirring about the camp; even the animals stood frozen, knowing that any movement sapped whatever energy they had left.

It's an eerie silence when approximately 2 million people won't move, talk, or make any commotion. A fly buzzed, a cow bell softly tinkled, while most of Israel dozed through a midday mid-summer torture. Moses sat at an Egyptian writing desk; he was transcribing what God told him on the mount. Empty scrolls were rolled up and stacked on one corner of the desk; a pile of unused quills lay ready. The only noise heard in the tent was the scratching of a quill on tanned leather.

"Moses," Aaron interrupted, "take a rest, finish your writing when the night air is cool. Sleep now."

Moses looked up and smiled at his older brother, then shook his head no. Then he said, "When the Lord God gives a message, I must write it as soon as possible. I don't know how long I'll live."

Aaron laughed at his brother. "Since God has given you a message, He will protect your life so you can write it down for everyone to know it."

Moses grinned broadly through his gray stringy beard.

Aaron told his older brother, "Since God told you what to write, He will not let you forget anything. God will give you His Spirit to write His Word, just as God gave His spirit to Bezalel and Aholiab to build the Tabernacle. The Word of God is just as important as the Tabernacle of God.

Moses nodded his head in approval and answered, "Yes, even though I am old, my heart is young. I am excited with what God tells me. I want to write it down as soon as possible—so He will tell me something more."

During the 40 years of wandering in the wilderness, Moses spent many days writing the Word of God. He recorded *Genesis*—the history of Creation and Abraham, Isaac, Jacob, and Joseph. Next Moses wrote the history of their *Exodus* out of Egypt and building the Tabernacle.

Today, Moses was writing the Torah—God's instructions how to offer sacrifices to God and how to live holy lives. Aaron asked,

"What will you name this third scroll?"

Moses quickly answered, "I don't write a name on a scroll until I'm finished, then I write the name on the outside. This scroll is all about the work of the priests, but I don't want to name it *priests*—that sounds so functional."

Moses thought for a moment, then said, "This scroll is about the family of Levi, the family of the priests. That's our family. I'll name it *Leviticus*."

Leviticus has more quotations of God speaking than any other book in the Bible. Over 90 percent of Leviticus contains the actual words of God. Because of this many Jewish children memorized the entire book—and if they memorized more than one Old Testament book, Leviticus was the first.

Because the Book of Leviticus contains more of the actual spoken words of God than any other book in the Bible, Jewish rabbis coined the phrase, "Let the pure read the pure." By this they meant children, who were thought to be pure, should be taught to read by reading the Book of Leviticus, which came to be known as the pure Word of God. This means the first book that received more attention from Jesus as He grew up in Nazareth is probably the last book to get the attention of Christians today.

The Book of Leviticus begins with instructions concerning the five major offerings in the Levitical system of worship. Most commentators agree the first of these, the whole burnt offering, is the model on which the apostle

Paul challenges the Romans to be "a living sacrifice" (cf. Rom. 12:1). This sacrifice involved burning the complete animal as an offering of worship to God and came to represent the highest expression of commitment a person could make to God in the Law. There is even greater agreement that Christ offered Himself as each of these five sacrifices in His death on Calvary.

The first seven chapters of the Book of Leviticus became the manual of sacrifice for Israel and her priests. The first part of this manual was addressed to the people and stressed their responsibility in the area of sacrifice (see Lev. 1:1–6:7). The second part of this section of the book was addressed to the priests and outlined their privilege regarding the sacrifices (see Lev. 8:1–27:34).

As you pray through Leviticus, remember you are praying the actual words of God. May you get close to God by using His words in intercession, and perhaps God will come closer to you than at any other time in your life.

Sincerely yours in Christ,
Elmer Towns
Written from my home
at the foot of the Blue Ridge Mountains

THE STORY OF JESUS COPYING LEVITICUS

Date: A.D. 2 ~ Place: Nazareth

"JESUS," Mary yelled out into the backyard of their humble home where Joseph's carpenter shop was located. Jesus had just turned six years old, and it was the spring of A.D. 2.

Jesus loved to play in the backyard, especially now that the grass was green and all types of wildlife were making their presence known around the city of Nazareth—deer, squirrel, rabbits, and birds, all kinds of birds. Mary did not realize the deep love of her son for animals. Maybe she didn't know that because she didn't yet realize He had created them in the original creation (see Col. 1:16). The young Jesus did not know every species of birds, because in the kenosis Jesus had voluntarily given up the independent exercise of His omniscience. He only knew what He was taught, or what He learned from His heavenly Father or the Holy Spirit.

"JESUS," again Mary called for Him to come in. "Today you begin to learn how to write."

Unknown to Jesus, two days ago Mary told Joseph to go to the small pond and cut some papyrus reeds. Then Joseph sliced the small reeds, taking out the inner white pulp. Then with a stone he rolled the papyrus pulp out on a large table, making large round pancake-like sheets of papyrus, still damp from their moist growth. Joseph cut away the edges, making a square sheet of paper. Then with the excess that he had cut away, he rolled it again into a ball and flattened it again with the stone to make more sheets of paper. He put all the square sheets out to dry in the sun. (The word *paper* comes from the papyrus plant.)

While Joseph was preparing paper, Mary was busy making ink. She went to the fireplace and took black coals, placing them on the kitchen table. She crushed them into black, sand-like granules. Then rolling the granules out into fine powder, she mixed them with olive oil, making black ink— black carbon ink.

Joseph brought a fistful of feathers from the carpenter shop into the kitchen. With knife he carefully cut the end off of each feather and scraped part of the feathers away, making a perfect quill for his son.

"The first letter in our Hebrew alphabet is aleph that looks like this א." Jesus copied a duplicate of the aleph, and then Mary told Him about the beth...ב, then the gimel...ג, on through the Hebrew alphabet.

Mary showed Jesus how to squeeze the barrel of the feather and dip it into the black ink. When Jesus released His grip, the black ink was sucked into the barrel. Then Mary instructed,

"Squeeze gently..."

Jesus followed His mother's instructions and formed the aleph, א. Then He continued writing what His mother showed Him.

Jesus copied the entire 22-letter Hebrew alphabet.

"Now..." Mary announced, "Let's get a Hebrew Bible. You must copy the entire Hebrew Scriptures.

"Jesus, You're going to be King of Israel," Mary explained to her son, "Every king is required to make his own copy of Scripture and keep it by his right hand to judge Israel." Then she quoted,

> When he [the King] *sits on the throne as king, he must copy for himself this body of instruction on a scroll in the presence of the Levitical priests. He must always keep that copy with him and read it daily as long as he lives. That way he will learn to fear the Lord his God by obeying all the terms of these instructions and decrees* (Deuteronomy 17:18-19 NLT).

Mary thought to herself, *The angel told me that Jesus would be the king of Israel, so I must prepare Him to be the king.* She believed the angel, and she knew that her son was born in the line of David. She knew that He could be the next David.

"Every boy in Rabbi school must memorize the Book of Leviticus," Mary told her son Jesus. "But we will do more than memorize Leviticus; we will make our own copy of Leviticus." So Mary guided the child Jesus to copy first Genesis, then Exodus, then Leviticus…

When Jesus began copying Leviticus, Mary promised, "This will be the first book of Scripture You will memorize from beginning to end." She wanted Jesus to be head and shoulders above all the boys in Nazareth.

In Jesus' ministry, He quoted from Leviticus more than any other book of Scripture. Because so much of Leviticus quotes the actual words that the Lord spoke to Moses, this book has been revered by the Jews.

Leviticus 1

THE BURNT OFFERING THE MEANING OF SACRIFICES IN THE CHRISTIAN LIFE

- **The Whole Burnt Offering**—Complete Consecration and Worship

- **The Meal Offering**—Expression of Practical Holiness

- **The Peace Offering**—Fellowship With God

- **The Sin Offering**—Restored Fellowship With Christ

- **The Trespass Penalty Offering**—Continued Forgiveness of Sins After Salvation

The Lord called to Moses to tell the people, "When you offer an offering to Me, bring one of the livestock as your offering. Or you may bring one of the sheep or the goats. When anyone offers a whole burnt offering from their livestock, it must be a male. It must have no physical defects. The person must voluntarily bring the animal to the entrance of the Meeting Tent into My presence. The person must put his hand on the animal's head to identify his sin with the animal. Then I will accept the burnt offering. It will make atonement for the person's sin."

Lord, just as the worshiper identified his sin with the animal,
So I confess I am a sinner

And identify with Christ, who became my sin
So I could be forgiven and cleansed.
Thank You for salvation.

Lord, by faith I accept Christ's substitution for me;
By faith I am justified with Christ's righteousness.

"That person must kill the young bull in My presence. (Note: The animal was tied by a rope to a ring on the north side of the altar. A prayer was said, the animal's throat was cut, and the blood was caught in a big bowl by a priest's assistant.) Then the priests must bring its blood to the altar. Sprinkle the blood on all sides of the altar at the entrance to the Meeting Tent. The skin must be cut from that animal. Then he will cut the animal into pieces. The priests must burn the sacrifice by laying wood upon the sacrifice. They must lay wood upon the fire. They must lay the head, the fat, and other pieces on the wood. The priest must wash the animal's internal organs and its legs with water. Then the priest must char the whole thing on the altar as incense, and the smell of it will be pleasing to Me."

Lord, the bull symbolizes Christ the Servant
Who was patient and enduring.

I accept the burnt offering of Christ
As my substitute for my sin.

"The burnt offering may be a sheep or a goat, but he must offer a male animal that has no physical defects. That person must kill the animal on the north side of the altar in My presence. Then the priests must sprinkle its blood on the altar, on all sides. That person must cut the animal into pieces. Then the priest must lay the pieces with its head and its fat on the wood. The wood will be on the fire on the altar. That person must wash the animal's internal organs and the legs with water. Then the priest must bring all of it and char it on the altar as incense, and the smell of it will be pleasing to Me."

Lord, the sheep signifies Christ the Innocent Lamb
  Who became poor and obedient for my sake.

Lord, may I learn from Christ's example
  That the pathway of poverty leads to Your riches.

"The whole burnt offering may be a bird, but he must offer a dove or a young pigeon. The priest will bring the offering to the altar. He will wring off the bird's head. Then he will char it on the altar as incense. The bird's blood must be drained out beside the altar. The priest must remove the bird's craw and its contents. He must throw them on the east side of the altar, next to where they put the ashes from the altar. Then the priest must split the bird open by its wings. But he must not divide the bird into two parts. Then the priest must char the bird on the altar as incense. The smell of it will be pleasing to Me."

Lord, the burnt offering typifies Christ offering Himself
  Without blemish or spot—perfect—for me.

The burnt offering seeks to worship You
  And praise You for Your blessings to the worshiper.

The thought of penalty is not prominent,
  But it does atone for the sinner
  And gives Him a perfect standing before God.

So Lord, I come to You, bringing the sacrifices of praise
  For all You've done for me.

Amen.

Hygienic Necessity

The way God dealt with the sacrifices was based on the necessity of
cleanliness and separation from germs, bacteria, and spreading
of infectious diseases. The sacrifices could have become a breed-
ing ground for disease and a very real danger from fly-borne diseases that could spread. Nothing was to be left lying around
exposed. After the sacrifice was made, it was to be entirely
burned upon the altar and anything left over could be eaten for
one or two days, then it had to be burned completely and taken
out of the camp and destroyed by fire. Probably this place outside the camp was where other garbage was burned.

The blood that was poured out at the base of the altar would have
drained into the sand of the earth. As this was done repeatedly,
probably new sand was placed over the blood-soaked sand, and
that prohibited a fly-borne disease epidemic.

When a sacrifice was made to God, if it could be eaten, it had to be
eaten as soon as possible (see Lev. 8:15-18). Even though the
food was roasted, the Israelites did not have means of preserva-
tion or refrigeration, so it could not be kept indefinitely. This
was God's way of protecting His people. As an illustration,
today pork can be eaten safely because of our refrigeration and
preservatives; however, in a desert environment pork would
quickly deteriorate and become dangerous. So the Law of Moses
banned pork altogether. Remember, when God moved from the
Dispensation of the Law to the Dispensation of Grace, He let
down a sheet from Heaven containing many ceremoniously
unclean animals. He told them, "Rise and eat" (Acts 10:13). So
what could not be eaten under the Law could be eaten under
grace—with proper hygienic and preservative conditions.

Leviticus 2

THE MEAL OFFERING

"When a person offers a food offering to Me, that offering must be
made from flour. That person must pour olive oil and incense on
it. Then he must take it to Aaron's sons, the priests. They must
get a handful of flour, along with the olive oil and all the
incense, and burn it as incense on the altar as a memorial offering. It will be an offering made by fire. The smell of it will be
pleasing to Me. The rest of the food offering will belong to
Aaron and his sons. This offering will be a most holy part of the
offerings made by fire to Me."

Lord, fine flour typified the evenness and balance of Christ.
  God enjoys His sense of smell
  When I worship Him from my heart.

Lord, fire typified the testing of Christ,
  That He was perfect in every way;
  I place myself on the altar to You,
  Praying You will be pleased with
  My sacrifice and worship to You.

"If you offer a food offering that was baked in an oven, it must be made
from flour, made without yeast and mixed with olive oil. It may
be wafers made without yeast with olive oil poured over them. If
your food offering is cooked on a flat pan used for baking, then
it must be made without yeast, made of flour mixed with olive
oil. Crumble it and pour olive oil over it as a food offering. If
your food offering is cooked in a frying pan, then it must be
made from flour and olive oil. Bring the food offering to Me and

hand it to the priest, and he will take it to the altar. The priest will separate the memorial offering from the food offering. He will burn it as incense on the altar. Its smell will be pleasing to Me. The rest of the food offering belongs to Aaron and his sons to feed their families."

Lord, the absence of leaven typified no sin in Christ,
The oil mingled typified Christ's perfection
Anointed with the Holy Spirit in life;

The oven typified Christ's temptation and suffering;
I accept all Christ did for me,
I worship Christ for all He is.

"Every food offering that you offer to Me must be made without yeast. You must not burn any yeast or honey as incense, since it is an offering made by fire to Me. You may bring yeast and honey to Me as an offering from the first harvest. But yeast and honey must not go up as a pleasing smell to Me on the altar. You must also put salt on all your food offerings. (Salt was, and still is, used as a preservative, symbolic for preserving peace and for loyalty. Here it represented a lasting covenant with Yahweh.) Salt represents your permanent covenant with God. You must add salt to all your offerings. If you offer a food offering from the first harvest to Me, then offer only crushed heads of new grain. Roast it in the fire, and put olive oil and incense on the grain as a food offering. The priest will burn the memorial offering of the crushed grain and olive oil as incense, in addition to frankincense as an offering to Me."

Lord, salt typified the enduring quality of Christ,
That He will present me and keep me;
I rejoice in this confidence.

*Lord, the absence of honey typified the solemnest of salvation;
I am serious in my worship to You.*

Amen.

Leviticus 3

THE PEACE OFFERING

"A person's peace-offering sacrifice must be brought into My presence
and is an offering that may come from cattle. It may be a male
or female animal, and it must have no physical defects. The person must put his hand on the animal's head and kill it at the
entrance to the Meeting Tent. Then the priests must sprinkle the
blood on all sides of the altar. The peace-offering sacrifice is
made by fire to Me. Offer the fat of the animal's internal organs,
everything that covers them. Offer both kidneys and the fat
which is on the loins. Also offer the fatty fold of the liver.
Remove it, along with the kidneys, then the priests will burn
these parts on the altar as incense. The smell of it will be pleasing to Me. Then they will put them on the smoldering ashes of
the fire that never goes out."

Lord, the peace offering typified the whole sacrifice of Christ;
  He made peace between us and God,
  Satisfying the judgment of God against our sin.

Then Christ gives me the indwelling peace of God
  In my heart as a result of salvation;
  Thank You, Lord, for peace.

Lord, the smell of the peace offering pleased You;
  Be pleased with my worship of You.

"A person's peace-offering sacrifice to Me may be sheep or goats, and it
may be male or female, but it must have no physical defects. If
he offers a sheep, then he must bring it into My presence, put

his hand on its head to emphasize the substitutionary aspect of the sacrifice. The worshiper must confess his sins and then kill the animal in front of the Meeting Tent. The priests will sprinkle its blood on all sides of the altar. Then this person has made a peace-offering sacrifice, an offering made by fire to Me. The person must bring its fat and the entire fat-tail by cutting off the tail close to the spine. He must also bring the fat of the internal organs, including the fat that is on them and whatever covers them. He must offer both kidneys and the fat which is on the loins and the fatty fold of the liver, removing it, along with the kidneys, and burn these parts on the altar as incense to Me."

Lord, burning fat has a pleasant aroma,
　　The peace offering was pleasing to Your smell.

Lord, I praise You for the inner peace;
　　May my inner character be pleasing to You.

Lord, I realize blood carries disease and germs and
　　Are stored in a person's fat;
　　Thank You for shielding us from disease and physical
　　harm.

"A person's peace offering may be a goat offered in My presence. He must put his hand on the goat's head and kill it in front of the Meeting Tent. Then the priests must sprinkle its blood on all sides of the altar. From this peace offering, that person makes an offering by fire to Me. The person must offer all the fat of the goat's internal organs, including the fat that is on them and whatever covers them. He must offer both kidneys and the fat which is on them and on the loins. And, he must offer the fatty fold of the liver, removing it along with the kidneys. Then the priest will burn these parts on the altar as incense, the smell of it will be pleasing to Me. All the fat belongs to Me.

"This law will continue for people from now on ("throughout your generations"). You must not eat any of the fat or the blood."
(Disease and germs are transported throughout the body by blood and reside in the fat. This prohibition contributed to the health of God's people.)

Amen.

Leviticus 4

THE SIN OFFERING

The Lord said to Moses, "Tell the people of Israel, 'When a person
might sin unintentionally—has done something that I have commanded not to be done and actually does commit a particular
sin (it may be the anointed priest who has sinned)—if so, he has
brought guilt upon all the people. Then he must offer a young
bull to Me that has no physical defects. This will be a sin offering for the sin he has done. He must bring the bull to the
entrance of the Meeting Tent, into My presence. Then he must
put his hand on the bull's head and kill the bull in My presence.
Then the anointed priest must take some of the bull's blood and
must bring it up to the Meeting Tent. The priest must dip his finger into the blood and sprinkle it seven times (symbolic of perfection) in My presence in front of the curtain that is in front of
the Holy of Holies. The priest must also put some of the blood
on the corners of the Altar of Burning Incense that stands in My
presence. Then the priest must pour out all the rest of the bull's
blood at the bottom of the Brazen Altar of Burnt Offering.'"

Lord, Christ typifies the Sin Offering because His death
Covers any and all sin I commit ignorantly;

You have said, "If I walk in the light...the blood of Jesus Christ
cleanses [me] from all sin" (1 John 1:7).

Thank You for forgiving my ignorant sin
Even when I don't know that I should confess it;
You are a merciful God and I worship you.

"The priest must remove all the fat from the bull of the sin-offering,
removing all the fat that is on and around the internal organs.
He must take out the kidneys and the fat that is on them and
the fat on the loins and extract the fatty fold of the liver, along
with the kidneys. You must do the same thing that you did for
the peace-offering sacrifice. The priest must burn as incense the
animal parts on the Brazen Altar of Burnt Offering. However,
the priest must carry out the skin (hide) of the bull and all of its
meat, including its head, its legs, its intestines, and its waste, taking these to the place where the ashes are poured out. He must
burn it upon a wood fire, on top of the pile of ashes."

Lord, the sin offering typified the work of
Christ as an advocate who intercedes
To You on behalf of sinning believers (me);

Jesus as my High Priest is "an advocate
With the Father, Jesus Christ, the righteous" (1 John 2:1);

Because Jesus is righteous (perfect), He is my
Propitiation (satisfaction) to forgive my sin;
Lord, You are a merciful God, I worship You.

"The whole community of Israel might sin without knowing it. They
might do something that I have commanded *not* to be done. If
this happens, they are guilty. When they learn about the sin they
have committed, the community must offer a young bull as a sin
offering. They must bring it in front of the Meeting Tent. The elders as representatives of the community must put their hands on
the bull's head in My presence. Then they must kill the bull in
My presence. The anointed priest must bring some of the bull's
blood into the Meeting Tent. The high priest must dip his finger
into the blood and sprinkle it seven times in My presence, in
front of the curtain. Then he must put some of the blood on the
corners of the burning incense altar, in My presence. The priest

must pour out the rest of the blood at the bottom of the Brazen Altar of Burnt Offering. That altar is at the entrance to the Meeting Tent. The priest must take away all the fat from the bull and burn it on the altar as incense. He must do the same thing with this bull that he had done to the first bull of the sin offering. In this way, the high priest covers the sins of the whole community, and I will forgive them. Then the priest must transport the bull outside the camp and burn it just as he did with the first bull. This will be a sin offering for the whole congregation.

"A ruler might sin, but he didn't mean to do it. He might do something which I, his God, have commanded must *not* be done. If he does, he is guilty. When his sin that he committed is pointed out to him, he must bring a male goat with no physical defects. That will be his sin offering. The ruler must put his hand on the goat's head and kill it as a whole burnt offering in My presence. The goat will be a sin offering. Then the priest must take some of the blood of the sin offering with his finger and put it on the corners of the Brazen Altar of Burnt Offering. He must pour out the rest of its blood at the bottom of the Brazen Altar. He must burn all of the goat's fat on the altar as incense in the same way that he burns the fat of the peace-offering sacrifices. This is how the priest cancels the ruler's sin. Then I will forgive him.

"Any common person might sin but didn't mean to do it. He might do something that I have commanded *must* not be done. He will be guilty. When that person has his sin pointed out to him, he must bring his sin offering, a female goat with no physical defects, and he must put his hand on the animal's head, killing it at the place where they offer the whole burnt offerings. Then the priest must take some of the goat's blood with his finger and put it on the corners of the Brazen Altar of Burnt Offering. He must pour out all the rest of the goat's blood at the bottom of the altar.

Then the priest must remove all the goat's fat in the same way that the fat was removed from the peace-offering sacrifices. The priest must burn it on the Brazen Altar as incense, and its smell will be pleasing to Me. In this way, the priest will make atonement for that person's sin. And I will forgive him.

"This person may bring a lamb as his sin offering, but it must be a female lamb with no physical defects. The person must put his hand on the animal's head and kill it as a sin offering where they offer the whole burnt offerings. The priest must take some of the blood of the sin offering with his finger and put it on the corners of the Brazen Altar of Burnt Offering. Then he must pour all the rest of the lamb's blood at the bottom of the altar. The priest must remove all of the lamb's fat in the same way that the lamb's fat was removed from the peace-offering sacrifices. He must burn it on the altar as incense to please Me. In this way, the priest will cancel that person's sins, and I will forgive him."

Lord, these animal sacrifices had no intrinsic value in themselves;
They prefigured the value in the sacrifice of Christ for me;

Thank You, Christ, for suffering for me,
Thank You, Father, for forgiving me all my sin.

Amen.

Leviticus 5

SINS REQUIRING A SIN OFFERING

The Lord said to Moses, "A person sins when: as a witness, he is ordered to tell what he has seen or knows, but he does *not* tell the court, then he *will* be held guilty of sin.

"When a person touches something that is 'unclean,' he is guilty. It might be the dead body of an unclean, wild animal; or an unclean, domesticated animal; or an unclean, crawling thing. He might not realize that he touched it and is unclean. Nevertheless, he will still be guilty of sin.

"When a person touches something that comes from a human being that is 'unclean,' it could be any type of uncleanliness which causes him to be unclean, and he does not realize it. However, he *will* become guilty of sin whenever he becomes aware that it is unclean.

"When a person makes a rash vow without really thinking it through, he is guilty when he doesn't do what he promises. The flippant vow could be about anything. He might even make a vow and forget about it. Nevertheless, when he remembers it, he will be guilty of one of these sins."

Lord, this sacrifice deals with the consequences of sin;
When a person is guilty of injuring You or another,
They must bring a sacrifice that deals with injury.

The person must first get forgiveness for his personal guilt,
And second he must deal with the injury he caused.

Lord, thank You for cleansing my conscience from sin and
Forgiving me so I can come worship You.

"When anyone is guilty of any of these things, he must admit how he
sinned, then bring a guilt offering to Me. It will be a penalty for
the sin that he committed. This sin offering must be a female
lamb or a goat from the flock. The priest will perform the ritual
to cancel (make atonement for) that person's sin. That person
might not be able to afford a lamb; if so, he must bring two
doves or two young pigeons to Me. These will be his penalty for
his sin. One bird will be for a sin offering; the other one will be
for a burnt offering. He must bring them to the priest. First, the
priest will offer the one bird for the sin offering. He will wring
the bird's head from its neck. However, he must not pull it off
completely. Then he must sprinkle the blood from the sin offering on the side of the Brazen Altar. Next, he must drain out the
rest of the blood at the bottom of the altar. It will be a sin offering. Then the priest must offer the second bird as a burnt offering. In this way, the priest will make atonement for the sin that
the person committed. Then I will forgive him.

"That person might not be able to afford two doves or two young
pigeons. If that is the case, the sinner must bring about two
quarts of flour for a sin offering. He must not put olive oil or
incense because it is a sin offering. He must bring the flour to
the priest. The priest will get a handful of the flour as a memorial offering and burn it on the altar as burning incense. By this
sin offering the priest will make atonement for the sin that the
person committed. And I will forgive him. And this will become
a food offering for the priest.'"

Penalty or Trespass Offering

The Lord said to Moses, "A person might sin unintentionally and do something inadvertently against My holy things. If so, that person must bring a male sheep from the flock with no physical defects as his penalty offering for Me. The value of the ram in silver shekels must be accurate! (Use the proper value for silver as set by the standard of the Holy Place for a penalty offering.) That person must pay for the sin which he committed against the holy thing. He must add 20 percent to its value and give it all to the priest. In this way, the priest will make atonement for his sin. And I will forgive him. The priest does this by offering a ram for the penalty offering.

"A person might sin and do something specific that I have commanded *not* to be done. It doesn't matter whether that person knew about it or not. The person strayed without knowing it or didn't realize it. He will still be guilty. He will be responsible for his sin. He must bring a ram from the flock to the priest with no physical defects. It must be worth the correct amount to be a penalty offering. With this offering, the priest will make atonement for his sin, and I will forgive him."

Lord, You require holiness in my inward life before You
    As well as holiness in my outward relations with others;

Thank You for Christ who cleanses me inwardly,
    I will make restitution with all I offend outwardly.

Amen.

Leviticus 6

SINS REQUIRING SACRIFICES

The Lord said to Moses, "A person might sin against Me in several ways: He might tell a lie about what happened to something that his friend left with him for safekeeping. Or he might steal something from him. Or he might have cheated him, or he might have found something that was lost and then lied about it. Or he might have sworn to God when he knew it was false. Or he might have committed some other sin. If he did any of these things, he would be guilty of sin. He must bring back whatever he stole. Or he must bring back whatever he took away by cheating. Or he must restore whatever was left to his care for safekeeping. Or he must return whatever he found and then lied about. Or he must repay what he swore to God was true but was false. He *must* pay the full price. Then he must add an extra 20 percent of its value. He must give the money to the true owner on the same day that he brings his penalty offering to God. He must also pay a penalty to the priest. It must be a male sheep from the flock with no physical defects, which is worth the correct amount. It is a penalty offering to Me. Then, in My presence, the priest will make atonement for that person's sin. And I will forgive him of all the sins that made him guilty."

The Lord gave these instructions to Moses, "The whole burnt offering is a burnt offering on the hearth (the part at the top of the Brazen Altar that is closest to the fire) all night until morning. The altar's fire *must* be kept burning. The priest must put on his linen robe and linen underwear next to his body. Then he must remove all the leftover ashes of the burnt offering that was on the altar, putting these ashes beside the altar. Then he must take off those clothes and put on different clothes and carry these ashes outside the camp to a special place."

Lord, the priest typified Jesus' offering outside the camp;
"Jesus...sanctified the people with his own blood,
Suffered outside the gate" (Heb. 13:12).

Lord, thank You that Jesus not only became our sin
But that He also suffered for me.
"I will go forth unto Him without the camp where He bore
my reproach" (Heb. 13:13 AMP).

The Lord said, "The fire must always be kept burning on the altar. It must *not* be allowed to go out. The priest must burn firewood on the altar every morning, as he arranges the whole burnt offering on the fire. And he must burn the fat of the peace offerings as incense. The fire must be kept burning on the altar all the time. It must *not* go out!

"These are the instructions about the meal offering: The priests must offer it into me in front of the altar. The priest must take a handful of the flour food offering and add olive oil and incense. The priest must burn the meal offering on the altar as incense. It will be a memorial offering to Me. Its smell will be pleasing to Me. Aaron and his sons may eat the rest of it, but it must be eaten without yeast in a holy place. They must eat it in the courtyard of the Meeting Tent. It must not be cooked with yeast. I have given it to the priest as their share of the offerings made to Me by fire. It is holy, like the sin offering and like the penalty offering. Any male descendant of Aaron may eat of the offerings made to Me by fire. This permanent rule will continue through your generations. Whatever touches these offerings will be considered holy." (This kind of holiness was ceremonial.)

The Lord said to Moses, "This is the offering that Aaron and his sons must bring to Me. They must do this on the day that they anoint Aaron as high priest. They must bring two quarts of flour for a continual food offering. They must bring half of it in the morning and half of it in the evening. The flour must be mixed with olive oil and cooked on a flat pan. After it is mixed well, take the batter and shape it into pieces and bake it. You must offer them as a meal offering to Me. It will produce a smell that will be pleasing to Me. One of the priests will be anointed to take Aaron's place as high priest. He must make the meal offering to Me. All food offering that is made when a man is consecrated into the priesthood must be completely burned; it must *not* be eaten!"

The Lord said to Moses, "Give Aaron and the priests these instructions about the sin offering. 'The animal must be killed in My presence in the same place that the whole burnt offering is killed, it is holy. The priest who offers the sin offering must eat it in a holy place; it must be eaten in the courtyard of the Meeting Tent. Anything that touches the meat of the sin offering will become holy. Whenever some of the blood gets on any of the clothes of the priests, then wash the clothes in a holy place. The clay pot where the meat is boiled must be broken. If a bronze pot is used for boiling the meat, the pot must be scrubbed and rinsed with water. Any male in a priest's family may eat the offering; it is holy. The blood of the sin offering may be taken into the Holy Place and used to make atonement for sin. It must be burned with fire. It must *not* be eaten!'"

Lord, thank You for practical insight into Your concerns
Because blood is a carrier of disease;
You instructed Your priests to wash old blood away;

Even the porous clay pots where disease might hide
You told them to break it lest they eat out of that pot
And expose themselves to viruses or diseases.

Lord, I will separate myself for sinful practices
To keep myself holy and healthy;

I will not drink alcoholic beverages
Lest I become addicted to it;

I will keep myself sexually pure
Lest I expose myself to AIDS or sexual diseases;

I dedicate anew my body to Your use;
Fill me with the Spirit of God
And let my body be the temple of the Holy Spirit.

Amen.

Leviticus 7

THE PENALTY OR TRESPASS OFFERING

"These are the instructions (Torah) for the penalty offering; it is holy. The priest must kill the animal in the same place where they kill the whole burnt offering animals. Then the priest must sprinkle its blood on all sides of the Brazen Altar. He must offer all the fat from the penalty offering, including the tail fat and the fat that covers the internal organs. He must take out both kidneys and the fat that is on them and the loins and extract the fatty fold of the liver and remove it, along with the kidneys. The priest must burn all these things on the altar as incense to Me, as a penalty offering. Any male among the priests may eat the meat of it. Since it is holy, it *must* be eaten in a holy place.

"The penalty offering is like the sin offering; the instructions for both are the same. The priest who makes atonement for sin with the animal shall take it to his family. And the priest who offers any man's burnt offering may also have the skin from it. It belongs to him.

"Every meal offering belongs to the priest who offers it. This includes those baked in an oven, cooked on a flat pan used for baking, or baked in a dish. All the meal offerings belong to all the priests. They will share and share alike."

Lord, I'm glad You provided food
*   For the priests who served You;*

I'll gladly tithe to my church
Knowing some of that money goes
To those who serve You fulltime in ministry.

"These are the instructions about the peace-offering sacrifices that a person may offer to Me. He may bring the peace offering to show that he is thankful to Me. If he does, then he should also bring loaves of bread, made without yeast. They must have olive oil poured over them. Also he should bring loaves of flour mixed with olive oil, made with yeast. These should be brought with his peace-offering sacrifice, which he gives to show thanksgiving to Me.

"He must offer one of each kind of offering—a wave-offering for Me. It will be given to the priest who sprinkles the blood of the peace offering. (According to Jewish tradition, there were to be ten cakes of each kind of bread in every thanksgiving offering. The other cakes were returned to the sacrificer.)

"The sacrifice of his peace offering is for thanking Me. The meat from it must be eaten on the same day that it is offered. None of it must be left over until morning. A person might bring a peace-offering sacrifice just to give a gift to Me. Or it may be done because of a special vow to Me. Then the sacrifice should be eaten on the same day he offers it. If there is any left over, then it may be eaten on the next day. If any meat from this sacrifice is left over on the third day, then it *must* be burned up! Any meat of the peace-offering sacrifice that is eaten on the third day will *not* be accepted. It will become unclean because anyone who eats any of the meat will be guilty of sin!"

Christ in the Offerings

There are five major offerings that the Levites brought to God. First, the *burnt offering* was a picture of Christ's perfect obedience whereby He offered Himself to God as a propitiation or satisfaction of our sins.

Second was the *meal offering* where bread and oil were perfectly blended before being offered to God. This is a picture of Christ's perfectly blended divine and human nature—the hypostatic union where He was completely God and completely man at the same time, perfectly blended into one personality. The meal offering presented Christ as the Bread of Life.

The third offering was the *peace offering,* which is a picture of worship or praise to God because the death of Christ was the basis of the believer's peace with God, and the indwelling presence of Christ becomes the basis of the believer's internal peace of God.

The *sin offering* shows Christ as the One who became sin for us (see Rom. 8:3), "For He made Him who knew no sin [to be] sin for us, that we might become the righteousness of God in Him" (2 Cor. 5:21). This offering was brought when a believer sinned against God.

Finally, the *penalty or trespass* offering indicates Christ's atoning work for the sins of the believer after he is saved. Christ the Intercessor prays for the forgiveness of the believer's sin (see Heb. 7:24-25), and Christ the Mediator prays to keep the believer from sin (1 John 2:1-2).

"People must *not* eat meat that touches anything 'unclean.' They must burn this meat with fire. But anyone who is 'clean' may eat other meat. But the person who is 'unclean' might eat the meat from the peace offering that belongs to Me. If he does, then that individual *must* be separated from his people."

"Someone might touch an unclean discharge that comes from people, or the unclean discharge from an animal, or some other creature. Touching it will make him unclean. If he comes into My presence and eats meat from the peace-offering sacrifice that belongs to Me, then that person *must* be separated from his people."

Lord, I will be clean inwardly and outwardly;
  I want to be holy in every area of life
  So You'll be glorified in all I do.

The Lord said to Moses, "Tell the people of Israel: 'You must not eat any of the fat from cattle, sheep, or goats (however, fat could be used for other purposes such as making soap or oiling a harness, etc.). If an animal is found dead or torn apart by wild animals, then you may use its fat for other purposes, but you must *not* eat it. If someone eats fat from an animal offering made by fire to Me, that person *must* be separated from his people. It does not matter where you live, you must *not* eat blood from any bird or animal. Anyone who eats blood *must* be separated from his people.'"

The Lord said to Moses, "If someone offers a peace-offering sacrifice to Me, he must carry that part of the gift in his own hands. It will be an offering made by fire to Me. He must carry the fat and the chest of the animal to the priest. It must be waved to and fro horizontally in a solemn gesture as being given to Me. Then it is for the priests. (It was waved toward the bronze altar to symbolize that is was offered to God and waved away from the altar to symbolize that it was being returned to the priest for them to eat.) Then the priest must burn the fat on the altar as incense. But the chest of the animal will belong to Aaron and the priests.

"You must also give the right thigh from the sacrifice of your peace offerings as a (heave) raised offering to Me, then give it to the priest. Then gather the whole community (the whole nation represented by all the elders who were present. This series of ceremonies was repeated every day during that week [see Lev. 8:33].

Some attended on one day, and others attended on other days)
together at the entrance to the Meeting Tent."

So Moses did as the Lord commanded him. All the community met
together at the entrance of the Meeting Tent. Then Moses spoke
to the people, "This is what the Lord has commanded to be
done to ordain priests to serve God."

Then Moses brought Aaron and his sons forward and bathed them in
the Laver with water. He put the inner robe upon Aaron. And he
tied the cloth belt around Aaron. Then he put on him the outer
robe. Next, he put the holy vest upon Aaron. Then he tied the
skillfully woven band around him. So, the special holy vest was
tied to Aaron. Then Moses put the chest pocket upon him, and
put the Urim and Thummin in the chest pocket. Moses also put
the turban upon Aaron's head and the strip of gold on the front
of the turban. This strip of gold is the holy crown. Moses did
this all just as the Lord commanded him to do.

Then Moses anointed the Holy Tent and everything in it with the special
olive oil. In this way, Moses made them holy for the Lord. Then
Moses sprinkled some oil on the altar seven times. He anointed
the altar and all of its tools. He also anointed the large Laver
and its base. In this way, Moses made them holy for the Lord.

Then Moses poured some of the special anointed oil upon Aaron's
head. Moses anointed Aaron to make him holy for the Lord's
service.

Then Moses brought Aaron's sons forward and put the inner robes
upon them. He tied cloth belts around them, and put headbands
upon them. He did these things just as the Lord had commanded him.

Then Moses brought forth the bull of the sin offering. Aaron and his
sons put their hands upon its head, and Moses killed the bull

and took some of the blood on his finger and put it on all the corners of the altar. In this way, Moses made the altar pure. Then he poured out the rest of the blood at the bottom of the altar. So, he made it holy and ready for service to God. Then Moses took all of the fat from the internal organs of the bull and the fatty fold of the liver, and both kidneys and their fat, and burned them on the altar as incense. Moses took the bull—its skin, its meat, and its waste—outside the camp. He burned them in a fire outside the camp. Moses did all these things just as the Lord had commanded him.

Next, Moses brought the ram of the burnt offering. Aaron and his sons put their hands on its head. Then Moses killed it. He sprinkled its blood on all sides of the altar. Then Moses cut the ram into pieces, and burned the head, the pieces, and the fat as incense. He washed the internal organs and legs with water. Then he burned the whole ram upon the altar as incense, as a burnt offering made by fire to the Lord. Moses did these things just as the Lord had commanded him.

Then Moses brought the other ram that was used when Aaron and his sons were consecrated into the priesthood. They put their hands upon its head. And Moses killed it. He put some of its blood upon the bottom of Aaron's right ear, and some upon the thumb of Aaron's right hand, and some on the big toe of his right foot. (The ram was raised up vertically to Heaven perhaps several times, showing that it actually belonged to God and that it was being offered *up* to God. But the act of lowering it symbolized that it was being returned from God to the priests as His divine gift to them.) The right thigh will belong to the priest who offers the blood and the fat of the peace offerings. I will receive the chests of the wave offerings and the thighs of the raised offering from the sons of Israel as the sacrifices of their peace offerings. And I will give these parts to Aaron the high priest and to his sons for them to eat. This is the portion that belongs to Aaron and his sons and is a gift from Me. Aaron and his sons were given this privilege on the day that they were ordained as priests to Me.

"On the day when I anointed the priests, I commanded the people of Israel to give this share to them. From now on, it is to be given to the priests as their share. So, these are the instructions about the whole burnt offerings, the meal offerings, the sin offerings, the peace offerings, and the penalty offerings. They are also the instructions for the priests."

The Lord gave these commands to Moses on Mount Sinai on the day that He commanded the Israelites to bring their offerings to Him.

Lord, I see Jesus in the various sacrifices
That were offered to You in the Tabernacle;

Thank You for this pre-figure of Jesus,
The Lamb of God who takes away the sin of the world.

Amen.

Leviticus 8

Aaron and His Sons Are Anointed

The Lord said to Moses, "Bring Aaron, along with his sons, and their clothes and the special olive oil used in anointing the bull of the sin offering and the two male sheep into My presence. Also bring the basket of bread made without yeast." (Rabbinical tradition says that there were eighteen pieces of bread, that is, six pieces of each of three kinds: (a) loaves of ordinary unleavened bread; (b) loaves of oiled bread (Lev. 2:1,4); (c) oiled wafers (Lev. 2:4,6).)

"Then gather the whole community (the whole nation represented by all the elders who were present. This series of ceremonies was repeated every day during that week [see Lev. 8:33]. Some attended on one day, and others attended on other days) together at the entrance to the Meeting Tent."

The Priesthood

The Book of Leviticus gets its name from the tribe of Levi, which was the priestly tribe of Israel. Though all Levites had priestly duties (singers, teachers, janitors, guards, etc.), only the certain descendants of Aaron were called of God to do the sacrificial ministry of a priest (see Heb. 5:4). Because the office of the priest is one of the three anointed offices of Christ (prophet, priest, and king), the details concerning the priesthood in this book are typical of our Great High Priest.

Old Testament Priest	Christ, our Intercessor
Earthly tabernacle	Heavenly temple

Once a year	Once for all
Veil kept people out	Rent veil
Covered sins	Forgave sins
Blood of bulls	His own blood

So Moses did as the Lord commanded him. All the community met together at the entrance of the Meeting Tent. Then Moses spoke to the people, "This is what the Lord has commanded to be done to ordain priests to serve God." Then Moses brought Aaron and his sons forward and bathed them in the Laver with water. He put the inner robe upon Aaron. And he tied the cloth belt around Aaron. Then he put on him the outer robe. Next, he put the holy vest upon Aaron. Then he tied the skillfully woven band around him. So, the special holy vest was tied to Aaron. Then Moses put the chest pocket upon him and put the Urim and Thummin in the chest pocket. Moses also put the turban upon Aaron's head with the strip of gold on the front of the turban. This strip of gold is the holy crown. Moses did this all just as the Lord commanded him to do.

Then Moses anointed the Holy Tent and everything in it with the special olive oil. In this way, Moses made them holy for the Lord. Then Moses sprinkled some oil on the altar seven times. He anointed the altar and all of its tools. He also anointed the large Laver and its base. In this way, Moses made them holy for the Lord. Then Moses poured some of the special anointed oil upon Aaron's head. Moses anointed Aaron to make him holy for the Lord's service. Then Moses brought Aaron's sons forward and put the inner robes upon them. He tied cloth belts around them and put headbands upon them. He did these things just as the Lord had commanded him.

Then Moses brought forth the bull of the sin-offering. Aaron and his sons put their hands upon its head, and Moses killed the bull and took some of the blood on his finger and put it on all the corners of the altar. In this way, Moses made the altar pure. Then he poured out the rest of the blood at the bottom of the altar. So, he made it holy and ready for service to God. Then Moses took all of the fat from the internal organs of the bull and the fatty fold of the liver, and both kidneys and their fat, and burned them on the altar as incense. Moses took the bull—its skin, its meat, and its waste—outside the camp. He burned them in a fire outside the camp. Moses did all these things just as the Lord had commanded him.

Next, Moses brought the ram of the burnt offering. Aaron and his sons put their hands on its head. Then Moses killed it. He sprinkled its blood on all sides of the altar. Then Moses cut the ram into pieces, and burned the head, the pieces, and the fat as incense. He washed the internal organs and legs with water. Then he burned the whole ram upon the altar as incense, as a burnt offering made by fire to the Lord. Moses did these things just as the Lord had commanded him.

Then Moses brought the other ram that was used in consecrating Aaron and his sons to become priests. They put their hands upon its head. And Moses killed it. He put some of its blood upon the bottom of Aaron's right ear, and some upon the thumb of Aaron's right hand, some on the big toe of his right foot. Then, Moses brought Aaron's sons to the altar. He put some of the blood upon the lobes of their right ears, some on the thumbs of their right hands, and, on the big toes of their right feet. Then, Moses sprinkled blood on all sides of the altar. Moses then placed on the altar the tail fat and the fat from the ram and the internal organs, the fatty fold of the liver, also the fat of both kidneys and the right thigh. He took a basket of bread made without yeast to place in the presence of the Lord each day. Moses took a loaf of bread from the basket, a loaf made with olive oil, and a wafer and put these pieces of bread on the fat and the right thigh of the ram. Moses put all these things in the hands of Aaron and his sons. The pieces were presented as a wave offering in the presence of the Lord. Then Moses took them from their hands and burned them on the altar on top of the burnt offering as incense. So, this was the offering for anointing Aaron and his sons when they became priests. The smell of it was pleasing to the Lord.

Lord, I know that worship is pleasing to You,
May You be pleased as I offer my life
As a sacrifice of sweet incense to You.

Moses took the brisket and presented it as a wave offering in the presence of the Lord. It was Moses' share of the ram used in anointing them as priests. This was just as the Lord had commanded him.

Next Moses took some of the special olive oil and some of the blood which was on the altar and sprinkled some of the oil on Aaron's clothes. He also sprinkled some of it on Aaron's sons, and their clothes. This made Aaron holy for the Lord, as well as Aaron's clothes, his sons, and their clothes.

Then Moses said to Aaron and his sons, "I gave you a command, 'Take the meat and the basket of bread from the offering for anointing priests, boil the meat at the door of the Meeting Tent, eat it there, along with the bread. If any of the meat or the bread is left over, burn it with fire! The time of anointing will last seven days. You must not go outside the entrance of the Meeting Tent until that time is up. Stay there until the time of your anointing is finished. The Lord commanded the things that we did today. These things will make atonement for your sins. You must stay at the entrance of the Meeting Tent for seven days, day and night. If you do not obey the Lord's commands, then you will die!'" So, Aaron and his sons did everything that the Lord had commanded them through Moses.

Lord, just as Your servants were anointed with oil for Tabernacle service,
> *I ask today your anointing of the Holy Spirit on me*
> *So I can serve You in wisdom and power.*

Lord, if I'm not filled and anointed with the Holy Spirit,
> *Then I can't serve You effectively;*
> *So, fill and anoint me today.*

Amen.

Leviticus 9

AARON OFFERS SACRIFICES

On the eighth day after his anointing, Moses summoned Aaron and his
sons, and the elders of Israel to the Tent of Meeting. Moses said
to Aaron, "Prepare a bull calf and a ram with no physical defects
for sacrifice. The bull calf will be a sin offering, and the ram will
be a whole burnt offering. Offer these animals to the Lord. Tell
the people of Israel, 'Take a male goat for a sin offering, and
take a calf and lamb for a whole burnt offering. Both the calf
and the lamb must each be 1 year old, with no physical defects.
Prepare a bull and a ram for peace offerings. Prepare these animals along with a food offering mixed with olive oil. Sacrifice
these things to the Lord. Why? Do this, because the Lord will
appear to you today.'"

So, the whole community came to the front of the Meeting Tent, bringing the things which Moses had commanded them to bring. As
they stood in the presence of the Lord, Moses said, "You have
done what the Lord has commanded. So, the Lord's splendor
(glory) will appear to you."

Lord, I know it's important for me to gather
With other believers to worship and serve You.

I will attend church every Sunday to worship You,
And serve You with other believers.

Then Moses told Aaron, "Go to the altar, offer your sin offerings and
your whole burnt offerings. Do this to make atonement for your
own sins and the people's sins. Offer the sacrifices for the peo-

ple. And do the rituals to atone for their sins. Do this just as the Lord has commanded." So, Aaron went to the altar and killed the bull calf as a sin offering for himself. Then his sons brought the blood to him, and he dipped his finger into the blood and put it on the corners of the Altar. Then he poured out the rest of the blood at the bottom of the Altar. Aaron took the fat, the kidneys, and the fatty fold of the liver and burned these things upon the altar as incense. He did this just as the Lord had commanded Moses. Then Aaron placed these offerings in a position where they would continue to burn and eventually be consumed. Instantly, God's fire consumed all the offerings.

Then Aaron killed the animal for the whole burnt offering. Aaron's sons brought the blood to him. And he sprinkled it on all sides of the Altar. Aaron's sons gave each of the pieces and the head of the burnt offering to Aaron. And, he placed them on the Altar as incense. Next, Aaron washed the internal organs and the legs of the burnt offering and placed them upon the Altar as incense.

Then Aaron brought the offering that was for the people. He took the goat of the people's sin offering, killed it, and offered the goat as a sin offering. He did this just as he had done for the first sin offering. Then Aaron brought the whole burnt offering and offered it according to God's command. He also brought the food offering to the altar. He took a handful of the grain and placed it upon the altar as incense. This was in addition to the morning's whole burnt offering. Aaron also killed the bull and the ram. These were the peace-offering sacrifices for the people. Aaron's sons presented the blood from these animals to Aaron. He sprinkled it on all sides of the Altar. Aaron's sons also presented to him the fat of the bull and of the ram. They brought the ram's tail fat and the fat covering the internal organs, along with the kidneys and the fatty fold of the liver. Aaron's sons placed these fat parts upon the chest of the bull and the ram.

Then Aaron placed these fat parts on the altar as incense. Aaron waved the briskets and the right thigh in the presence of the Lord. This was the priests' share of the offering. He did this just as Moses had commanded.

Then Aaron lifted up his hands toward the people and blessed them. When Aaron had finished offering the sin offering, the burnt offering, and the peace offering, he stepped down from the Altar. The Altar was elevated above the level of the floor, and the ascent was a gentle slope (see Exod. 20:26). Moses and Aaron went into the Meeting Tent. After they came out and blessed the people, the Lord's splendor appeared to all the people. Fire came out from the Lord and burned up the whole burnt offering and the fat on the altar. When all the people saw this, they shouted with joy and then bowed their faces to the ground.

Lord, it's important that You accept the offering of my life
That I sacrifice to You;

Let the fire of Your presence fall in my life and
Burn up all sin and chaff within me;

May my life be reverent and focused on You;
May my life be a gift offering to You.

Amen.

Leviticus 10

NADAB AND ABIHU WERE KILLED

Each of Aaron's sons, Nadab and Abihu, got their pans for burning incense (ceremonial vessels that contained hot coals that were used for burning incense). They put their own fire (not the fire from the Altar that was in the presence of Yahweh) in them and put incense on it. However, they used unauthorized fire that God had commanded them *not* to use. Then they brought it into the presence of the Lord in the Tent of Meeting. So fire came out from the presence of the Lord, and Nadab and Abihu died instantly. They died in the presence of the Lord. This was the first instance of contempt for sacred things.

Then Moses said to Aaron, "This is what the Lord was talking about when He said, 'I AM HOLY, I MUST be respected by those who come near Me.'"

Aaron was silent.

Uzziel, Aaron's uncle, had sons named Mishael and Elzaphan. They were first cousins to Nadab and Abihu. Moses summoned them and told them, "Come pick up the corpses of your cousins and carry them outside the camp, away from the Holy Place."

Mishael and Elzaphan came and carried the corpses of Nadab and Abihu outside the camp. Nadab and Abihu were still wearing their special priestly robes. Then Moses told Aaron and his remaining sons, Eleazar and Ithamar, "Do *not* show any grief. Do *not* tear your clothes or leave your hair uncombed. If you do, you will *die*, and the Lord will be angry with the entire community. All the people of Israel are your relatives. *They* are permitted to cry openly over Nadab and Abihu, whom the Lord destroyed by fire, but not you! *You* must not even leave the entrance of the Meeting Tent. If you go outside, then you will *die*! This is because the Lord has anointed you to His service." So, Aaron, Eleazar, and Ithamar obeyed Moses.

Lord, teach me to fear You. May I never
Take Your Word and commandments lightly.

Lord, I worship You as a burning fire that consumes all sin;
I will separate myself from everything I know is sin,
I want to be holy, acceptable by You (see Rom. 12:1-2).

Rules for the Priests

Then the Lord said to Aaron, "You and your sons must not drink wine or beer when you go into the Meeting Tent. Otherwise, you will die! This law will continue from now on. You must distinguish what is holy from what is not holy, between what is 'clean' from what is 'unclean.' You must teach the people of Israel all the laws I have spoken to them through Moses."

Moses talked to Aaron and his remaining sons, Eleazar and Ithamar saying, "Some of the meal offering is left over from the sacrifices offered by fire to the Lord. Eat that part of the meal offering, but do not add yeast to it. Eat it near the altar, because it is holy. This part belongs to you and your sons. However, you must eat it in a holy place. It is part of the offerings made by fire to the Lord. He commanded me to tell you this.

"Also, you, your sons, and daughters may eat the brisket of the wave offering and the thigh of the raised offering that was presented to God. However, you must eat them in a 'clean' place. They are your share of the peace-offering sacrifices given by the Israelites.

"The people must bring the fat from their animals that is part of the offerings made by fire. They must also bring the thigh of the raised offering and the brisket of the wave offering. These will be presented to the Lord. They will always be your share of the offerings for you and your children. The Lord has commanded it."

Moses asked about the goat of the sin offering that had already been burned up. Moses became very angry with Eleazar and Ithamar, Aaron's remaining sons, saying, "You were supposed to eat that goat in the sanctuary area in the presence of the Lord! It is holy! God gave it to you to take away the sins of the people. You did not bring the goat's blood inside the Holy Place. You were supposed to eat the goat in the sanctuary area, as I commanded!"

Aaron said to Moses, "Eleazar and Ithamar brought their sin offering and their whole burnt offering into the presence of the Lord. But today these terrible things have happened to *me*! Do you think the Lord would be any happier if I *ate* the sin offering today?" And when Moses heard this, he was satisfied (after learning that Aaron had acted sincerely and not out of rebellion or negligence, Moses was content).

Lord, thank You for overlooking unintentional sin
While judging premeditated sin;

Forgive me all my unintentional sins.
I promise You I will not plan to sin
Or disobey You.

Amen.

Leviticus 11

CLEAN AND UNCLEAN FOODS

The Lord spoke to Moses and Aaron, "Tell the people of Israel: there are living, land animals that you may eat. You may eat any animal that has a split hoof or completely divides the cleft of the hooves and chews the cud. Don't eat animals that only chew the cud or that only have the split hoof. The camel chews the cud, but it does not have a split hoof; it is unclean for you. The rock badger chews the cud, but it does not have a split hoof; it is unclean for you. The rabbit chews the cud, but it does not have a split hoof; it is unclean for you. The pig has a split hoof that is completely divided, but it does not chew the cud; it is unclean for you. You must not eat meat from these animals. Don't even touch their dead bodies. They are unclean for you."

Lord, You are concerned with my inner physical health,
As well as my outward spiritual testimony.

May I please You with the things I eat,
Make me physically strong and free from sickness.

May my inner private life influence the outer,
So I can be a testimony to others.

"You may eat creatures that live in water and have fins and scales. Do not eat creatures that live in the sea or in a river that do *not* have fins and scales. This includes the things that swarm in the water, and all other things that live in the water. You should avoid them; their meat is forbidden. Avoid their dead bodies.

You must avoid frogs, crabs, eels, oysters, and all types of shell-fish (including mollusks, crustaceans).

"Also, some birds should not be eaten. You must not eat any of these birds: eagles, vultures, black vultures, red kits, or any kind of black kite, raven, horned owls, screech owls, seagulls, or any kind of hawk, little owls, cormorants, great owls, white owls, desert owls, or ospreys, storks, heron, hoopoes, or bats.

"Don't eat insects that have wings and walk on all four feet; they are to be avoided. However, you may eat certain insects that have wings and walk on four feet. You may eat those that have legs with joints above their feet, so that they can hop on the ground. These are the insects which you may eat: all kinds of locusts, winged locusts, crickets, and grasshoppers. But all other insects that have wings and walk on four feet are to be avoided; they will make you unclean. Anyone who touches the dead body of one of these insects will become unclean until evening. If some-one picks up one of these dead insects, then he must wash his clothes. He will be unclean until evening.

"Some animals have a split hoof, but the hoof is not completely split. And, some animals do not chew the cud. They are unclean for you. Anyone who touches the dead body of one of these animals will become unclean. Of all the animals that walk on all four feet, some walk on their paws (canines, the dog family; and felines, the cat family, are included here). They are unclean for you. Anyone who touches the dead body of one of these animals will become unclean. He will be unclean until evening. Anyone who picks up their dead bodies must wash his clothes. He will be unclean until evening. These animals are unclean for you.

"These creatures that crawl on the ground are unclean for you: moles, rats, all kinds of big lizards, geckos, monitor lizards, (possibly crocodiles) wall lizards, sand reptiles, and chameleons. These crawling animals are unclean for you. Anyone who touches them after they have died will be unclean until evening. If any unclean animal dies and falls on something, then that thing will also become unclean. The animal might fall on something made of wood, cloth, leather, or burlap. It doesn't matter what the article was used for. It must be washed with water. It will be unclean until evening. Then it will become clean again."

Treatment of Vessels (Leviticus 11:32-37)

God was concerned that any type of infection or disease might contaminate a person from a dead body, or any other dead animal. When anything touched a dead body or blood, it had to be washed or on some occasions, destroyed. No food or drink could be used that had been in contact with a dead animal. Certain porous pots of clay could not be washed because germs could have seeped into the pores and then passed to another person. That pot was to be broken. Notice that a bronze vessel could be re-used when it was washed in warm, running water, probably pouring water over them to wash away any germs or bacteria.

There are several passages where God commands people to not touch dead bodies. Because of the warm conditions of the desert, decomposition set in much quicker than any other place in the world. So in Leviticus 11:32, God had certain restrictions on a person who touched a dead body to prevent further contamination and/or spreading of disease. Notice that in Leviticus 11:39-40, where personal contact was made with a dead body—even by a clean animal. There must be a time of temporary isolation, and the person or the animal was cleansed by thorough washing. Again, God's prevention of the spread of disease among His people.

"If a dead, unclean animal falls into a clay bowl, anything inside the bowl will become unclean. And you must break the bowl. When water from an unclean, clay bowl gets on any food, then that food will become unclean. Any liquid that may be ingested from any such bowl will be unclean. If any dead, unclean animal falls on something, then that thing becomes unclean. If an animal falls on an oven or a cooking pot, it must be broken into pieces. These things will be unclean for you.

"Now a spring or well that collects water remains clean. It can be used to cleanse.

"Anyone who touches the dead body of any unclean animal will become unclean. A dead, unclean animal might fall on some seed to be planted. That seed is still clean. But if you put water on some seeds, and a dead, unclean animal falls on those seeds, then they will be unclean for you."

"Also, if an edible animal dies on its own, anyone who touches its dead body will be unclean until evening. Anyone who eats meat from its dead body must wash his clothes; he will be unclean until the evening. Anyone who picks up its dead body must wash his clothes; he will be unclean until the evening."

"Everything that crawls on the ground is unclean; it must not be eaten (including all kinds of snakes, worms, maggots, moles, rats, mice, caterpillars, and centipedes). You must not eat any of the creatures that crawl on the ground (including all reptiles that have no feet, mollusks, snakes, snails, slugs, and worms). This includes creatures that crawl on their bellies or walk on all four feet or on many feet (including lizards and all insects). You must not eat them because they are unclean. Do not pollute yourselves by these crawling creatures or become defiled by them, so that you could be made unclean. I am the Lord your God.

"Consecrate yourselves to be holy for Me, for I am holy. I am the Lord who brought you out of the land of Egypt. I did it so I could be your God. Therefore, you *must* be holy, because I am holy. These are the instructions about all of the domesticated animals, the birds, all creatures that move in the water, and every creature that crawls on land. These instructions will help you know the difference between unclean creatures and clean creatures. They help people to know which creatures may be eaten and which ones must not be eaten."

Lord, thank You for Your concern for my health.
    I again dedicate my body to Your service.

Help me make right choices about the food I eat;
    And after that, protect me from unknown food dangers.

Lord, I want to be healthy to Your glory
    Help me discipline my physical life to that end.

        Amen.

Why Dietary Laws

God listed many animals that the people of Israel couldn't eat. There was one common denominator with them all; they couldn't eat predator or scavenger animals. This included certain types of animals in their livestock, fish and seafood, rodents, birds, and insects.

With the sin by Adam and Eve, death came and with it decay, germs, disease, and bacteria. Every dead body produces an enormous amount of potential disease and was life threatening in some cases. A scavenger animal spreads diseases. As an example, many insects feed off garbage, feces, and food that is spoiled, rotten, or contaminated. God didn't want His people ingesting animals that possibly had disease in their bodies.

There was one criterion that God could be given to describe clean animals; they are vegetarians. Those that eat the leaf of trees, grass, or bushes do not normally have bacteria in their system as do scavenger creatures. The issue was much more than eating an unclean creature or eating things that seem repulsive, poisonous, or obnoxious. God wanted His people to be holy in their bodies or total lifestyle; He didn't want His people associated with creatures that were dirty, or creatures that depended upon garbage or rotting things for its livelihood. The issue was holiness of mind and body as well as health and physical wholeness. The dietary laws protected God's people from sickness and disease.

When God did away with the dietary laws (see Acts 10:9-16; Col. 2:14-17), He allowed humans to eat those creatures previously called "unclean." Usually, cooking the creatures over 220° will kill any bacteria and make the food safe to eat today.

When God promised, "I will put none of the diseases on you which I have brought on [you]" (Exod. 15:26), their health involved obedience to all of God's dietary instructions about removing garbage and anything that would defile them, physically or spiritually.

Blood that was poured beside the Brazen Altar would be absorbed into the sand. Immediately the priest would cover the spot with clean sand. The insect-borne disease couldn't be spread to the people.

Amen.

Leviticus 12

CLEANSING AFTER CHILDBIRTH

The Lord said to Moses, "Tell this to the people of Israel: 'If a woman gets pregnant and gives birth to a son, then she will become ritually unclean for seven days (the uncleanness came from the bleeding of the birth process, not from the birth itself). This will be similar to her being unclean during her monthly period. On the eighth day, the little boy must be circumcised. Then it will be 33 days before she becomes cleansed of her bleeding. She must not touch anything that is holy. She must not enter the sanctuary area until her time of cleansing is complete. But if a woman gives birth to a daughter, then the mother will be 'unclean' for two weeks. This is like her being 'unclean' during her monthly period. Then, it will be 66 days before she becomes cleansed from her bleeding.

"After she has a son or daughter, the new mother must bring certain sacrifices to the entrance of the Meeting Tent. She must bring a year-old lamb for a whole burnt offering to the priest, and a dove or a young pigeon for a sin offering. The priest will offer them in the presence of the Lord to make her clean. Then she will be 'cleansed' from her bleeding. These are the instructions for a woman who gives birth to a boy or a girl.

"And, if she cannot afford a sheep, then she must bring two doves or two young pigeons (Mary and Joseph were so poor that they could not afford a lamb [see Luke 2:24]). One bird will be for a whole burnt offering and one for a sin offering. In this way, the priest will make atonement for her and she will be cleansed. (Luke's birth story of Jesus of Nazareth quotes the special ceremonies of Leviticus 12 prophetically. God was revealing the nature of the relationship of Christ to all making, that salvation would soon come to humanity through this baby boy [compare Luke 2:30; Rev. 12:5].)

Lord, You give salvation to all who call on You,
Thank You for saving my soul.

Lord, thank You for this glance into salvation coming,

For in this instance we see salvation prophetically.

Amen.

Leviticus 13

THE RULES ABOUT SKIN DISEASES

The Lord said to Moses and Aaron, "When someone has a swelling on his skin, or a rash, or a bright spot, bring the person to Aaron the priest, or one of his sons. (The priests acted as medical examiners to prevent the spread of disease among the people. They prescribed an environment of isolation and quarantine until more observable facts were known.) The priest must examine the sore on the person's skin. The hair in the sore may have become white, and the sore may seem deeper than the person's skin. If so, it is leprosy. (The term leprosy covered a wide variety of disease that destroyed human flesh. This chapter describes several types of possible skin disorders—incurable forms of leprosy, anesthetic leprosy, tuberculated leprosy [Elephantiasis], Hansen's disease, different kinds of skin eruptions [which resembled leprosy but eventually disappeared spontaneously], herpes, ringworm, eczema, psoriasis, etc.) When the priest has finished examining the person, the priest must pronounce him to be ritually 'unclean.'

"Sometimes there is a white spot on a person's skin, but the spot does not appear to be deeper than the skin. If that is true, and if the hair from the spot has not turned white, then the priest must separate (quarantine) that person from other people for seven days. On the seventh day, the priest must examine the person again to see if the sore has changed; it might not have spread over the skin. If it has not spread, then the priest must keep the person isolated for seven more days. On the seventh day, the priest must examine the person again. If the sore has not faded nor spread over the skin, then the priest will pronounce that person clean. That sore is only a rash. The person must wash his clothes. Then he will become ritually 'clean' again. But if the sore spread again after the priest has pronounced him to be 'clean,' then the person must come to the priest again. The priest must examine him to see if the rash has spread over the skin. Then the priest must pronounce that the person is 'unclean.' It is leprosy."

Lord, there is so much disease in this sinful world.
Protect me as I protect myself.

May my body be a clean temple
Where You live and You are glorified.

"If a person has leprosy, then he must be brought to the priest to examine him. If he sees a white swelling in the skin, and the hair has become white, or the skin looks raw inside the swelling, then it is leprosy. It is a chronic disease that he has had for a long time. The priest must pronounce that the person is 'unclean.' He will not need to separate that person from other people, because everyone knows that the person is unclean. Sometimes a skin disease spreads all over a person's body, covering that person's skin from his head to his feet. Then the priest must examine the person's entire body. The priest might see that the disease covers the whole body. It might have turned all of the person's skin white. Then the priest must pronounce that the person is 'clean.' But when the person has an open sore, he is not clean. When the priest sees the open sore, he must pronounce that the person is 'unclean.' It is leprosy. If the open sore becomes white again, then the person must go to the priest. The priest must examine him to see if the sores have become white. Then the priest must pronounce that the person with the sores is 'clean.' After that, he will be 'clean.'"

Leprosy

Leprosy was a dangerous disease that had no known cure. To keep it from spreading, people were kept in isolation. It was the task of the priest to be the medical examiner to determine when a person had leprosy. The person with the disease has been kept in isolation from the time of Moses to today. Leprosy was stamped out in Britain several centuries ago by keeping the leper in isolation. However, even then, the leper was treated humanely as a human being who can worship and praise God.

"Someone may have a boil on his skin, but it has been healed. In the place where the boil was, there might be a white swelling, or a bright, reddish-white spot. The priest must examine it to see if the spot might seem deeper than the skin. If the hair on it has become white, the priest must pronounce that the person is 'unclean.' The spot is leprosy and has broken out from inside the boil. If the priest examines the spot, and there are no white hairs in it, and the spot is no deeper than the skin, and it has faded, then the priest must isolate the person for seven days. If the spot spreads in the skin, then the priest must pronounce that the person is 'unclean.' It is a disease that will spread. However, the bright spot may not spread or change. If so, it is only a scar from an old boil. Then the priest must pronounce that the person is 'clean.' If a person gets a burn on his skin from fire, and the open sore becomes white or reddish-white, then the priest must examine it to see if the white spot has become deeper than the skin. If the hair at that spot has become white, it is leprosy; the disease has broken out in the burn. Then the priest must pronounce that the person is 'unclean.' It is leprosy. However, the priest must examine the spot to see if there is any white hair in the bright spot. The spot may be no deeper than the surrounding skin. If so, the priest must isolate the person from other people for seven days.

"On the seventh day, the priest must examine him again. If the spot has spread farther in the skin, then the priest must pronounce that the person is 'unclean.' It is leprosy. But if the bright spot has not spread but it is faded, then it is swelling from the burn. The priest must pronounce that the person is 'clean.' The spot is only a scar from the burn. If someone gets a sore on his scalp or on his beard, a priest must examine that sore to see if it is deeper than the skin and if the hair around it is thin and yellow. If these things are true, then the priest must pronounce that the person is 'unclean.' It is an itch of the head or chin—a type of leprosy. But when the priest examines it to see if the sore might not seem deeper than the skin, there may not be any black hair in it. If that is true, the priest must isolate the person who has itch from other people for seven days. On the seventh day, the priest must examine the sore again, because the itch may not have spread. If there are no yellow hairs growing in it, and the itch does not appear to be deeper than the skin, then the person must shave himself, but he must not shave the itch. The priest must separate that person who has the itch from other people for seven more days. On the seventh day, the priest must examine the itch again to see if the itch has spread. If it does not appear to be deeper than the skin, the priest must pronounce that the person is 'clean.' So, the person must wash his clothes and become clean. But the itch may have spread farther in the skin after the person has become clean. Then the priest must examine him again to see if the itch has spread, then the priest does not need to look for the yellowish hair. That person is 'unclean.' But the priest might think the itch has stopped spreading, and black hair may be growing in it, then the itch has been healed. That person is 'clean,' therefore the priest must pronounce that he is 'clean.' When a person has white spots all over his skin, the priest must examine them to see if the spots on his skin are pale-white, then the disease is only a harmless rash. It may have been a type of eczema which lasted from two months to two years. That person is 'clean.'

"A man might lose hair from his head and be bald; he is 'clean.' He might lose hair from his forehead and his temples and have a bald forehead; he is 'clean.' But if there is a reddish-white sore on his scalp, it is leprosy. A priest must examine that person to see if the swelling of the sore might be reddish-white on his scalp. If it looks like leprosy that has already spread in the skin, that person has leprosy. He is unclean. The priest must pronounce that the person is 'unclean' because of the sore on his head.

"If a person has leprosy that spreads, then he must warn other people. He must shout, 'Unclean! Unclean!' His clothes must be torn at the seams. He must let his hair stay uncombed. And he must cover his mouth. That person will be unclean during the whole time that he has the disease. And he must be isolated to a home outside the city limits, living in a leper camp.

"Some clothing (linen or wool) might have mildew in it. The mildew might be in a piece of leather or in something made of leather. The mildew might be in the clothing, in the leather, or in the woven or knitted material. If the mildew is greenish or reddish, then it is spreading and must be shown to the priest. The priest must examine the mildew and put that garment in an isolated place for seven days. On the seventh day, he must examine the mildew. It doesn't matter whether the cloth is woven or knitted. It doesn't matter whether the mildew is in leather or in anything that is made of leather. If the mildew has spread, the priest must burn the garment. If the mildew is spreading, it must be burned! But if the priest does the examination, and sees the mildew has not spread throughout the garment, or in the fabric of anything that is cloth or leather, then the priest must order the people to wash that suspected piece of cloth or leather. Then he must isolate the garment for seven more days. Then the priest must examine it again. If the mildew still looks the same, then that thing is 'unclean.' It doesn't matter whether the mildew has spread or not. It doesn't matter if the mildew is on the inside or on the outside. You must burn it. But when the priest looks at that garment, and sees that the mildew might have faded, the priest must cut the mildew out of the piece of leather or cloth. It doesn't matter whether the cloth is woven or knitted. But the mildew might come back to that piece of leather or cloth. If that happens, the mildew is spreading. And that piece of leather or cloth must be burned! If mildew is in the cloth, the woven or knitted material, or the leather article, it must be washed. When the mildew is gone, then it will be 'clean.'"

Lord, thank You for preventative measures
        To keep me from disease and sickness.

I praise You for Your concern for my health.
        May I do all I can to stay healthy.

Lord, I renew the dedication of my body to You.
        Live in me and be glorified in me.

                Amen.

Leviticus 14

Cleansing From Skin Disease

The Lord said to Moses, "These are the instructions for persons who had leprosy but who have become well. First, he must be brought to the priest. A priest must examine the person who had leprosy, going to that person outside the camp to see if the leprosy is healed. Then the priest must order the person to get two live, clean birds, a piece of cedar wood, a piece of red cloth, and a hyssop plant (using the piece of string, the hyssop was tied to the wood to make a primitive brush). One bird must be killed on a clay bowl under running water. Then the priest must take the other bird that is still alive and dip the live bird and the other things into the blood of the first bird. Then the priest must sprinkle the blood seven times on the person who is being cleansed using the brush. He must pronounce that the person is 'clean.' Then the priest must go to an open field and release the live bird.

"Next, the one to be cleansed must wash his clothes, shave off all of his hair, and bathe with water. After that, he will be 'clean' and may come into the camp. However, he must first stay on the outside of his tent for seven days. On the seventh day, he must shave off all of his hair—from his head, his beard, and his eyebrows—all of it. He must wash his clothes and bathe his body in water. Then he will be 'clean.' On the eighth day, the person who had the skin disease must offer two male lambs with no physical defects. He must also offer a 1-year-old female lamb with no physical defects. And that person must offer 6 quarts of flour mixed with olive oil as a food offering. He must also offer two-thirds of a pint of olive oil. The priest who is doing the cleansing must position the person who is to cleanse himself, along with these items, in My presence at the entrance of the Meeting Tent."

Lord, medical technicians have demonstrated with good reason
Laws of cleanliness and uncleanliness given by You;
These were not superstitious taboos.

God wanted the Israelites to be in the best health possible
With a strong intellect, emotion, and will in their physical
bodies.

Lord, that meant they had to exercise self-discipline in their diets,
So help me do the same to keep healthy.

Lord, You told them what they could eat and not eat to prevent
disease and infection,
I will obey healthy dietary rules to glorify You.

"The priest will take one male lamb and offer it and the quantity of olive oil as a guilt offering. Then he will wave them in My presence as a wave offering. Then he will kill the male lamb where they kill the sin offerings and the whole burnt offerings. The guilt offering is like the sin offering; the meat belongs to the priest. It is holy. The priest will take some of the blood of the guilt offering and put some on the bottom of the right ear of the person and on the big toe of that person's right foot. The priest will then take some of the olive oil and pour it into his own left hand. Then the priest will dip a finger of his right hand into the olive oil that is in his left hand, and sprinkle some of the olive oil seven times in My presence. The priest will put some olive oil from his hand on the bottom of the right ear of the person who is cleansing himself. He will put some on the thumb of that person's right hand and on the big toe of that person's right foot. The olive oil will go on these places on top of the blood of the guilt offering. He will put the rest of the olive oil that is in his left hand on the head of the person who is cleansing himself. In this way, the priest will pronounce that person as 'cured' in My presence."

Lord, I know the blood must be applied first to my life,
      To cleanse me from sin.

Then the oil of the Holy Spirit must anoint me
      For refreshing, spiritual illumination, power, and assurance.

"Next, the priest will offer the sin offering. He will pronounce that person as 'cured' of his 'unclean' state. After this, the priest will kill the animal for the whole burnt offering. Then offer the whole burnt offering and the food offering on the altar. In this way, the priest will pronounce that person as 'cured.' However, that person may be poor and unable to afford these offerings. If so, then he must take one male lamb for a guilt offering and present it to Me. Then the priest can pronounce that person as 'cured.' That person must offer two quarts of flour mixed with olive oil as a meal offering. He must also offer two-thirds of a pint of olive oil. He must offer two doves or two young pigeons that he can afford. One bird will be a sin offering. The other will be a whole burnt offering. On the eighth day, that person will bring them to Me and to the priest at the entrance of the Meeting Tent, so that the person can become 'clean.' Then the priest must take the lamb for the guilt offering and the quantity of olive oil and present them as a wave offering in My presence. Then he will kill the male lamb for the guilt offering, take some of its blood for the guilt offering and put it on the lobe of the right ear and on the thumb and on the big toe of that person's right foot. The priest will also pour some of the olive oil into his own left hand. Then with a finger of his right hand, he will sprinkle some of the olive oil seven times in My presence. Then the priest will take some of the olive oil that is in his hand and put it on the right ear lobe and on the thumb of that person's right hand, on the big toe of that person's right foot. The olive oil will go over these places on top of the blood from the guilt offering. The priest must put the rest of the olive oil that is in his hand upon the head of the person and pronounce that person as 'cured' in My presence.

"Then the priest will sacrifice one of the doves or the young pigeons; what the person can afford. He must offer one of the birds as a sin offering and offer the other bird as a whole burnt offering. He must offer them along with the meal offering. In this way, the priest will pronounce that person as 'cured' in My presence.

"These are the instructions (Torah) for the cleansing of someone who had leprosy and was cured but couldn't afford much."

Lord, the cleansed leper brought offerings to You
Because he was healed of his leprosy.

Next the person brought the normal sacrifice to You
Because he wanted to thank You and worship You.

Lord, in the same way I first pray for forgiveness of sin,
Then I thank You for cleansing of sin.

Next I come to You to worship You for Your guidance
And for Your providential leading in my life.

The Lord also said to Moses and Aaron, "I am giving the land of Canaan to your people to own it for themselves. When they enter that land, mildew may grow in someone's house. If that happens, then the owner must come and tell the priest. He should say, 'I have seen something that looks like mildew in my house!' Then the priest must order the residents to move everything out of that house before he goes in to examine the mildew. This should be done so that he may not have to declare that everything in the house is 'unclean.' After the people have emptied the house, the priest will go back in to inspect it. If he sees the spots of the outbreak on the walls of the house (greenish or reddish), then the priest must go out of that house through the door and close it up for seven days. On the seventh day, the priest must come back to check that house. If the mildew has spread into the walls of that house, then the priest must order the residents to tear out the contaminated stones and throw them away in a special 'unclean' place outside the town. Then the priest must have all the inside walls of the house scraped, and they must dump the plaster in a special, unclean place outside the town. Then they must put new stones into the walls, replacing the old stones. And they must get new plaster and replaster the house. If the mildew re-appears in his house, then the priest must come back and check the house again to see if the mildew has spread again in the house. If so, then it is a mildew that destroys things, so the house is 'unclean.' The owner must tear down the house, remove its stones, all of its plaster, and its wood, and take it to the 'unclean' place, outside the town. Anyone who goes into that house while it was closed will be 'unclean' until the evening. Anyone who eats in that house or lies down there must wash his clothes. After new stones and the plaster have been put into a house, the priest must check it thoroughly again to see if mildew has spread in the house. Then the priest will pronounce that the house is 'clean' because the mildew is gone.

"Then, to make the house 'clean,' the priest must get two birds, a piece of cedar wood, a piece of red cloth, and a hyssop plant (to make a primitive brush). He will kill one bird on a clay bowl over running water, then take the other live bird and dip the live bird and the other things into the blood of the first bird. Then, the priest will sprinkle the blood on the house seven times using hyssop, tied to cedar wood with a red cloth. He will make the house ceremonially 'clean' with these things. The priest will then go to an open field outside the town and release the live bird. This is how the priest pronounces the house 'safe.' It will then be ceremonially 'clean.' These are the instructions about any kind of leprosy; for the itch, for mildew, and for swellings, rashes, or bright spots on the skin."

Lord, you speak to us through symbols, such as the
> *Live bird that is released and given its freedom.*

Thank You for Your freedom given to me
> *After You have forgiven my sins and made me clean.*

But Lord, You also had the health of your people in mind,
> *In many cultures people had not recognized the*
> *Airborne diseases caused by mildew in their houses,*

Thank You for protecting my health,
> *When I didn't even understand what You were doing.*

> *Amen.*

Leviticus 15

RULES ABOUT UNCLEAN DISCHARGES

The Lord said to Moses and Aaron, "Tell the people of Israel: 'When an emission comes from any male's body, he is "unclean" (the Greek Septuagint renders this as gonorrhea), whether the emission flows freely or it has stopped flowing, it is his "uncleanness." The man who discharges body fluid may be lying on a bed, then that bed becomes "unclean." Everything he sits on becomes "unclean." Anyone who touches that man's bed must wash his clothes and bathe himself in water. And that person will be "unclean" until the evening. If anyone sits on something that that person has sat on, he must wash his clothes and bathe himself in water. He will be "unclean" until evening. Anyone who touches the skin of that person must wash his clothes and bathe himself in water. That person will be "unclean" until the evening. If the emitter spits on a "clean" person, then the person who was clean must wash his clothes and must bathe himself in water. And that person will be "unclean" until the evening. Anything upon which the "unclean" man has ridden will also become unclean. If anyone touches something that was underneath that person, then he will be "unclean" until the evening. If anyone carries anything that was underneath that person, he must also wash his clothes and bathe himself in water. He will be "unclean" until evening. If the emitter touches another person, then he must wash his clothes and bathe himself in water. He will be "unclean" until the evening. If the emitter touches a clay bowl, it must be broken. If he touches a wooden bowl, then that bowl must be washed in running water.'"

Lord, You are deeply concerned when Your people
Are guilty of sexual sins.

Therefore, You tell us to be sexually pure.
Lord, I will be sexually holy to please You.

"If an emitter becomes 'clean,' he must count off seven days for himself for his cleansing. He must wash his clothes and bathe his body in running water. (By divine revelation, Moses had special knowledge about germs thousands of years ahead of time.) Then he will be 'clean.' On the eighth day, he must sacrifice for himself two doves or two young pigeons. He must come into My presence at the entrance of the Meeting Tent. He will give the two birds to the priest. The priest will offer the birds. One bird is for a sin offering; the other bird is for a whole burnt offering. So, in My presence, the priest will pronounce that man 'clean' from his emission.

"If semen comes out from a man, then he must bathe his entire body in water. He will be 'unclean' until the evening. If semen gets on any garment or on leather, then it must be washed with water. It will be 'unclean' until evening.

"If a man has sex with his wife, and semen comes out, then both persons must bathe in water. They will be 'unclean' until the evening.

Lord, You said sex is not dirty,
But holy between a husband and wife (see Heb. 13:4).

I will keep Your commandments and
Bring glory to You in all things.

"When a woman has her monthly period, she is 'ceremonially impure' for seven days. Anyone who touches her will be 'unclean' until the evening. Anything that she lies on during this time will be 'unclean.' Everything she sits on during that time will be 'unclean.' Anyone who touches her bed must wash his clothes and bathe himself in water. That person will be 'unclean' until the evening. Anyone who touches anything that she sat on must wash his clothes and bathe himself in water. That person will be 'unclean' until evening. It doesn't matter whether the person touched the woman's bed or anything else that she sat on. That person will be 'unclean' until the evening.

"A man might have sex with a woman in her monthly period (unknown to him the period was beginning). If he does, he himself will be 'unclean' for seven days. And, every bed he lies on will also be 'unclean.'

"A woman might have a discharge of blood for many days, not during her regular monthly period, or she may continue to have a loss of blood after her regular period. If she does, she will be 'unclean,' as she is during her monthly period. She will be 'unclean' for as long as she continues to bleed. During all the time of her bleeding, any bed that she lies on will be like her bed during her regular monthly period. Everything she sits on will be 'unclean.' It will be like the time of her regular, monthly period. If anyone touches those things, he must wash his clothes and bathe himself in water. He will be 'unclean' until the evening.

"When the woman becomes cleansed from her bleeding, she must wait for seven days. After that, she will be 'clean.' Then on the eighth day, she must sacrifice for herself two doves or two young pigeons. She must bring them to the priest at the entrance of the Meeting Tent. Then the priest must offer one bird for a sin offering and the other bird for a whole burnt offering. The priest will pronounce her 'pure' in My presence. So, you (Moses and Aaron) must warn the people of Israel to stay separated from things that make them 'unclean.' If you don't warn the people, then they might pollute My Holy Tent, and then they would have to die!"

These were the instructions for the man who discharges a substance, or one who becomes 'unclean' from semen, or for women who become 'impure' from their monthly period, or for anyone who becomes 'unclean,' or a man who has sex with an 'unclean' woman.

Lord, the Old Testament laws are done away in Christ,
But I will continue to obey the principles
So I can be healthy and disciplined in body.

Lord, may I please You in all my physical habits.
May I worship You in a strong, healthy body.

Amen.

Leviticus 16

THE DAY OF ATONEMENT

Since two of Aaron's sons had died while offering incense to the Lord, this time the Lord spoke to Moses, saying, "Tell your brother Aaron there are times when he must *not* go behind the curtain into the Holy of Holies. The Ark of the Covenant is in the room behind that curtain. The Mercy Seat is on top of the Ark of the Covenant where I promised to appear and fellowship with Israel. There I will appear in a cloud over that lid. (The cloud veiled God's holy presence.) If Aaron goes in at a time of his choosing, he will die!

"Aaron may enter the Holy of Holies only on the Day of Atonement. Before he enters, he must offer a young bull for a sin offering and a male sheep for a whole burnt offering. He must put on special clothes, instead of the full regalia of the high priest. He must dress in the ordinary clothing of a common priest. He will put on the inner robe made of holy linen. The linen underwear will be next to his body. His sash will be a cloth belt. And he will wear the linen turban. These are holy clothes. He must bathe his whole body in water before he puts them on. Aaron must receive two male goats from the community of the people of Israel for a sin offering, and one male sheep for a whole burnt offering.

Lord, clothe me with the garments of righteousness
So I can come properly into Your presence.

"Then Aaron must offer the bull for the sin offering, which is for himself. Next, Aaron must perform the ritual to atone for his sins and for his family. Next, Aaron must get the two goats and stand them in My presence at the entrance to the Meeting Tent. Aaron must seek My will by choosing lots for the two goats. One lot will be for an offering to Me; the other will be for the scapegoat that is to be taken far away. Aaron will take the goat that was chosen for Me and offer this goat as a sin offering. The other goat—the scapegoat—must be brought into My presence. The priest will sanctify it, to atone for Israel's sins. Then this goat must be released into the desert.

"Next, Aaron must offer the bull as a sin-offering for himself. This will atone for his sins and for the sins of his family. Then he must kill the bull for the sin offering. Then he must take a pan full of burning coals from off the altar into My presence. Aaron must take two handfuls of sweet incense that has been ground into powder. He must bring it into the room behind the curtain. He must put the incense on the fire in My presence. Then the cloud of incense will obscure the Mercy Seat on top of the Ark of the Covenant. When Aaron comes in, he will *not* die!

"Also, Aaron must get some of the blood from the bull and sprinkle it with his finger on the front of the Mercy Seat, toward the east. Then with his finger he will sprinkle the blood seven times in front of the lid.

"Next, Aaron must kill the goat of the sin offering on behalf of the people. He must bring this goat's blood into the room behind the curtain. (This was the second time that the high priest went into the Holy of Holies.) He must sprinkle the goat's blood on the Mercy Seat and in front of it. Because the people of Israel have been polluted by all their sins and rebellions, Aaron is canceling their sins in the Holy of Holies. During that time, no one else is allowed inside the Meeting Tent. No one will go in until Aaron comes out. So, Aaron will perform the rituals to atone for the sins for himself, and his family, and the sins of the whole congregation of Israel.

"Afterward, he will go out to the Brazen Altar that is in My presence. He will make the altar ready for Me. Aaron will get some of the bull's blood and some of the goat's blood and put it on the corners of the altar on all sides. Then, using his finger, he will sprinkle some of the blood on the altar seven times. In this way, Aaron will make the altar 'clean' for Me. And it will be 'pure' from all the pollutions of the people of Israel."

Lord, when many deny the efficacy of the blood,
 I believe in the blood and apply it to my life.

There's an old hymn that says, "There's power in the blood";
 I reaffirm that power and claim it for my life.

The Scapegoat

"Aaron will make the Holy of Holies, the Meeting Tent, and the altar ready for Me. He will bring the goat to Me. He will put both of his hands on the head of the live goat and confess all the violations and rebellions of the people of Israel over the goat. In this way, Aaron will put the people's sins on the goat's head. Then he will send the goat away into the desert (symbolizing the removal of sin and its guilt). A man who has been appointed will take the goat away. So, the goat will carry all the people's sins on itself. The man will release it in a lonely place in the desert. Then Aaron will go into the Meeting Tent and take off the linen clothes. He must leave those clothes there. He must bathe his whole body with water. Then he will put on his regular clothes. He will come out and offer the whole burnt offering for himself and a whole burnt offering for the people, making atonement for himself and for the people. Then, he will burn the fat of the sin offering on the altar.

"The man who released the goat into the desert must also wash his clothes. Then he must bathe his whole body with water. After that, he is allowed to come back into the camp. The bull and the goat for the sin offerings must be taken outside the camp. (This typified Jesus Christ as our sin offering dying outside the camp [see Heb. 13:11-13].) The blood from these animals was brought into the Holy of Holies, to make the Holy Place ready for God. And the priests must completely burn up the animals' skins, bodies, and waste in the fire. Then the one who burns them must wash his clothes and bathe his whole body with water. After that, he is allowed to come back into the camp."

Lord, the scapegoat tells me you have separated my sins,
As far as the east is from the west.

You have eliminated my sins
And will remember them no more.

Observe the Day of Atonement

"On the tenth day of the seventh month each year, you must not eat (a fast including complete penitence and total self-humiliation— The Day of Atonement [Yom Kippur] is the only public fast which was commanded by the Law of Moses). You must not do any work. The travelers or foreigners who live among you must not work, either. In this day, the priests will make you 'clean.' All of your sins will be atoned for you in My presence. This is a very important day of rest for all of you, so you must fast. So, the anointed priest will perform the rituals for making things ready for Me. He is ordained to take his father's place. That priest must put on the holy linen clothes and make the Holy of Holies ready. He must also make the Meeting Tent and the altar ready for Me. He must make atonement for his sins and for all of the people of the congregation. You will do these things once each year." (Contrariwise, Christ's sacrifice was "once for all.") So, Aaron did the things the Lord had commanded Moses.

Lord, every Israelite had to fast on the Day of Atonement
To identify with cleansing for his/her sins.

When the High Priest atoned for the sins of all Israel,
It did not apply to a faithless Israelite.
A person demonstrated his/her faith by fasting.

Lord, I fast to identify with Jesus who fasted 40 days,
But I also identify with His atoning death.

Finally, I fast not to get something from You.
I fast to know Your heart and have You know mine.

Amen.

Leviticus 17

THE IMPORTANCE OF BLOOD

The Lord said to Moses, "Tell Aaron, his sons, and all the people that
this is the word that I have commanded: 'If an Israelite tries to
sacrifice an ox, a lamb, or a goat inside the camp or outside the
camp, but he does *not* bring that animal to the entrance of the
Meeting Tent, then that man is guilty of a very serious offense.
He *should* have offered the animal as a gift to Me in front of the
Holy Tent. His sins will be imputed to him—he has shed unauthorized blood! He *must* be separated from his people.' (This
could have been either excommunication or the death penalty.)

"Why? So that the people of Israel will bring their sacrifices to Me. In
the past, they killed animals in the open fields. Now they must
always bring those animals to Me, at the entrance of the Meeting
Tent. They must bring them to the priest and sacrifice them as
peace offerings to Me."

Lord, just as it was important for an Israelite
To sacrifice to You in the Tabernacle,

So I know it's imperative for me to meet
With other believers in a local church every Sunday.

Lord, I will meet each Lord's Day to worship You
And fellowship with a congregation of believers.

"Then, the priest will sprinkle the blood from those animals upon My
Brazen Altar. And the priest will burn the fat from those animals
as incense. This smell will be pleasing to Me. They must not
offer sacrifices to the goat idols of heathen nations (a goat was a

symbol of satan or other gods). When they chased after those other gods, they have acted like whores! These rules will continue for the people from now on!"

Lord, the blood was applied to my sin
When I accepted Christ as Savior.

Now You have promised to me life.
"The blood of Jesus Christ His Son
Cleanses us from all sin" (1 John 1:7).

I praise You for the cleansing blood of Christ,
And I promise to walk in the light.

"Anyone (any man of the household of Israel) might offer a whole burnt offering or a sacrifice to Me. Or the worshiper might be a foreigner who lives with you. However, that person must take his sacrifice to the entrance at the Meeting Tent. There he may offer it to Me. If he does not do this, then he must be separated from his people."

"I will be against anyone who eats blood! It doesn't matter whether he is a citizen of Israel or a foreigner who lives among you. If he eats any blood, then I will separate that person from his people. This is because the life of the body is in the blood." (This verse emphasizes the sanctity of life. *Blood* represents a living sacrifice that was killed to substitute an animal's life for the worshiper's.)

"And I have given you special rules for pouring that blood on the altar to make atonement for your sins. Why? Because it is the *blood* that makes atonement for sins. That is why I tell the people of Israel: 'None of you are permitted to eat blood! And no foreigner who lives among you may eat blood, either.' Someone might hunt a wild animal or a bird that can be eaten. Or it might be a foreigner who lives among you. But he must pour out its blood on the ground and cover it with dirt. Because if any of its blood is still in the meat, then the animal's life is still in it. So, I give this command to the people of Israel: 'Do *not* eat any meat that still has blood in it. Anyone who eats blood must be separated from his people. It is forbidden for any person to eat an animal that has died on its own or to eat an animal that was killed by another animal. (Such dead animals would *not* have had their blood drained from them properly.) That person might be a native son of Israel or a foreigner who lives among you. If he eats such an animal, he will be "unclean" until the evening. He must wash his clothes and bathe himself with water. Then he will be 'clean.' However, if he does not wash his clothes and bathe his body, then he will be guilty of sin."

Amen.

The Transfer and Storage of Infectious Diseases

The Lord is omniscient. He knew all about germs and infections long before scientific discovery tells us disease is transferred by blood and resides in fat. So God told us not to drink the blood or eat the fat. God didn't want any type of potential health threat to be ingested by His people.

Leviticus 18

LAWS ABOUT SEXUAL PRACTICES

The Lord said to Moses, "Tell the sons of Israel: 'I am the Lord, your
God. In the past you lived in Egypt and were influenced by their
culture, now you must *not* do the deeds of that country. And you
must not bring their practices into the land of Canaan where I
am bringing you. You must obey My laws and My rules. Follow
them! I am the Lord, your God.'"

Lord, I yield my body to Your use,
 May my life bring glory to You.

Lord, I will be sexually pure,
 I will be a good testimony for You.

"A person who obeys My laws and rules will *live* by them, for I am the
Lord. You must never have sex with your close relatives. You
must not shame your father or mother by having sex with your
mother. She is your mother. Do *not* have sex with her! You must
not have sex with your father's wife. That would shame your
father. You must not have sex with your sister (this could be a
full-blooded sister, a half-sister, or a step-sister). She is the
daughter of your father or your mother. It doesn't matter if she
was born in your house or born somewhere else. You must not
have sex with your granddaughter. She is your son's daughter or
your daughter's daughter. That would bring shame on you. If
your father and his wife have a daughter, then she is your sister.
You must not have sex with her. You must not have sex with
your father's sister, (a paternal aunt); she is your father's close
relative. You must not have sex with your mother's sister (a

maternal aunt); she is your mother's close relative. You must not have sex with the wife of your father's brother. This would shame him. His wife is your aunt. You must not have sex with your daughter-in-law. She is your son's wife. You must not have sex with your brother's wife. That would shame your brother. You must not have sex with both a woman and her daughter. And do not have sex with this woman's granddaughter. It may be the daughter of her son or the daughter of her daughter. They are close relatives. It would be evil to do this. While your wife is still living, you must not take her sister as another wife (polygamy—plural marriage—was wrong); do not have sex with her.

"You must not go near a woman to have sex with her during her monthly period. She is 'unclean' during this time.

"You must not have sex with your neighbor's wife and make yourself 'unclean' with her.

"You must not offer any of your children to be sacrificed to Molech (the abominable god of the Ammonites; they sacrificed children to the fire-god). This would show that you don't respect your God. I am the Lord, your God.

"You must not have sex with a man as you would have sex with a woman. That is a terrible sin" (This abomination led to the total destruction of Sodom and Gomorrah [see Gen. 18:20-21; 19:4-29; Matt. 10:15; 11:23-24; Luke 17:29; Rom. 9:29; 2 Peter 2:6; Jude 1:7; Rev. 11:8]. All homosexuality [sodomy, lesbian-ism, and other same-sex, sexual perversions] is condemned in Scripture with the penalty of death [Rom. 1:18-32]).

Lord, this is a growing modern-day sin.
I will be separate from this sin.

I pray for homosexuals and lesbians
That they may use Your standard for purity,
And obey You in sexual purity.

I pray for the salvation of all homosexuals
And lesbians and their growth in Christ.

"You must not have sex with an animal and make yourself unclean with it. Also, a woman must not have sex with an animal. It is not natural (literally, it is a perversion). Don't make yourselves unclean with any of these evil things." (Incest [1 Cor. 5:1], adultery [Rom. 13:9], and homosexuality [Rom. 1:27,32; 1 Cor. 6:9] are just as sinful today as they were when Moses wrote the words of this chapter.)

Lord, I pray for the growing sin of my nation,
Send a growing spirit of conviction
Against all sexual sins.

Lord, save my nation from Your judgment,
God bless my nation.

"I am driving nations out of their land because they did these sins. The land has become 'unclean.' So, I punished them for their sins. And the land vomited out those people who live there. You must obey My laws and My rules. You must not do any of these terrible sins. These instructions are for the native-born of Israel and for the people who live among you. Before you came, the men of the land did all of those terrible sins. The nations became 'unclean.' If you do the same things, then you will also become 'unclean.' And the land will vomit you out as it vomited out the nations before you. Anyone who does all these terrible sins must be separated from his people. The people who lived in the land ahead of you have done those terrible sins, but you must not do them. You must obey My laws. Do not make yourself 'unclean' by these terrible sins. I am the Lord, your God."

Lord, I commit myself to be sexually pure.
I will not violate my sexual purity,
Nor the sexual purity of another person.

Keep me in the hour of temptation;
I want to be a clean vessel for Your use.

Amen.

Leviticus 19

OBEY GOD'S LAWS

The Lord said to Moses, "Tell all the people of Israel: 'I am the Lord, your God. You must be holy, because I am holy. (Living a holy life has always been a part of God's law for His people.) Each person among you must respect his mother and his father. And you must keep My Sabbaths. I am the Lord, your God. Do not worship idols. Do not make statue-gods for yourselves. I am the Lord, your God. When you sacrifice peace offerings to Me, it must be voluntary. You may eat it on the same day that you offered it, or you may also eat it on the next day. However, if any of it is left over on the third day (the food would be spoiled by this time), you must burn it all up; it is unclean. If any of it is eaten on the third day, it will not be accepted. Anyone who eats it on the third day will be guilty of sin. That is because he desecrated the holy thing that belonged to Me. That person must be separated from his people.

"'As you harvest your crops on your land, don't completely finish harvesting to the corner of your field. Don't gather the gleanings (the leftover kernels of grain that were missed by the first harvesters) after you harvest. Don't pick up all the grapes in your vineyards. And don't pick up the grapes that fall on the ground. You must leave those things for the poor people. You must also leave them for people who are staying in your country. I am the Lord, your God.

"'You must not steal. You must not tell lies. You must not cheat each other. You must not make a false promise by My Name. If you do, you will show that you do *not* respect your God. I am the Lord.

"'You must not extort your neighbor or rob him. You must not keep a hired worker's salary all night until morning. Pay him when he finishes working. You must not curse a deaf man. And you must not put something in front of a blind person to cause him to fall. Instead, you must revere your God; I am the Lord. Be fair (literally, "Do not do evil") in your judging. You must not give special treatment to poor people or to important people. You must be fair when you judge your neighbor.

"'You must not spread false stories against other people. You must not do anything that would put your neighbor's life in danger; I am the Lord. You must not hate your brother in your heart. If your neighbor does something wrong, then rebuke him. If you do not tell him, you yourself will be partly to blame. Forget about the bad things that people do to you. You must not try to get even (revenge). Love your neighbor as you love yourself; I am the Lord.'"

Lord, You gave us certain instructions on how to treat others.
I will always treat others
As I want them to treat me.

I will follow the rule of "love."
I will love others as I love myself.

Give me a heart for other people.
Help me treat them as You would.
Then I can be Your follower.

Amen.

"'Obey My laws. You must not breed two different kinds of cattle together. You must not sow your field with two different kinds of seed.

322

You must not wear clothing made from two different kinds of material mixed together. If a man has sex with a slave girl engaged to another man and this slave girl has not been purchased or given her freedom, there must be an investigation. But the two of them are not to be put to death. That is because the woman was not free. The man must bring a male sheep as his penalty offering to the Lord at the entrance of the Meeting Tent. The priest will offer the ram for the man as a penalty offering in My presence. It will be for the man's sin which he committed. The priest will do this to make atonement for the sins of the man. Then the man will be forgiven for the sin that he did.

"'In the future, you will plant various kinds of trees for food when you enter that land. After planting a tree, wait three years before eating its fruit. (Farmers pluck the blossoms of the trees in the early years to cause the tree to bear more fruit in the later years.) Eating the fruit will be forbidden to you at the beginning. In the fourth year, all the fruit from the tree will belong to Me. It will be holy offerings of praise to Me. Then, in the fifth year, you may eat the fruit from the tree. Then the tree will produce more fruit for you. I am the Lord, your God.

"'You must not eat any meat with blood still in it.

"'You must not try to predict the future by using so-called signs or black magic (imagining omens, astrology, spells, charms, divinations). You must not cut the hair on the sides of your heads. And you must not cut the edges of your beard. (The Egyptians were clean-shaven. The Hebrews were not to follow any idolatrous practices or customs which were current at that time.)

"You must not gash your body to show sadness for someone who has died. Do not put tattoo marks on yourselves. Any self-imposed disfiguration of the body is an outrage to God! It is an insult to the One who originally designed the human body. I am the Lord.

"'You must not cause your daughter to become a whore. (Pagan priests paid a high price to the parents who would sell their girls to become temple prostitutes.) Otherwise, the land would become full of prostitution. If you do this, then the country will be filled with all kinds of evil.

"'Obey the laws about My Sabbaths. You must respect My sanctuary; I am the Lord. Do not go to mediums or fortune-tellers for advice. If you do, you will become "defiled." I am the Lord, your God.

"'Give respect to old men. Stand up when they come into the room. By this you revere your God; I am the Lord.

"'Do not oppress foreigners who live in your country. Treat them just as you would treat your own citizens. Love foreigners the same way you would love yourselves, because you were once foreigners in the land of Egypt. I am the Lord, your God.

"'Be fair when you judge people. And be fair when you measure and weigh things. Your baskets for weighing should be the correct size. And your jars should contain the accurate amount to measure liquid. Your weights and scales should weigh accurately. I am the Lord, your God. I brought you out of the land of Egypt. Remember and observe all of My laws and My rules. I am the Lord.'"

Lord, You have rules and expectations for my life.
May I always follow Your principles

May I be a testimony to others
And show them that Christ lives in me.

Lord, help me be a dedicated disciple of Jesus
And keep me obedient to You.

Amen.

Leviticus 20

Punishment for Disobeying God's Laws

The Lord said to Moses, "You must also tell the people of Israel these things: 'A Jewish man or a foreigner staying in Israel might offer one of his children to Molech. That person *must* be killed! The common people must stone him.' (This public act of repudiation of sin by the entire Jewish congregation committed them to God's high standard of discipline.)

"I will be against him and cut him off from his people because he offered his children to Molech. He polluted My Holy Name, and he defiled My sanctuary. The common people may ignore that person and *not* execute the one who offered his children to Molech. But I will be against a sympathizer and his family. I will cut him off from his people. I will do this to *anyone* who is unfaithful to Me and who worships Molech.

"I will be against anyone who goes to mediums (those who claimed to communicate with dead people) or fortune-tellers for advice. He is being unfaithful to Me. (Only the true God was to be consulted. And God spoke to His people through His prophets, and they worshiped God through His priests.) So, I will cut him off from his people. Be My holy people. Be holy because I am holy. I am the Lord, your God. You must keep My rules and practice them. I am the Lord, and I am making you holy."

Lord, I will be faithful in these things.
My nation has a growing tolerance
To seek these demon-influenced practices.

Forgive my nation its sin, and don't judge us.
I pray for national revival.
May my nation fear and worship You.

"Anyone who curses his father or mother *must* be put to death. He has cursed his father or his mother, so he must be punished.

"A man might have sex with his neighbor's wife. If he does, then both the man and the woman are guilty of adultery. So, they *must* both be put to death! A man might have sex with his father's wife. If he does, both the man and his father's wife *must* be put to death! They have brought their blood upon themselves. That man has shamed his father. A man might have sex with his daughter-in-law. If he does, both of them must be put to death! What they have done is not natural. It must be punished. They have brought it upon themselves. A man might have sex with another man, as a man does with a woman. If he does, these two men have done a terrible sin. They *must* be put to death! They have brought it upon themselves. A man might have sex with both a woman and her mother. This is evil. The people must burn that man and the two women in a fire. (After being stoned to death, the bodies of the sinners would be burned. Compare Joshua 7:25.) There must be *no* such evil thing among you. A man might have sex with an animal. (The sin of bestiality.) If he does, he *must* be put to death! And you must also kill the animal! A woman might have sex with an animal. If she does, you must kill the woman and the animal! They *must* be put to death. They have brought it upon themselves.

"It is shameful for a brother to marry his sister and have sex with her. In front of everyone, they must both be cut off from their people. The man has shamed his sister. And he is guilty of sin. A man might have sex with a woman during her monthly period. If he does, both the woman and the man must be separated

328

from their people. They have sinned because they exposed the source of her blood.

"Do not have sex with your mother's sister or your father's sister. That would shame a close relative. Both would be guilty of this sin. A man must not have sex with his uncle's wife. That would shame his uncle. That man and his uncle's wife will die without children. (Any children who were born to such illegal unions would *not* be recorded in the official genealogical rolls to the natural father. Instead, they would summarily assign the child to a dead brother or a dead uncle! Thus, such offspring would not be regarded as lawfully belonging to the sinful parents, nor would they be entitled to any hereditary privileges.) They are guilty of sin. It is wrong for a man to marry his brother's wife. He has shamed his brother. You must keep all of My laws and My rules and practice them. I am leading you to your own land to live there. If you obey My laws and My rules, then that land will not vomit you out."

Lord, Your laws are exact
  And when I break them, Your punishment is sure.

If not punished in this life,
  Then You will deal with my sin in final judgment.

Lord, I thank You for the blood of Jesus Christ
  Who cleanses me from all sin,
  And delivers me from future judgment.

"I am expelling the people who live there from that country, because they did all of these same sins. I am disgusted with them. Do not live the same way those people lived! I have told you that you will get their land. I will give it to you as your very own. It is a land flowing with milk and honey. I am the Lord, your God. I have set you apart from other people. So, you must make a distinction between 'clean' animals and birds, and 'unclean' animals and birds. Do not make yourselves 'unclean' by eating any of these unclean animals or birds or things that crawl on the ground. I have set you apart from other people to belong to Me, so you must be holy to Me. I am the Lord, and I am holy.

"If there is among you a man or a woman who is a medium (one who claims to be able to communicate with dead people) or a fortune-teller, they *must* be put to death. You must execute them by stoning them. They have brought it upon themselves!"

Lord, I will obey Your laws
And I will honor You in all I do.
Use me for Your glory.

Amen.

Leviticus 21

Rules for the Priests

The Lord told Moses to tell these things to the sons of Aaron, the
priests: "A priest must not make himself ceremonially 'unclean'
by touching a corpse. But if the dead person was one of his
close relatives, he may touch his mother or father, son or daughter, brother or an unmarried sister who would be close to him
because she had no husband. (The priest's wife was *not* men-
tioned because she was already 'one flesh' with her husband). A
priest must not make himself 'unclean,' thus, polluting himself.
He is a leader among his people. Priests must not shave their
heads, nor shave off the edges of their beards. They must not cut
their bodies. (This was a pagan custom.) Priests must be holy
for their God. They must *not* profane God's name, because they
present the offerings made by fire to the Lord. This is the food
(not to be understood literally, only metaphorically) of their
God. So, priests *must* be holy.

"A priest serves God in a special way, so he must not marry a prostitute
or a woman who was divorced from her husband, because he
offers up the food of your God. The priest is holy. I am the
Lord. I make you people holy, and I am holy.

"If a priest's daughter makes herself 'unclean' by becoming a whore,
then she shames her father. She must be burned with fire!

"The high priest was chosen from among his priestly brothers, and special olive oil is poured on his head. He is ordained to wear the
priestly clothes. He must not let his hair go uncombed. He must
not rip his clothes (an outward sign of great sorrow).

"He must not go wherever there is a corpse, even if it is his own father or mother. (He must not interrupt his immediate sacred duties to God on behalf of the whole nation of Israel.) If he does, then he would make the sanctuary 'unclean.' The special crown of olive oil used by Me to anoint priests was poured on his head. I am the Lord.

"The high priest must marry a woman who is a virgin, and not marry a widow, a divorced woman, a woman who has been defiled, or a prostitute. He must marry only a virgin from his own people." (It was also required that she *must* come from the tribe of Levi.)

"He must *not* profane his children by marrying outside the Levitical family, as all of his descendants would have been disqualified to ever serve as priests. I have set the high priest apart for his special job."

The Lord said to Moses, "Tell Aaron: 'Some of your descendants might have something physically wrong with them. If they do, they must never offer the special food of their God. Those who have something physically wrong may be blind, crippled, or have damaged faces, deformed, crippled feet or hands, hunchbacks, dwarfs, men who have something physically wrong with their eyes, men who have an itching disease or scabs, or men who have damaged testicles. If a priest has any of these, he *cannot* offer the food of his God! However, he is allowed to eat the food of his God, the holy food, but he may *not* go inside the curtain into the Holy of Holies, nor desecrate My sanctuary, because I am the Lord. I make these things holy.'" So, Moses told these things to Aaron and Aaron's sons, and to all the people of Israel.

> *Lord, the rules for priests were more strict*
> *Than the rules for average Israelites.*

You want Your servants to be set aside
To wholly serve and glorify You.

Today, Christ is our High Priest who sacrificed for me,
And today, He is interceding for me.

In a special way, every believer is a priest;
We all minister for You in worship and prayer.

I will be separate from sin because I'm Your priest.
I will serve You in worship and intercession.

Amen.

Leviticus 22

BE HOLY

The Lord told Moses, "Tell Aaron and his sons: 'The people of Israel will dedicate offerings to Me. These things are holy. The people must keep their distance. They must not profane My holy name. I am the Lord.' Tell them: 'One of your future descendants might be "unclean," and approach the dedicated, holy things. Whoever does that must be separated from ever appearing in My presence (excluded from the sanctuary). I am the Lord. One of Aaron's descendents might be a leper, or he might discharge a fluid from his body. He cannot eat the holy offerings until he becomes "clean."

"'He might become "unclean" from touching a corpse or from his own semen. Or he might become "unclean" if he touches anything unclean, crawling, or a dead animal, or an unclean person. It doesn't matter what made him "unclean," anyone who becomes "unclean," that person must not eat of the holy offerings. However, he must bathe his whole body with water. He will become "clean" only after the sun goes down. Then he may eat some of the holy things. The offerings are his food.

"'A priest might find an animal that died on its own or one that was killed. He must not eat that dead animal. If he eats it, he will become "unclean." I am the Lord. The priests must keep all the rules that I have given. In that way, they will not become guilty. If they defile the altar, they will die! I am the Lord, I have made it holy.

"'Only people in a priest's family may eat the holy offerings that the priest brings home from the Tent of Meeting. A visitor staying with the priest or a hired worker must *not* eat it. If the priest buys a slave with his own money, that slave is permitted to eat some of the holy offerings. Slaves who were born into the priest's household may also eat the priest's food.

"'A priest's daughter might marry a person who is not from the Levitical line. If she does, she must not eat any of the holy offerings. The husband of a priest's daughter might die, and she becomes a widow. Or the priest's daughter might become divorced. So she might go back to her father's house where she lived as a child. If that happens, she may eat some of her father's food. But only people from a priest's family may eat this food. If someone eats some of the holy offering by mistake, that person must repay the priest for that holy food. He must also pay the priest another 20 percent of the price of that food.

"'The people of Israel will present offerings to Me. These gifts become holy. So the priest must not treat these holy things as though they were *not* holy (by giving these holy things to laymen as food). If they allow this, they are treating those offerings as though they were *not* holy. The person who eats it will become guilty and must pay a penalty offering. I am the Lord; I make these offerings holy.'"

The Lord said to Moses, "Tell Aaron and his sons and all the people that if a citizen of Israel or a foreigner who lives in Israel wants to bring a whole burnt offering, or make a voluntary vow, or present a special gift; he must bring a male animal with *no* physical defects. The gift might be a bull, a ram, or a goat. He must *not* bring an animal that has something physically wrong with it. If so, you must *not* accept it. Someone might bring a peace-offering sacrifice to Me that might be a donation for a special vow the person has made. Or it may be a special gift the person wanted to give to Me. It might be a bull or a ram. However, it *must* be healthy, with *no* physical defects. Then it will be acceptable. You must not offer to Me any animal that is blind. It must not have broken bones or be crippled. It must not have running sores or any sort of skin disease. You must not offer to Me any questionable animals. They cannot be used as an offering by fire to Me. However, I will accept a bull or a lamb that may be smaller than normal, or not perfectly formed. If someone wants to donate that animal as a special gift or a free-will offering to Me, then it will be accepted. But it will *not* be accepted for a vow. Some animals have bruised, crushed, torn, or severed testicles (literally, castrated), you must *not* offer such an animal to Me. You must not receive such animals as a sacrifice to Me, your God."

The Lord said to Moses, "When a calf, a lamb, or a goat is born, it must stay with its mother for seven days. But after the eighth day, this animal would be acceptable as a sacrifice. It may be offered by fire to Me. However, you must not kill that animal and its mother on the same day. You might want to offer some special offering of thanksgiving to Me. However, you must do it in a way that I accept. You must eat the entire animal on that same day. You must not leave any of the meat until the next morning (the rules for the priests were more strict than for ordinary Israelites). I am the Lord. Keep my commands and obey them. I am the Lord. Do *not* defile My holy name. You *must* regard Me as holy! I am the Lord, who has made you holy. I brought you out of the land of Egypt to become your God. I am the Lord your God."

Lord, the priest had strict rules for the animals
They brought as a sacrifice to You.

Christ was a perfect fulfillment of these types,
Christ was the lamb of God who took away
The sins of the world.

Thank You for cleansing my sin
  By the blood of Jesus Christ.

In appreciation I will live a holy life to You
  And I will serve You with my whole heart.

  Amen.

Leviticus 23

THE FESTIVALS

The Lord said to Moses, "Announce My appointed feasts as holy gatherings. These are My special feasts. There are six days for you to work, but the seventh day will be a Sabbath rest. It is a day for a holy summoning. You must not do any work. It is a Sabbath (The Sabbath was the sign of the covenant God made with Israel for the dispensation of the Law at Mount Sinai [Exod. 31:16-17]) to Me in all your homes.

"These are My appointed feasts. Announce these holy summonings at the times set for them."

The Yearly Feasts or Festivals

The Book of Leviticus gives the religious calendar of Israel as expressed in the seven feasts of the year (Lev. 23:1-44). Each of these feasts has a spiritual fulfillment in the historic roots of Christianity or its future anticipations. The annual calendar of Israel was for many centuries a prophetic witness to the ministry of Christ in our new dispensation of grace. The fourth feast represents the coming rapture of Christ. The last two feasts in the calendar are references to Israel and are yet to be fulfilled.

The Feasts of Israel

Feast	Fulfillment in the New Testament
Passover	Death of Christ
Firstfruits	Resurrection
Pentecost	Holy Spirit
Trumpets	Rapture
Atonement	National conversion of Israel
Tabernacles	Messianic kingdom or Millennium

The Passover and the Festival of Unleavened Bread

The Lord's Passover is celebrated on the fourteenth day of the first
month (Nisan). It begins at twilight. The Feast of Unleavened
Bread begins on the fifteenth day of the same month. You must
eat bread made without yeast (Christians are commanded symbolically to "purge out the old leaven") for seven days. On the
first day of this feast, you will have a holy summoning. "You
must *not* do work of any kind. For seven days, you must bring
an offering made by fire to Me. There will be a holy summoning
on the seventh day, and on that day you must not do work of
any kind."

Lord, thank you for Passover, for on this day
Jesus died for my sins,
And the sins of the whole world.

Lord, I pray for the solution of lost family
So they will come to know you.

The Festival of First Fruits

The Lord said to Moses, "When you enter the land that I will give you, gather its harvest. At that time, bring to the priest the very first sheaf of grain from your harvest. The priest will wave the sheaf in My presence. Then it will be accepted on your behalf. The priest will present the bundle of grain on the day after the Sabbath. On the day when you present the bundle of grain, sacrifice a male lamb. It must be 1 year old with no physical defects. It will be a whole burnt offering to Me. You must also offer a food offering of 4 quarts of flour mixed with olive oil to Me. It is an offering made by fire to Me, and the smell of it will be appealing to Me. You must also offer about 1 quart of wine as a drink offering. The first thing you do is bring your offering to Me. Until you do this, do *not* eat the new grain, or roasted grain, or the bread made from new grain. This law will always continue from now on, wherever you live."

Lord, You raised up Jesus on the Sunday after Pentecost.
Jesus' resurrection was a foreshadow of my resurrection;
I will appear before You, just as Jesus enters Heaven.

Jesus' resurrection was the first-fruits
Of all those who would be resurrected after Him.

Lord, I praise You for Jesus' resurrection,
For I will be raised, because of Him.

Pentecost—The Harvest Festival

"Count seven full weeks after the Sabbath that you bring the bundle of grain to present as a wave offering to Me at the Feast of First Fruits. On the 50th day, you will bring a new food offering to Me. That is the first day (Sunday) after the seventh week.

"On that day, bring two baked loaves of bread from your homes. That bread will be presented (or waved) as an offering. Use yeast and 4 quarts of flour to make those loaves of bread. They will be your gift to Me from the first wheat of your harvest.

"Besides the bread, offer one bull, two male sheep, and seven male lambs. The lambs must be 1 year old, with no physical defects. Offer them with the food offerings and drink offerings. They will be a whole burnt offering to Me, an offering made by fire. The smell will be pleasing to Me.

"You must also offer one male goat for a sin offering, and you must offer two male lambs as a peace offering. The priest will present the two lambs as an offering. He will present them with the bread from the first wheat of the harvest. They are holy to Me, and they belong to the priest. On that same day, call a holy meeting. You must not do work of any kind on that day. This law will continue from now on, wherever you live.

"You will harvest your crops on your land. But do not harvest all the way to the corners of your field. If some grain falls onto the ground, do not gather it up. Leave it for the poor people and the foreigners in your country. I am the Lord, your God."

Lord, Pentecost was fulfilled when the Holy Spirit
Came on Pentecost to fill every believer.

I am indwelt with Your Holy Spirit
To live a holy life and serve you acceptably.

The Festival of the Trumpets

Again the Lord said to Moses, "Tell the people of Israel: 'On the first day of the seventh month, you must have a special day of rest that will be a holy meeting (Rosh Hashanah). Blow the trumpet for a special time of remembering (trumpet blasts across the land signaled the end of their agricultural year and the beginning of a new season). Do not do any work of any kind, and bring an offering made by fire to Me.'"

Lord, the feast of trumpets predates the return of Christ.
   He will return with the sound of a trumpet.

Lord, my saved family and friends will be raised,
   And if I die before the rapture,
   I too will be raised with them.

Lord, thank you for the hope of the rapture.
   I look for Jesus coming in the clouds.

The Day of Atonement

The Lord said to Moses, "The Day of Atonement will be on the tenth day of the seventh month. This will be a holy meeting where you humble your souls and fast. You must bring an offering made by fire to Me on that day. Do not do any work on that day; because it is the Day of Atonement to cover your sins in My presence; I am your God. If anyone refuses to quit eating food on this day, then he must be separated from his people. If anyone does work on that day, then I will destroy him from among his people. You must not do any work! This law will continue from now on, wherever you live. It will be a Sabbath of rest for you. And you must fast, starting your fast at sundown on the evening of the ninth day of the month and continue from that evening until the next evening."

Lord, You have a future prayer for Israel.
   I look forward to that special day when
   "All Israel will be saved."

The Festival of Tents

The Lord said to Moses, "Tell the people of Israel: 'On the fifteenth day of the seventh month is the Feast of Tabernacle. (The people of Israel lived in temporary shelters—tents—when God brought them out of Egypt. This feast was celebrated from the fifteenth through the twenty-second days of the seventh month. It was the end of the Jewish agricultural year.) This feast to Me will continue for seven days. There will be a holy meeting on the first day. Do not do work of any kind. For seven days, you will bring an offering made by fire to Me each day. On the eighth day, you will have another holy meeting, and will bring an offering made by fire to Me. This will be a special gathering. Do *not* do work of any kind!

"'These are My special feasts. You must announce the holy meetings on these feast days to bring offerings made by fire to Me—whole burnt offerings, food offerings, sacrifices, and drink offerings. You must bring these gifts at the proper time (on its own day).

"'In addition to those offerings, you must bring special offerings as payment for special vows. They are also in addition to the special offerings that you want to give to Me. So, on the fifteenth day of the seventh month, be sure to celebrate My festival for seven days. By then, you will have gathered in the crops of the land. You must rest on the first day and on the eighth day. On the first day, you will take good fruit from the fruit trees, branches from palm trees, and willow branches and other leafy branches to celebrate in My presence for seven days. Every year, you must celebrate in My presence for seven days. Every year, you must celebrate this festival to Me for seven days on a continual basis. All the people born in Israel must live in booths for seven days. This is so that all of your descendants will

344

*remember that I brought them out of the land of Egypt. I
am the Lord, your God."' So Moses told the people of
Israel about the Lord's appointed feasts.*

*Lord, the festival of tents looks back to Your deliverance
    Of Israel from the land of Egypt.*

*It also looks forward to the coming millennium,
    When Israel will live in the Promised Land
    And enjoy Your special presence in peace.*

Amen.

Leviticus 24

CARE OF THE LAMPS

The Lord said to Moses, "Command the people of Israel to bring to you
pure oil from crushed olives for the lamps in the Tabernacle.
These lamps must never go out. Aaron will keep the lamps burning in the Meeting Tent. They will burn from evening until morning in My presence. They will burn in front of the curtain of the
Ark of the Covenant. This law will continue for people from
now on. They must keep the lamps burning on the lamp stands
(Menorah) of pure gold in My presence."

Lord, I will let my light shine
In a dark world for You.

I will be constant in my testimony
So others will see Christ in me.

The Holy Bread

"Take flour and bake 12 loaves of bread, using four quarts of flour. Put
the loaves in two rows on the pure gold Table of Showbread of
My presence. Six loaves will be in each row (12 loaves represented the 12 tribes of Israel). Pour pure olive oil incense on each
row. It is an offering made by fire to Me. Every Sabbath day,
Aaron will set the Bread of My Presence in order, in My presence. Thus My covenant with the people of Israel will always
continue. That bread will belong to Aaron and to his sons, and
will always be their share; they will eat it in a holy place,

because it is a very holy part of the offerings made by fire to Me."

Lord, I will fellowship constantly with Jesus, the Bread of Life,
He will be my strength,
And I will serve You.

The Punishment for Violating the Laws

Now there was a son of an Israelite woman and an Egyptian father who was walking among the Israelites when a fight broke out in the camp between him and an Israelite man. The son of the Israelite woman began cursing and blaspheming the name of the Lord, so the people took him to Moses. The mother's name was Shelomith, the daughter of Dibri, from the tribe of Dan. The people held him as a prisoner until the Lord's will was declared to them.

Then the Lord said to Moses, "Take the one who cursed Me outside the camp, along with all the people who heard him. They must put their hands on his head (symbolically laying the guilt of the crime upon his head). Then all the people must stone and kill him. If anyone curses his God, he is guilty of sin. Anyone who blasphemes My name must surely be put to death! All the people must certainly stone him. Foreigners must be punished just like the person born in Israel. If someone blasphemes My Name, then he *must* be put to death!"

Lord, I will guard my speech
So I don't blaspheme You.

I want to be a good testimony with
My speech so others will glorify You.

"If someone takes the life of another human being, then he must surely be put to death! Someone might kill an animal that belongs to another person. If he does, he must give that person another animal to take its place. If someone causes an injury to his neighbor, the same kind of injury must be paid back to him. A broken bone must be paid for a broken bone—an eye for an eye, and a tooth for a tooth (symbolically, the penalty was to fit the crime, not to exceed it). In the same way, when someone injures another human being, he must be injured in return. So, when anyone kills another person's animal, he must give that person an animal to take its place. But the person who kills another human being must be put to death! The law will be the same for the foreigner as for those from your own country. I am the Lord, your God."

Then Moses spoke to the people of Israel, and they took the man who had cursed outside the camp and stoned him. So, the people of Israel did as the Lord had commanded Moses.

> *Lord, I will not intentionally harm another person,*
>> *If I do so intentionally, forgive me.*

> *May I glorify you with all my actions.*
>> *Help me be kind to other people,*
>> *And keep me from hurting anyone.*

> *Amen.*

Leviticus 25

THE YEAR OF SOLEMN REST

The Lord spoke to Moses at Mount Sinai, "Tell the people of Israel, 'I
will be giving you land. When you enter it, let it have a special
time of rest (a Sabbath) for Me. You may plant seed in your field
for six years and prune your vineyards for six years and gather
in their fruit. However, during the seventh year, you must let the
land rest. (This was a Sabbath year. And after a series of seven
of these Sabbath years [7 x 7 = a total of 49 years], there would
be the year of jubilee. God sent the whole nation into captivity
for a period of 70 years to make up for the 490 years [in round
numbers] in which they had failed to observe the years of
Sabbath rest [2 Chron. 36:20-21].) This will be a Sabbath to
honor Me. You must *not* plant seed in your field or prune your
vineyards. You must not reap the crops that grow on their own
after harvest, nor gather into barns the grapes from your vines
that are not pruned. The land will have one year of rest. You may
eat whatever the land produces during that year. It will be food
for your male servants and your female servants. It will be food
for your hired workers and the foreigners who live in your country. It will also be food for your livestock and the wild animals
in your land. Whatever the land produces may be eaten.'"

A Year of Jubilee

"'Count off 7 groups of 7 years. This will be 49 years. (This meant that
would have been back-to-back sabbatical years. So, the year of
Jubilee occurred every 50th year.) On the Day of Atonement you

must blow the horn (shofar, the Hebrew "yobal"; hence, the word "jubilee" was an onomatopoetic word, imitating the joyful shout or cry of joy that pervaded the countryside during that 50th year). This will be blown throughout the whole country on the tenth day of the seventh month.

"'Make the 50th year a special year. Announce freedom for all people who live in your country; this is a Jubilee. Each of you will go back to his own property. And each of you will go back to his own family group.

"'The 50th year will be a special time for you to celebrate. Do not plant seeds. Do not harvest into barns the crops that grow by themselves. Don't gather into barns grapes from the vines that are not pruned in the year of Jubilee. It will be a holy time for you. You may eat the bounty that comes from the field.

"'In this year of Jubilee, each of you must return to the land that was owned by his ancestors. If you sell land to your neighbor or buy from him, then don't cheat him. If you want to buy your neighbor's land (The Lord owned the land; the people were only tenants who were leasing the land until the Year of Jubilee.), then count the number of years since the last Jubilee. Use that number to decide the pro-rated price. If he sells the land, then count the number of years remaining for harvesting crops to decide a fair price. If there are many years remaining until the next Jubilee, then the price will be high. If there are only a few years left, the price must lower. That is because your neighbor is really selling only a few crops to you. You must not cheat each other. You must revere Me, the Lord, your God.'"

Obey the Lord and You Will Be Blessed

"'Remember My laws and My rules, and obey them. Then you will live
in the land in peace. The land will yield good crops, and you
will eat as much as you want, and you will live in peace. But
you might ask: "What if we do not plant seeds or gather crops,
then what will we eat during the seventh year?" I will send a
great blessing upon you during the sixth year so that the land
will produce bumper crops for three years! When you plant
seeds in the eighth year, you will still be eating from the old
crop, until the harvest of the ninth year.

"'The land belongs to Me! So, you can never sell it. You are only pilgrims and travelers who live for awhile on My land. Some people might lease their land, but their family will always get its
land back. If a Jewish person in your country becomes very
poor, so that he has to "sell" his land, a redeemer (his close relative) must come and buy it back for him (compare Ruth 3:10-
18; 4:1-10). A person might not have a redeemer to buy back
his land for him. However, if he makes enough money to buy it
back himself, then he must count the years since the land was
sold. He must use that number to decide how much to pay for
the land. Then he is allowed to buy it back. So, the land will
belong to him again. But if he does not get enough money to
buy it back for himself, then the one who bought it will keep it
until the year of Jubilee. But during that celebration, the land
will go back to the first owner's family.

"'If someone sells a home in a walled city, he has the right to buy it
back for one year. But if the owner does not buy the house back
before one full year is over, then the house in the walled city
belongs to the one who bought it, and to his future sons. The
house will *not* go back to the first owner at Jubilee (most of the
houses in walled cities were occupied by craftsmen and traders;

their wealth was not tied up in lands). However, houses in small towns without walls are like open country. They can be bought back. And, they must be returned to their first owner at Jubilee.

"'The Levites may always buy their houses back. This is true in the towns that belong to them. If someone buys a house from a Levite in the Levite's town, it will return to the Levites in the Jubilee. Also, the fields and pastures around the towns of the Levites cannot be sold. They will always belong to the Levites.

"'If someone from your country becomes too poor to support himself, help him live among you, as you would help a stranger or a foreigner. Do not charge him any interest or increase on the money that you loan him. Revere your God! And respect the life of your brother among you. Do not lend him money for interest. Do not try to make a profit from your food. I am the Lord, your God. I brought you out of the land of Egypt to give the land of Canaan and become your God.

"'Some Jewish brother might become very poor, even selling himself as a slave. If he does, then you must not make him work like a slave. (No Jew would ever be reduced to the same type of oppressive slavery from which they had escaped in Egypt.) He will be like a hired worker, or like a visitor with you until the year of Jubilee. Then he is allowed to leave you. He may take his children and go back to his clan, even to the land of his ancestors. This is because the Israelites are My servants. I brought them out of the land of Egypt. They must not be sold as slaves again!

"'You must not be overbearing or cruel with this person; you must revere your God! You are allowed to buy men-slaves and women-slaves from other nations that surround you, and you may buy children as slaves. These children might come from the families of native-born foreigners who live in your land. These child-slaves will belong to you. You may even pass (bequeath) these foreign slaves on to your children after you die. You can make them permanent slaves, but you must not enslave your own brothers, the Israelites.

"'A foreigner or a visitor among you might become rich, and some Jewish brother might become poor. The poor man sells himself as a slave to a foreigner who lives among you, he has the right to be bought back and become free. One of his Jewish relatives may buy him back (redeem him). His uncle or his uncle's son may buy him back. Or one of his other close relatives may buy him back. Or if he gets enough money, then he may pay the money himself. Then he will be free again.

"'How do you decide the price? You must count the years from the time that he sold himself to the next year of Jubilee. Use that number to decide the fair price. This is because the person really only hired himself out for a specified number of years. There might be many years remaining before the year of Jubilee, and then the person must pay a small part of the first price. ("He must pay in silver for his redemption by paying the original purchase price.") There might be a few years left until the year of Jubilee. Then he must calculate according to the years of service due from him. He shall refund the money for his redemption. However, he will live like a hired man with the foreigner; don't let the foreigner rule over him harshly in your sight. That person and his children will eventually become free at the year of Jubilee. That is because the people of Israel are My servants. I brought them out of the land of Egypt. I am the Lord, your God.'"

Lord, you blessed your people with rest in the Sabbatical year,
And the year of Jubilee.

Thank you for Sunday, my day of rest,
The day I will worship and serve You.

Amen.

Leviticus 26

Blessings of Obedience and Curses of Disobedience

"Do not make idols for yourselves. Do not set up statues or an upright pillar either. Do not put stone images in your land to bow yourselves down to them, because I am the Lord your God. Remember My Sabbaths, and you must revere My sanctuary. I am the Lord. If you live by My rules and obey and practice My commands, then I will give you rains in their season (The former heavy rain at the end of autumn and the latter light rain in the spring). The land will produce crops, and the trees of the field will produce their fruit. Your threshing will continue until the grape harvest. And your grape harvest will continue until it is time to plant. Then you will have plenty to eat, and you will live in your land in peace.

"I will give peace to your country, and you will be able to settle down. No one will terrorize you. I will eliminate savage animals from your country. And foreign armies will not pass through your country. You will chase your enemies and defeat them. You will kill them with your sword. Five of you will chase 100 men, and 100 of you will chase 10,000 men. You will defeat your enemies and kill them with your swords. Then I will show kindness to you. I will let you have many children. I will keep My covenant with you. And you will have enough crops to last for more than one year. You will harvest the new crops, and you will have to throw out the old crops to make room for the new ones.

"Also, I will place My Holy Tabernacle among you. I will not feel disgusted with you but will walk among you and be your God, and
you will be My people. I am the Lord, your God. You were once
slaves in the land of the Egyptians, bent low under their heavy
weights which you carried. But I broke the yoke that was on
your shoulders. I caused you to walk proudly again."

Obey or Be Punished!

"Now if you do not listen to Me nor obey all these commands, and if
you reject all of My laws and My rules because you hate con-
forming to any of them, then you have broken My covenant. I
will cause terrible things to happen to you. I will cause you to
have a severe disease and a high fever, destroying your eyesight
and draining your strength. You will not have success when you
plant your seeds. Your enemies will eat your crops. I will be
against you, and your enemies will defeat you. The enemies who
hate you *will* rule over you. You will run away even when no
one is chasing you!

"If you still do not obey Me and still will not listen to Me, then I will
punish you seven times more for your sins. I will break the great
cities that make you proud. The skies will not give rain. The
earth will not produce crops. You will work hard, but it will not
help. Your land will not grow any crops. Your trees will not produce their fruit. If you still turn against Me and refuse to listen
to Me, then I will hit you seven times harder. The more you sin,
the more you will be punished! (Literally, 'as many as your sins
deserve'), and I will send wild animals to attack you. They will
snatch your children away from you. They will destroy your livestock. They will make you so little in number that the roads will
seem deserted.

"And if you don't learn your lesson after all these things, and if you *still* turn against Me, then I will also turn against you. I will punish you seven times harder for your sins because you broke My covenant. I will bring foreign armies against you, and you will go into your cities for safety, but I will cause disease to spread among you there. Then your enemy will defeat you. There will be very little bread to eat, they will weigh each piece of bread you will eat, but you will still be hungry. And after all of that, if you still refuse to listen to Me, and if you still turn against Me, then I will truly oppose you, showing my anger. I will punish you for your sins seven times harder!

"You will eat the bodies of your sons and daughters. And I will destroy your high places (where false gods are worshiped). I will cut down your incense altars. And I will pile your corpses on top of the lifeless carcasses of your idols. I will be disgusted with you, and I will destroy your towns. I will make your so-called 'holy places' a wasteland. I will not be delighted in the scent of your offerings. I will devastate the land. Even your enemies who come to settle in it will be shocked at it. I will scatter you among the nations. I will pull out My sword and chase you. Your land will become empty. Your towns will become wastelands. Then you will live in your country of your enemies. And so, your land will finally get its rest. It will enjoy its times of Sabbaths, and all the time that it lies desolate, it will have the rest (Sabbaths) that you should have given it while you lived in it. Those of you who are still left alive will lose your courage in the lands of your enemies. You will even be scared by the sound of a leaf that is blown by the wind. You will run away as if someone were chasing you with a sword. You will fall down, even when no one is chasing you, falling over each other. You will have *no* strength to stand up against your enemies. You will die among other nations and disappear in the countries of your enemies. So, those who are still left alive will rot away in their sins and the sins of their ancestors in the lands of your enemies.

"However, perhaps the people might confess their sins and the violations of their ancestors, which they have committed against Me. Maybe they will admit that they have turned against Me. If these disobedient people are sorry for what they did, they will accept punishment for their sin. If they do, then I will remember My covenant with Jacob. I will also remember My covenant with Isaac and My covenant with Abraham. And I will remember the land that was abandoned as it enjoys its times of rest. Then those who are still left alive will accept their punishment for their sins. They will learn that they were punished because they rejected My laws and My rules and they hated to conform to any of them. Yet, even after all that, when they are in the land of their enemies, if they come to Me for help, I will not turn away from them. I will not be disgusted with them anymore. I won't completely destroy them. I will *not* break My covenant with them, because I am the Lord, their God!

"For their sake, I will remember My covenant with their ancestors that brought them out of the land of Egypt. I did it so that I could become their God. The other nations saw these things that I, the Lord, did for you. These are the laws, the rules, and the instructions that I gave to the people of Israel through the hand of Moses on Mount Sinai."

Lord, I will learn from the disobedience of Israel,
I will keep Your commandments of instruction;
I will bring glory to You.

Forgive my sins and the sins of my people;
Have mercy on me and my people.

Amen.

Leviticus 27

THE LAWS ABOUT GIFTS
OFFERED TO THE LORD

The Lord said to Moses, "Tell the people of Israel: 'When someone might make an extraordinary vow to Me, or he promises to give himself as a servant to Me, the priest must set a specified price for that person. The specified price for a man who is 20 to 60 years old is 1¼ pounds (50 pieces) of silver. You must use the standard as set by the sanctuary. The specified price for a woman who is 20 to 60 years old is 12 ounces (30 shekels) of silver. The specified price for a young male who is 5 to 20 years old is 8 ounces (20 shekels) of silver. The specified price for a young female who is 5 to 20 years old is 4 ounces (10 shekels) of silver. The specified price for a baby boy is 1 month old to 5 years old is two ounces (5 shekels) of silver. For a baby girl, the specified price is 1½ ounces (3 shekels) of silver. The specified price for a man who is 60 years old or older is 6 ounces (15 shekels) of silver. The specified price for a woman who is 60 years old or older is 4 ounces (10 shekels) of silver. However, if a person is too poor to pay the specified price, then bring him to the priest who will decide how much money the person who vowed can afford to pay.

'"Some animals may be used as an offering to Me. If someone promises to donate them to Me, then it will become holy. That person must not try to put another animal in its place, replacing a good animal for a bad animal. If he tries to change animals, then *both* animals will become "holy"!

"'Unclean animals cannot be donated as a sacrifice to Me. If someone does that, then that animal must be brought to the priest who will decide on a price for that animal. The price will be according to whether the animal is good or bad. If the priest decides on a set price, then *that* is the price for the animal. If the person wants to buy back the animal, then he must add an additional 20 percent to the specified price.

"'A person might dedicate his house to Me. If he does, then the priest must decide its specified value. The price will be according to whether the house is good or bad. If the priest decides on a specified price, then *that* is the price for the house. But the person who dedicates his house might want to buy it back. If he does, then he must add an additional 20 percent to the specified price. Then the house will belong to him again.

"'A person might dedicate part of his fields to Me. The value of those fields will depend on how much seed is needed to plant them. It will cost 1¼ pounds (50 shekels) of silver for each six bushels of barley seed needed. The person might dedicate his field starting from the year of Jubilee. Then its specified value will be whatever the priest decides. However, a person might dedicate his field *after* the Jubilee. If he does, the priest must decide the exact price. He must count the number of years until the next year of Jubilee. Then he will use that number to decide the exact price. The person who dedicated the field might want to buy it back. If he does, he must add 20 percent to that price. Then the field will belong to him again. If he does not buy the field back, then it can never be redeemed. If it is sold to someone else, then the first person can never buy it back. Now the field when it is released at the year of Jubilee will be "holy" to Me.

"'The field will *always* belong to Me. It will become the property of the priests. Someone may dedicate to Me a field that he has purchased, but it may not be a part of his family estate. If he dedicates such a field, then the priest must count the years until the next Jubilee. He must decide the specified price for the land. Then that land will belong to Me. At the year of Jubilee, the field must go back to its original owner; it must go back to the family who sold the land. You must use the standard set by the sanctuary in paying these specified prices.

"'People may dedicate cattle or sheep to Me. But if an animal is the first one born, it already belongs to Me. So, people may not dedicate these animals a second time. If the animal is ceremonially "unclean," the person must buy it back. The priest will decide the specified price of the animal, and the person must add 20 percent. If he does not buy it back, then the priest must sell it for the price that was set.

"'There is a special kind of gift that people dedicate to Me. It may be a person, an animal, or a field from the family property. That kind of gift cannot be repurchased or sold. It is "holy" to Me. If a person is devoted for the purpose of being destroyed, he cannot be repurchased. He *must* be put to death!

"'Ten percent of all crops belong to Me. This includes the produce from fields and the fruit from the trees. That 10 percent is "holy" to Me. A person might want to get back his 10 percent, if he does, then he must add 20 percent to its price to buy it back.

"'The priest will take every tenth animal from a person's cattle or sheep. It will be "holy" to Me. The owner should not pick out the good animals from the bad. He should not exchange one animal for another. If he does exchange it, *both* animals will become "holy." They cannot be repurchased.'"

These are the commands which the Lord commanded Moses at Mount Sinai. They are for the people of Israel.

Lord, You have spoken in the Book of Leviticus;
  Help me understand your commandments
  And instructions.

Lord, I want to obey you and keep your commandments,
  Give me strength to always obey You.
  When I am weak, forgive me.

    Amen.

EPILOGUE

The Tabernacle is perhaps the fullest Old Testament type (pre-figure) of New Testament salvation. Technically, *Tabernacle* means tent, which was 45 feet long, by 15 feet wide, by 15 feet tall. While Moses was on Mount Sinai getting the stone tablets of the Ten Commandments written by the finger of God, he also received the pattern for the Tabernacle. The Book of Hebrews makes it abundantly clear that access into the Tabernacle is a picture of spiritual truth of how we go to the Father through Jesus Christ. The following chart parallels some truths of the Tabernacle with New Testament fulfillment.

Old Testament Tabernacle	New Testament Tabernacle
Gate (Exod. 27:16)	Jesus the Way (John 14:6)
Brazen Altar (Exod. 27:1-8)	Altar of Salvation (Heb. 13:10)
Laver (Exod. 30:18-20)	Washing of the Word (Eph. 5:26)
Gold-plated Board (Exod. 26:15-30)	Humanity and Deity of Jesus (John 1:14)
Door (Exod. 26:36-37)	Jesus is the Door (John 10:7)
Table of Showbread (Exod. 25:23-30)	Jesus the Bread of God (John 6:33-35)

Altar of Incense (Exod. 30:1-10)	Jesus High Priestly Prayers (John 17, Heb. 7:25).
Golden Candlestick (Exod. 25:31-40)	Jesus the Light (John 8:12)
Ark of the Covenant (Exod. 25:10-22)	Dwelling Place of God (1 Cor. 6:19)
Mercy Seat (Exod. 37:6-9)	Jesus the Propitiation (1 John 2:2)
Aaron's Rod that Budded (Heb. 9:4)	Resurrection (Matt. 28:6)
Jar of Manna (Heb. 9:4)	Hidden Manna (Rev. 2:17)
Ministering Priest (Exod. 28:1-2)	Ministry of Jesus (Heb. 8:1)
Shekinah Cloud (Exod. 40:34-37)	Glory of Christ (James 2:1)
Sacrifice of Animals (Lev. 1–7)	Jesus the Lamb of God (John 1:29)

The Tabernacle was constructed according to the plan and pattern of God and atoned (covered) the sins of Israel until the blood of Jesus took them away (see Rom. 3:25-26). "So Moses finished the work" (Exod. 40:33). Perhaps it was then when Moses prayed his words we find in Psalm 90:1, 16-17, "Lord You have been our dwelling place in all generations...Let Your work appear to Your servants, and Your glory to their children. And let the beauty of the Lord our God be upon us, and establish the work of our hands for us; yes, establish the work of our hands."

ABOUT THE AUTHOR

DR. ELMER TOWNS is an author of popular and scholarly works, a seminar lecturer, and dedicated worker in Sunday school. He has written over 125 books, including several best sellers. He won the coveted Gold Medallion Book Award for *The Names of the Holy Spirit*.

Dr. Elmer Towns also cofounded Liberty University with Jerry Falwell in 1971 and now serves as Dean of the B.R. Lakin School of Religion and as professor of Theology and New Testament.

Liberty University is the fastest growing Christian university in America. Located in Lynchburg, Virginia, Liberty University is a private, coeducational, undergraduate and graduate institution offering 38 undergraduate and 15 graduate programs serving over 39,000 resident and external students (11,300 on campus). Individuals from all 50 states and more than 70 nations comprise the diverse student body. While the faculty and students vary greatly, the common denominator and driving force of Liberty University since its conception is love for Jesus Christ and the desire to make Him known to the entire world.

For more information about Liberty University, contact:

Liberty University
1971 University Boulevard
Lynchburg, VA 24502
Telephone: 434-582-2000
Website: www.Liberty.edu

Additional copies of this book and other
book titles from DESTINY IMAGE are
available at your local bookstore.

Call toll-free: 1-800-722-6774.

Send a request for a catalog to:

Destiny Image® Publishers, Inc.
P.O. Box 310
Shippensburg, PA 17257-0310

*"Speaking to the Purposes of God for This
Generation and for the Generations to Come."*

**For a complete list of our titles,
visit us at www.destinyimage.com.**